IFRS
PRINCIPLES OF ACCOUNTING

With Keywords In Korean

5th Edition

IFRS PRINCIPLES OF ACCOUNTING

With Keywords In Korean

YOON, KIM & JOHNSON

신영사

PREFACE

The universal business language of IFRS (International Financial Reporting Standards) connects the current global business environment despite differences in business environments such as culture, business practices, languages, and legal systems. Moreover, the widespread adoption of or convergence toward IFRS by more than 160 jurisdictions leads to the removal or minimization of geopolitical and cultural differences across countries. As a result, accounting students, who can command good accounting knowledge in IFRS and English, can land a decent job in the global accounting market that is ever more short-staffed in competent accountants in public and private accounting professions.

The authors of '*IFRS Principles of Accounting with Keywords in Korean*' are grateful for the continued support from the readers. The slim volume of the book with keywords in Korean will significantly help students easily read and understand complex accounting concepts. Despite its slim volume, the book covers most of the key concepts and principles of financial accounting. Our goal is to guide students in their quest to acquire basic concepts and competencies of financial accounting in English and Korean. We also hope this book raises a global mindset amongst students, lecturers of accounting, and accounting professionals. The book will help students taking an accounting course in English for the first time successfully learn Accounting in English and pursue their accounting career with a global mindset.

In the 5th edition, we have

- Added Chapter 14 on revenue recognition,
- Deleted outdated accounting issues on petty cash,
- Updated new developments in IFRS Conceptual Framework and standards, and
- Rewritten most of the chapters by using easy and clear explanations.

The readers will find it interesting that the book uses the names of various animals, flowers, and plants in the examples, multiple-choice questions, and exercises. Finally, the authors thank the accounting professors, students, and other readers for your patronage.

January 25, 2023

Soon Suk Yoon (Western Illinois University)
Hyo Jin Kim (Jeonju University)
Grace Johnson (Marietta College)

CONTENTS

CHAPTER 3 RECORDING TRANSACTIONS

CHAPTER 4 ADJUSTING AND CLOSING ENTRIES

CHAPTER 5 PREPARATION OF FINANCIAL STATEMENTS

CHAPTER 6 ACCOUNTING FOR MERCHANDISING FIRMS

CHAPTER 7 CASH AND FINANCIAL ASSETS

CHAPTER 10 PROPERTY, PLANT AND EQUIPMENT, AND INTANGIBLE ASSETS

CHAPTER 11 LIABILITIES

CHAPTER 12 SHAREHOLDERS' EQUITY

CHAPTER 13 STATEMENT OF CASH FLOWS

CHAPTER 14 REVENUE RECOGNITION

CHAPTER

1

INTRODUCTION TO FINANCIAL ACCOUNTING

1.1 SCOPE AND PURPOSE OF FINANCIAL ACCOUNTING

1.2 OTHER BRANCHES OF ACCOUNTING

1.3 TYPES OF BUSINESS ENTITY

1.4 BUSINESS ACTIVITIES

1.5 UNDERLYING CONCEPTS OF FINANCIAL ACCOUNTING

1.6 THE ACCOUNTING EQUATION

CHAPTER 1

INTRODUCTION TO FINANCIAL ACCOUNTING

1.1 SCOPE AND PURPOSE OF FINANCIAL ACCOUNTING

Financial accounting(재무회계) is the language of business. It is concerned with assisting economic entities(경제실체) like business firms(영리기업) in processing business transactions and events(사업상의 거래 및 사건) into financial statements (재무제표), showing the operating performance(영업성과) for a period of time(일정기간) and the financial position(재무상태) at a specific point in time(특정시점). The primary purpose of financial accounting is to help financial statement users(재무제표이용자) make rational economic decisions(합리적 경제의사결정). Thus, financial accounting may be defined as an information-providing process(정보제공과정) through recording, classifying, summarizing, and reporting business transactions and events in the financial statements(재무제표) with the purpose of showing the operating performance and financial position of an entity.

The financial statement users are interested in knowing about a company's activities, financial status, and operating results. They are providers of resources(자원제공자) to the company, and hence users of accounting information(회계정보) or financial information(재무정보).[1]

The users of accounting information are also called stakeholders(이해관계자) and make diverse economic decisions with respect to the company. The purpose of financial accounting is to provide useful information for rational decision-making by diverse stakeholders. The stakeholders use financial information generated by the accounting process. The stakeholders of a business typically include owners, managers, creditors, tax authorities, regulatory agencies, suppliers, customers, employees, and other users. The stakeholders and their information needs are summarized in Table 1-1.

Table 1-1 Accounting Information Users and Their Information Needs

Stakeholders (이해관계자)	Information Needs (정보요구사항)
Investors (Owners) (투자자, 소유주)	To evaluate the risk inherent in and return(이익) provided by their investment.
Creditors (채권자)	To evaluate a firm's financial capacity to meet its obligations when they become due.
Managers (경영자)	To evaluate the business's financial strengths and weaknesses in planning, organizing, and running the business.
Tax Authorities (과세당국)	To determine tax revenue based on the company's profitability and whether the company is complying with the tax laws.
Regulatory Agencies (감독기관)	To monitor whether the company is operating within prescribed rules(감독규범). The regulators are interested in the efficient allocation of resources.
Suppliers (납품업자)	To evaluate whether amounts owed to them will be paid when due.
Customers (고객)	To evaluate the company's continuing ability to honor product warranties(제품보증) and support the product lines.
Employees (종업원)	To evaluate the company's financial ability to pay increased wages and benefits.
Other users	Security exchanges(증권거래소), trade associations(산업연합회), the general public(일반대중), financial analysts(재무분석가) and the business media (business newspapers and global business information sources such as Reuters and Bloomberg), and others for various reasons.

1 "Financial" is synonymous with accounting in the sense that all accounting information is expressed in terms of monetary unit. Therefore, "financial" implies "of monetary."

1.2 OTHER BRANCHES OF ACCOUNTING

Other major branches of accounting are cost accounting, managerial accounting, auditing (public accounting), tax accounting, and governmental accounting.

Cost accounting(원가회계) is mainly concerned with measuring, recording, and reporting the costs of products or services. From the data accumulated, both the total cost and the unit cost of each product are determined. Cost information is also vital for effective performance evaluation(성과평가) of products, employees, divisions, and others.

Managerial accounting(관리회계), also called management accounting, is a field of accounting that provides economic and financial information for managers and other internal users. Specifically, managerial accounting provides information for (1) explaining manufacturing and non-manufacturing costs and how they are reported in the financial statements, (2) assisting managers in profit planning and formalizing these plans in the form of budgets, (3) providing a basis for controlling costs and expenses by comparing actual results with planned objectives and standard costs(표준원가), (4) accumulating and presenting relevant data for management decision making, and (5) determining the relationship among activity levels, costs, and profits.

Auditing(회계감사), also called public accounting(공공회계), refers to work done by independent public accountants who audit the financial statements of client companies to ensure that the financial statements are properly stated in accordance with accounting standards(회계기준). A license called a "CPA" (certified public accountant, 공인회계사) is required to work as a public accountant.

Tax accounting(세무회계) refers primarily to the determination of corporate income taxes(법인세). Corporate income taxes are based on accounting earnings(회계이익) from which taxable income(과세소득) is derived by adjusting additions and deductions. Other taxes like municipal taxes(지방세), excise taxes(내국세 또는 소비세), value-added-taxes(부가가치세) and the like are also areas of tax accounting.

Governmental accounting(정부회계) focuses on the specific accounting needs of central and local governmental institutions. However, some not-for-profit organizations(비영리조직), such as charitable organizations, schools, and hospitals, also fall into this category.

1.3 TYPES OF BUSINESS ENTITY

There are different types of business entities(기업실체), such as sole proprietorships, partnerships, and corporations.

In the sole proprietorship(개인기업), there is only one owner. In the event the business fails, the owner is personally liable for all debts incurred, i.e., unlimited liability(무한책임). Small owner-operated businesses such as small retail stores, auto-repair shops, beauty salons, and copy centers are often sole proprietorships.

A partnership(파트너십) has more than one owner. The partnership contract spells out the rights of each partner in such matters as profit distribution and withdrawal of funds. Personal liability exists in partnerships. Partnerships often are formed because one individual lacks the economic resources to establish the business. Sometimes, partners bring unique skills or licenses to the partnership. The most common partnerships are law firms, accounting firms, and hospitals.

In a corporation(주식회사), the equity interest(지분) belongs to investors who own the shares of stock(주식) in the business. Only limited liability(유한책임) exists for shareholders(주주) if the corporation fails, in that they will lose only what they have invested. No personal liability exists in corporations. Most of the large and listed firms(상장회사) are corporations because corporations offer many advantages: limited liability, transferability of ownership, and ease of raising funds, among others.

A business entity provides goods(재화) or services(용역) or both to customers to generate a profit (net income) for its owners. Profit or loss(순손익, net income or loss) is the difference between revenues and expenses. Revenues(수익) are the inflow of resources that the firm receives from its customers for the goods or services delivered to them. Expenses(비용) are resources used or consumed to produce and deliver goods or to provide services to customers. For example, for a manufacturing firm(제조회사) or retail firm(소매회사), revenues consist of the sales price charged. In contrast, revenue for a service business (e.g., an accounting firm) is the fee for services rendered. Expenses are incurred in the process of generating revenue. Examples of expenses are cost of goods sold(매출원가), wage or salary expense (임금), rent expense(임차료), and utility expense(공공요금). Revenues and expenses resulting from the profit-generating activities of business over a period of time are shown in the income statement(손익계산서).

A company must be financially sound to satisfy its debts at maturity(만기). A measure of financial health is the degree to which assets(자산) exceed liabilities(부채). A picture of a company's financial position at the end of an accounting period is shown in the statement of financial position(재무상태표), also called balance sheet(대차대조표).

A business entity must have sufficient cash flows to carry out its business activities. The flow of cash into and out of the entity is described in the statement of cash flows(현금흐름표).

1.4 BUSINESS ACTIVITIES

All businesses are involved in three types of activity: financing, investing, and operating.

Financing activity(재무활동) has to do with raising external funds to run the business. The two primary sources of external funds are borrowing money from financial institutions and issuing shares of stock in stock exchanges(주식시장) or bonds in bond markets(사채시장). A stock or share(주식) represents an equity certificate(지분증서), while a bond(사채) represents a debt certificate(채무증서). Stocks and bonds are collectively called securities(증권).

Investing activity(투자활동) involves the purchase of resources a company needs to run the business. Investing activities involve how to apply or invest funds raised from financing activities for operating purposes. Those resources purchased to run the business are called assets(자산). For example, a company obtains assets such as land, buildings, equipment, machinery, delivery trucks, and so forth.

Operating activity(영업활동) has something to do with how to run the business using the assets obtained through investing activities. Through operating activities, business entities generate revenues and incur expenses. Revenues(수익) are increases in assets or decreases in liabilities resulting from the sale of products or services in the ordinary course of business. Revenues arise from different sources and are identified by various names depending on the nature of the business. Common types of revenues are sales revenue(매출수익, 매출액), service revenue(용역수익), interest revenue(이자수익), and rent revenue(임대수익). Depending on the types of assets consumed or services used, expenses take many forms and are identified by various names. Common types of expenses are cost of goods sold(매출원가), selling expenses(판매비), administrative expenses(관리비), interest expenses(이자비용), and income tax expenses(법인세비용). Operating activities regularly involve assets and liabilities such as accounts receivable(매출채권), inventory(재고자산), prepaid expenses(선급비용), accounts payable(매입채무), accrued liabilities(미지급부채), and income taxes payable(미지급법인세).

1.5 UNDERLYING CONCEPTS OF FINANCIAL ACCOUNTING

(1) Objective of Financial Reporting

The objective of general-purpose financial reporting(일반목적재무보고) is to provide financial information(재무정보) about the reporting entity(보고실체) that is useful to the current and potential investors, lenders and other creditors in making decisions about providing resources to the entity. Investors, lenders, and other creditors are collectively called capital providers(자본제공자). Capital providers rely on general-purpose financial statements(일반목적재무제표) for much of the financial information they need. Capital providers are the primary users to whom general-purpose financial statements are directed.

General-purpose financial statements do not, and cannot, provide capital providers with all the information they need. They need to consider other pertinent information, such as general economic and political conditions. General-purpose financial statements are focused on meeting the needs of the maximum number of primary users, who may have different, and possibly conflicting information needs.

(2) Qualitative Characteristics of Accounting Information

For financial information to be useful in making economic decisions, financial reporting should provide capital providers with the types of information which meet various qualitative characteristics(질적특성). Decision-useful accounting information should possess two 'fundamental qualitative characteristics'(근본적 질적특성) and four 'enhancing qualitative characteristics'(보강적 질적특성).

The fundamental qualitative characteristics are relevance(목적적합성) and faithful representation(충실한 표현). The enhancing qualitative characteristics are comparability(비교가능성), verifiability(검증가능성), timeliness(적시성) and understandability(이해가능성). Decision-useful financial information must be relevant and faithfully represent what it intends to represent. The enhancing qualitative characteristics may help determine which alternative to use to depict economic phenomena(경제적 현상) if both alternatives are considered equally relevant and faithfully represented.

The qualitative characteristics of accounting information are summarized in Table 1-2.

Financial information has predictive value(예측가치) if it can help users predict future outcomes. In addition, financial information has confirmatory value(확인가치) if it confirms or changes previous expectations.

Completeness(완전성) refers to a complete depiction that includes all information necessary for a user to understand the phenomenon depicted. Neutrality(중립성) refers to a neutral depiction with no bias in the selection or presentation of financial information. Free from error(무오류) refers to the presentation of financial information with no errors or omissions in the selection or application of the process used to produce reported information.

Table 1-2 Qualitative Characteristics of Financial Information

Relevance (목적적합성)	Relevant financial information can make a difference in the decisions made by users. Financial information can make a difference in decisions if it has predictive value, confirmatory value, or both.
Faithful representation (충실한 표현)	Financial information must faithfully represent the economic phenomena it intends to represent. A faithful representation would be complete, neutral, and free from error.
Comparability (비교가능성)	Comparability enables users to identify and understand similarities and differences among items. For example, information about a reporting entity is more useful if it can be compared with similar information about other entities, or the same entity for another period or at another date.
Verifiability (검증가능성)	Verifiability means that different knowledgeable and independent observers could reach a consensus, although not necessarily complete agreement, that a particular depiction is a faithful representation. Verifiability helps assure users that information faithfully represents the economic phenomena that it intends to represent.
Timeliness (적시성)	Timeliness means that information is available to decision-makers in time to be capable of influencing their decisions.
Understandability (이해가능성)	Information is understandable by classifying, characterizing and representing it clearly and concisely.

(3) The Elements of Financial Statements

Financial statements portray the financial effects of transactions and other events by grouping them into broad classes according to their economic characteristics. These broad classes are termed the elements of financial statements(재무제표의 요소). The elements directly related to the measurement of financial position in the statement of financial position(재무상태표) are assets, liabilities, and equity. The elements directly related to the measurement of performance in the income statement(손익계산서) are income (or revenues) and expenses. These broad elements are sometimes called the five major categories of accounts(계정의 5대 범주).

Financial statements are prepared on the assumption that the reporting entity is a going concern(계속기업) and will continue to be in operation for the foreseeable future. Hence, the entity is assumed to have no intention nor the need to liquidate or curtail materially the scale of its operations.

Table 1-3 briefly defines the elements of financial statements.

Table 1-3 The Elements of Financial Statements

Assets (자산)	An asset is a present economic resource(경제적 자원) controlled by the entity as a result of past events. An economic resource is a right that has the potential to produce economic benefits(경제적 효익).
Liabilities (부채)	A liability is a present obligation(현재의무) of the entity to transfer an economic resource as a result of past events.
Equity (소유주지분)	Equity is the residual interest(잔여지분) in the assets of the entity after deducting all its liabilities. As such, equity is also called 'net assets(순자산).'
Income or Revenues[2] (수익)	Income is increases in assets, or decreases in liabilities, that result in increases in equity, other than those relating to contributions from equity holders(지분보유자로부터의 출자).
Expenses[3] (비용)	Expenses are decreases in assets, or increases in liabilities, that result in decreases in equity, other than those relating to distributions to equity holders(지분보유자에 대한 분배).

1.6 THE ACCOUNTING EQUATION

An entity's financial position represents the relationship between assets, liabilities, and equity. The accounting equation(회계등식) reflects these elements by expressing the equality of assets to the sum of liabilities and equity as follows:

$$\text{Assets} = \text{Liabilities} + \text{Equity}$$

The equation, in effect, says that a company's assets are subject to the claims of debt holders and equity holders (owners).

The accounting equation is the basis of the double-entry bookkeeping

2 'Income' is the term used by the IFRS Conceptual Framework, while 'revenue' is the term used by the U.S. Conceptual Framework. It should be noted that 'income' encompasses both revenues and gains.

3 'Expenses' under the IFRS Conceptual Framework include both 'expenses' and 'losses', while they are defined separately by the U.S. Conceptual Framework.

system(복식부기제도), which means that each transaction has a dual effect. A transaction(거래) affects either both sides of the equation by the same amount or one side of the equation only by increasing and decreasing it by identical amounts and thus netting to zero.

EXAMPLE 1-1 *Accounting Equation*

Zinnia Company has the following transactions in January 20×1:

1. Greg Woodruff started his business, Zinnia Company, with a cash investment of $10,000 and office equipment worth $5,000.
2. Purchased office supplies for $800 and paid cash.
3. Bought a laptop computer for $500 on account from Eden Digital Company.
4. Paid $400 of salary to his staff.
5. Received a bill for electricity consumed during the period for $300.
6. Earned service revenue of $2,000, of which $1,200 was received in cash, and $800 is to be received later from the clients.
7. Paid $300 to Eden Digital Company.
8. Greg Woodruff, the owner, withdrew $100 from the business for personal use.
9. Received $100 on account from one of the clients in Transaction 6.
10. Office supplies on hand at month's end are $600.

Analyses of the Transactions: Equip, OS, AR, and AP represent, respectively, Equipment, Office Supplies, Accounts Receivable, and Accounts Payable.

Transaction 1 Greg Woodruff started his business, Zinnia Company, with a cash investment of $10,000 and office equipment worth $5,000.

Analysis: The assets Cash(현금) and Office Equipment(비품) are increased, and Capital (자본금) is also increased for the total investment by the owner.

		A		=	L	+	E
Cash	Equip	OS	AR		AP		Capital
$10,000	$5,000						$15,000

Transaction 2 Purchased office supplies for cash, $800.

Analysis: The asset Office Supplies(사무용소모품) increases by $800 with a corresponding reduction in the asset Cash. The transaction is an example of using one asset to acquire another one.

A				= L	+ E
Cash	Equip	OS	AR	AP	Capital
$10,000	$5,000				$15,000
−800		$800			
$9,200	$5,000	$800			$15,000

Transaction 3 Bought a laptop computer for $500 on account from Eden Digital Company.

Analysis: An asset, Office Equipment(사무용비품), is acquired on account(외상), thereby creating a liability for future payment called Accounts Payable(외상매입금). Accounts payable are the amount owed to suppliers.

A				= L	+ E
Cash	Equip	OS	AR	AP	Capital
$9,200	$5,000	$800			$15,000
	500			$500	
$9,200	$5,500	$800		$500	$15,000

Transaction 4 Paid $400 of salary.

Analysis: Cash and capital are both reduced because of the salary expense(급여). Equity is reduced because expenses decrease equity.

A				= L	+ E
Cash	Equip	OS	AR	AP	Capital
$9,200	$5,500	$800		$500	$15,000
−400					−400
$8,800	$5,500	$800		$500	$14,600

Transaction 5 Received an electricity bill for $300 (not paid).

Analysis: Liabilities are increased by $300 since the business owes the payment for electricity consumed. Equity is reduced for the expense.

A				= L	+ E
Cash	Equip	OS	AR	AP	Capital
$8,800	$5,500	$800		$500	$14,600
				300	−300
$8,800	$5,500	$800		$800	$14,300

Transaction 6 Earned service revenue of $2,000, of which $1,200 was received in cash and $800 is to be received later from the clients.

Analysis: Cash increases by $1,200 and Accounts Receivable(외상매출금) (amounts owed to the business by the clients) increase by $800. Service revenue(용역수익) increases the owner's equity. Thus, equity is increased by $2,000.

		A		= L	+ E
Cash	Equip	OS	AR	AP	Capital
$8,800	$5,500	$800		$800	$14,300
1,200			$800		2,000
$10,000	$5,500	$800	$800	$800	$16,300

Transaction 7 Paid $300 to Eden Digital Company (in partial payment of the amount owed to Eden Digital Company).

Analysis: The payment reduces Cash and Accounts Payable by the same amount.

		A		= L	+ E
Cash	Equip	OS	AR	AP	Capital
$10,000	$5,500	$800	$800	$800	$16,300
−300				−300	
$9,700	$5,500	$800	$800	$500	$16,300

Transaction 8 Greg Woodruff, the owner, withdrew $100 for personal use.

Analysis: The withdrawal reduces Cash and Owner's equity. Personal withdrawal is a disinvestment in the business, reducing the owner's equity. Personal withdrawal is not related to running the business. Therefore, it is not an expense of the company.

		A		= L	+ E
Cash	Equip	OS	AR	AP	Capital
$9,700	$5,500	$800	$800	$500	$16,300
−100					−100
$9,600	$5,500	$800	$800	$500	$16,200

Transaction 9 Received $100 from one of the clients.

Analysis: The transaction increases Cash and reduces Accounts Receivable. One asset is being substituted for another one.

		A		= L	+ E
Cash	Equip	OS	AR	AP	Capital
$9,600	$5,500	$800	$800	$500	$16,200
100			−100		
$9,700	$5,500	$800	$700	$500	$16,200

Transaction 10 Office supplies on hand (determined by the count of supplies) at month's end are $600.

Analysis: Since the amount of office supplies acquired initially was $800, and $600 is left on hand, the firm must have used $200 of supplies during the period. As a result, Office Supplies and owner's equity decreased by $200. Therefore, the supplies consumed represent Office Supplies Expense(사무용소모품비).

		A		= L	+ E
Cash	Equip	OS	AR	AP	Capital
$9,700	$5,500	$800	$700	$500	$16,200
		−200			−200
$9,700	$5,500	$600	$700	$500	$16,000

From the change in owner's equity, we can determine the firm's net income, which is equal to revenues minus expenses.

Zinnia Company
Income Statement
For the Month of January 20×1

Service Revenue		$2,000
Less: Expenses		
Salary Expense	$400	
Utility Expense	300	
Office Supplies Expense	200	
Total Expenses		900
Net Income		$1,100

CHAPTER 1 Multiple Choice Questions

1.1 Financial accounting:

a Provides information primarily for external decision makers.
b Provides information primarily for a company's employees.
c Provides information primarily for the use of managers of the company.
d Is primarily used to compute a company's tax obligation.

1.2 The accounting equation is defined as:

a Assets = Liabilities + Owners' Equity.
b Assets = Liabilities − Owners' Equity.
c Net Income = Revenues − Expenses.
d Liabilities + Revenues = Assets.

1.3 The form of business organization that is legally separate from its owners is a:

a Partnership.
b Sole proprietorship.
c Corporation.
d Separation entity.

1.4 The accounts which represent the resources of the company are called:

a Liabilities.
b Revenues.
c Expenses.
d Assets.

1.5 Net income can best be described as:

a. Net cash received by a company during the year.
b. Revenues minus expenses.
c. The amount of profits retained in a company for the year.
d. Resources owned by a company.

1.6 The costs associated with producing revenues are referred to as:

a. Dividends.
b. Assets.
c. Liabilities.
d. Expenses.

1.7 If accounting information is considered to have faithful representation, then which of the following is true?

a. The information represents to users what it claims to represent.
b. The information follows conservatism principles and is also material.
c. The information is considered pertinent to or affects decisions.
d. The information will have predictive value, feedback value, and is timely.

1.8 For accounting information to be relevant, it must have which of the following characteristics?

a. Predictive value or confirmatory value
b. Large in amount and timely
c. Comparability or consistency
d. Freedom from material error, neutrality, or completeness

1.9 Fundamental qualitative characteristics of accounting information are:

a. Relevance and comparability.
b. Comparability and consistency.
c. Relevance and faithful representation.
d. Faithful representation and consistency.

1.10 Enhancing qualitative characteristics of accounting information include:

ⓐ Relevance and understandability.
ⓑ Comparability and consistency.
ⓒ Relevance and faithful representation.
ⓓ Cost effectiveness and materiality.

CHAPTER 1 Exercises

1.1 Effect of transactions on assets

For each of the following transactions, show the effect (increase=+ ; decrease=− ; no effect=0) on assets.

		+, −, 0
ⓐ	Owner withdrew cash for personal use.	______
ⓑ	Purchased land on credit.	______
ⓒ	Made a cash sale.	______
ⓓ	Purchased a delivery truck for cash.	______
ⓔ	Paid a telephone bill.	______
ⓕ	Paid an account payable.	______
ⓖ	Sold merchandise on account.	______
ⓗ	Discussed plans with the bank for a future loan.	______

1.2 Accounting equation (1)

Write the missing amount for each of the following cases based on the accounting equation:

	Assets	Liabilities	Equity
ⓐ	$4,000	$2,500	$?
ⓑ	12,800	?	5,700
ⓒ	?	2,800	3,900
ⓓ	5,560	?	2,820
ⓔ	57,000	28,000	?

1.3 Accounting equation (2)

Compute the missing amount for each of the following cases based on the accounting equation:

	A	B	C
Cash	$5,970	$5,500	$8,000
Accounts Receivable	15,500	30,000	13,000
Office Supplies	2,700	5,000	2,500
Office Equipment	30,000		12,000
Land	14,000	2,500	10,000
Accounts Payable		5,000	2,000
Capital	49,000	57,500	

1.4 Accounting equation (3)

The liabilities of a company increased by $35,000 during a month and the owner's equity decreased by $21,000 during that same month.

Required:

How much did assets change during the month?

1.5 Accounting equation (4)

Answer questions for the following three independent situations.

ⓐ A company reports total assets of $2,500 and total liabilities of $900. What is the amount of owners' equity?

ⓑ A company reports total liabilities of $2,400 and owners' equity of $1,100. What is the amount of total assets?

ⓒ A company reports total assets of $2,800 and total owners' equity of $800. What is the amount of total liabilities?

1.6 Accounting equation (5)

Provide answers for the following two independent situations.

- ⓐ A company reports an increase in assets of $1,700 and an increase in liabilities of $400. What is the amount of the change in owners' equity?
- ⓑ A company reports an increase in liabilities of $500 and a decrease in owners' equity of $800. What is the amount of the change in total assets?

1.7 Business activities (1)

Below are typical transactions for a company.

Transactions

- ⓐ Purchase office building
- ⓑ Pay building insurance premium
- ⓒ Pay property taxes to the local government
- ⓓ Provide services to customers
- ⓔ Borrow money from the bank
- ⓕ Pay salaries to employees
- ⓖ Sell equipment used in operations
- ⓗ Sell ordinary shares (common stocks) to shareholders

Required:

Indicate whether each transaction is classified as an operating, investing, or financing activity.

1.8 Business activities (2)

Indicate whether a company would classify the transaction as financing, investing, or operating.

Transactions

- ⓐ Receive cash from investors
- ⓑ Pay rent for the current period
- ⓒ Pay cash dividends to shareholders
- ⓓ Purchase office equipment
- ⓔ Provide services to customers

1.9 Effect of transactions on accounting equation (1)

Charles Pryor invested his savings in a small laundry shop. Record the transactions listed below in the form provided; then total and prove the results.

a. Opened the shop by investing $15,000 in cash.
b. Bought $1,500 of supplies on account from Woodchuck Company.
c. Bought cleaning equipment for $8,500 cash.
d. Received cash for cleaning services, $1,550.
e. Paid salaries and other expenses of $450.
f. Bought additional $2,500 of supplies from Woodchuck Company; paid $1,500 cash, remainder on account.
g. Charles Pryor withdrew $500 for personal use.

	Assets					=	Liabilities	+	Equity
	Cash	+	Supplies	+	Equipment	=	Accounts Payable	+	C. Pryor, Capital
a									
Balance									
b									
Balance									
c									
Balance									
d									
Balance									
e									
Balance									
f									
Balance									
g									
Balance									

1.10 Effect of transactions on accounting equation (2)

Analyze the transactions of a business described below and indicate their effect on the accounting equation. Use a plus sign (+) to indicate an increase and a minus sign (−) to indicate a decrease.

	Assets	=	Liabilities	+	Equity
ⓐ Received cash for services rendered.	______		______		______
ⓑ Purchased office equipment on credit.	______		______		______
ⓒ Paid employees' salaries.	______		______		______
ⓓ Received cash from customer in payment of accounts receivable.	______		______		______
ⓔ Paid a telephone bill for the month.	______		______		______
ⓕ Paid for office equipment purchased in transaction ⓑ.	______		______		______
ⓖ Purchased inventory on credit.	______		______		______
ⓗ Paid dividends to shareholders.	______		______		______
ⓘ Obtained a loan from the bank.	______		______		______
ⓙ Billed customers for services rendered.	______		______		______

1.11 Effect of transactions on accounts

Following are transactions of Grackle Inc., a new company, during the month of January 20×2:

ⓐ Issued 10,000 shares of ordinary share for $15,000 cash.
ⓑ Purchased land for $12,000, signing a note payable for the full amount.
ⓒ Purchased office equipment for $1,200 cash.
ⓓ Received cash of $14,000 for services provided to customers during the month.
ⓔ Purchased $300 of office supplies on account.
ⓕ Paid employees $10,000 for their first month's salaries.

Required:

1. What is the balance of Grackle's Cash account following these six transactions?
2. What is the total amount of Grackle's liabilities following these six transactions?

1.12 Qualitative characteristics

Match each qualitative characteristic with its definition.

Qualitative characteristics

- ⓐ Completeness
- ⓑ Neutrality
- ⓒ Verifiability
- ⓓ Confirmatory value
- ⓔ Timeliness
- ⓕ Predictive value

Definitions

1. _____ Information provides feedback on past activities.
2. _____ All information necessary to describe an item is reported.
3. _____ Information is presented in time to make useful decisions.
4. _____ Measurements that independent parties would agree upon.
5. _____ Information that does not bias the decision maker.
6. _____ Information is useful in helping to forecast future outcomes.

ACCOUNTING TERMINOLOGY IN CHAPTER 1

a period of time 일정기간
a specific point in time 특정시점
accounting earnings 회계이익
accounting equation 회계등식
accounting information 회계정보
accounting standards 회계기준
accounts payable 외상매입금, 매입채무
accounts receivable 외상매출금, 매출채권
accrued liabilities 미지급부채
administrative expenses 관리비
assets 자산
auditing 회계감사
balance sheet 대차대조표
bond market 사채시장
bonds 사채
business entity 기업실체
business events 사업상의 사건
business firms 영리기업
business transactions 사업상의 거래
capital 자본금
capital providers 자본제공자
cash 현금
certified public accountant (CPA) 공인회계사
comparability 비교가능성
completeness 완전성
confirmatory value 확인가치
contributions from equity holders 지분보유자로부터의 출자
corporate income tax 법인세
corporation 주식회사
cost accounting 원가회계
cost of goods sold 매출원가
creditors 채권자
customers 고객
debt certificate 채무증서
distributions to equity holders 지분보유자에 대한 분배
double-entry bookkeeping system 복식부기제도
economic benefits 경제적 효익
economic decisions 경제의사결정
economic entity 경제실체
economic phenomena 경제적 현상
economic resources 경제적 자원
elements of financial statements 재무제표의 요소
employees 종업원
enhancing qualitative characteristics 보강적 질적특성
equipment 비품
equity 소유주지분
equity certificate 지분증서
equity interest 지분
excise tax 내국세, 소비세
expenses 비용
faithful representation 충실한 표현
financial accounting 재무회계
financial analysts 재무분석가

financial information 재무정보
financial position 재무상태
financial statement users 재무제표이용자
financial statements 재무제표
financing activities 재무활동
five major categories of accounts
계정의 5대 범주
free from error 무오류
fundamental qualitative characteristics
근본적 질적특성
general public 일반대중
general-purpose financial reporting
일반목적재무보고
general-purpose financial statements
일반목적재무제표
going concern 계속기업
goods 재화
governmental accounting 정부회계
income statement 손익계산서
income tax expense 법인세비용
income taxes payable 미지급법인세
information needs 정보요구사항
information-providing process 정보제공과정
interest expense 이자비용
interest revenue 이자수익
inventory 재고자산
investing activities 투자활동
investors 투자자
liabilities 부채
limited liability 유한책임
listed firm 상장회사
managerial accounting 관리회계
managers 경영자
manufacturing firm 제조회사
maturity 만기
municipal taxes 지방세
net assets 순자산, 소유주지분
net income or loss 당기순손익
neutrality 중립성
not-for-profit organization 비영리조직
office equipment 사무용비품
office supplies 사무용소모품
office supplies expense 사무용소모품비
on account 외상
operating activities 영업활동
operating performance 영업성과
ordinary shares (common stocks) 보통주
owners 소유주
owners' equity 소유주지분
partnership 파트너십
performance evaluation 성과평가
predictive value 예측가치
prepaid expenses 선급비용
present obligations 현재의무
profit or loss 당기순손익
public accounting 공공회계
qualitative characteristics 질적특성
rational economic decisions
합리적 경제의사결정
regulatory agencies 감독기관
relevance 목적적합성
rent expense 임차료
rent revenue 임대수익
reporting entity 보고실체
residual interest 잔여지분
resource providers 자원제공자
retail firm 소매회사
revenue 수익
salary expense 급여
sales revenue 매출수익, 매출액
securities 증권
security exchanges 증권거래소
selling expenses 판매비
service revenue 용역수익

services 용역
shareholders 주주
shares (stocks) 주식
sole proprietorship 개인기업
stakeholders 이해관계자
standard costs 표준원가
statement of cash flows 현금흐름표
statement of financial position 재무상태표
stock exchange 주식시장
suppliers 납품업자
tax accounting 세무회계
tax authorities 과세당국
taxable income 과세소득
timeliness 적시성
trade associations 산업연합회
transactions 거래
understandability 이해가능성
unlimited liability 무한책임
utility expense 공공요금
value-added tax 부가가치세
verifiability 검증가능성
wage 임금

CHAPTER

2

FINANCIAL STATEMENTS

2.1 INTRODUCTION

2.2 CASH BASIS VERSUS ACCRUAL BASIS OF ACCOUNTING

2.3 INCOME STATEMENT

2.4 STATEMENT OF FINANCIAL POSITION

2.5 CLASSIFIED FINANCIAL STATEMENTS

CHAPTER 2

FINANCIAL STATEMENTS

2.1 INTRODUCTION

There are four primary financial statements. They are the income statement, the statement of financial position, the statement of changes in equity, and the statement of cash flows. The income statement provides information on a company's operating performance during the current accounting period. The statement of financial position provides information on a company's financial position at a point in time. The statement of changes in owners' equity shows changes in various components of owners' equity during the current accounting period.[1] The statement of cash flows shows changes in cash from three business activities (operating activities, investing activities, and financing activities) during the current accounting period.

Operating performance is measured by profit or loss(당기순손익, net income). Net income is measured by subtracting expenses(비용) from revenues

1 The components of owners' equity comprise share capital(자본금, capital stock), share premium(주식할증발행차금, additional paid-in capital), retained earnings(유보이익, 이익잉여금), accumulated other comprehensive income(기타포괄손익누계액) and capital adjustments(자본조정).

(수익). These are shown in the income statement(손익계산서), also called the statement of financial performance or profit or loss (PL) statement. Details showing the sources and amounts of revenues and expenses are provided in the income statement.

Assets, liabilities, and owners' equity are reported in the statement of financial position(재무상태표), also called the balance sheet(대차대조표). Financial position or financial condition(재무상태) is measured by the relationship among an entity's assets, liabilities, and owners' equity. Owners' equity(소유주지분), also called net assets(순자산), is the difference between the entity's total assets and total liabilities at the end of the current reporting period. The statement of financial position lists the types and amounts of each asset, liability, and owners' equity account at the end of the reporting period. This listing is necessary so that the owners know what the business entity owns or controls (cash, inventory, machinery, and so forth), what is owed by the entity (accounts payable, accrued liabilities, loans payable, and so forth), and the ending balance of owners' equity in the business entity.

All the transactions(거래), events(사건), or circumstances(상황) that bring about changes in revenues, expenses, assets, liabilities, and owners' equity are either summarized in the income statement or statement of financial position. Net income, as measured by the difference between revenues and expenses, gives rise to changes in owners' equity. As a result, the income statement and statement of financial position are interrelated. In other words, changes in financial position (through changes in owners' equity) are partially explained by revenues and expenses reported on the income statement.

Changes in owners' equity may also arise from investments by owners(소유주에 의한 투자) or distributions to owners(소유주에 대한 분배). Investments by owners increase owners' equity, and distributions to owners decrease owners' equity. Transactions with the owners of the company are called capital transactions(자본거래). Capital transactions do not affect net income but owners' equity, thus the statement of financial position. The statement of changes in owners' equity shows changes in equity resulting from profit or loss and capital transactions.

Profit or loss can be determined by changes in the financial position that occurred during the period after reconciling capital transactions by using the relationship between the statement of financial position and the income statement. Namely, profit or loss (net income or loss) for a period can be determined as follows:

Profit or loss = Ending balance of owners' equity
− Beginning balance of owners' equity
− Investments by owners during the period
+ Distributions to owners during the period

EXAMPLE 2-1 ***Relationship between Income Statement and Statement of Financial Position***

At the end of September 20×1, the accounting records of Zinnia Company show the following account balances (see Example 1-1 of Chapter 1).

Accounts	Assets	Liabilities and Owners' Equity
Cash	$9,700	
Accounts Receivable	700	
Office Supplies	600	
Office Equipment	5,500	
Accounts Payable		$500
Owners' Equity		16,000
Total	$16,500	$16,500

Zinnia's assets increased from the original investment of $15,000 to the ending balance of $16,500. However, the increase of $1,500 does not reflect profit or loss for the period. In addition, changes in liabilities and withdrawals by the owner (representing a distribution to the owner) also cause changes in assets.

The initial net assets (assets minus liabilities) were $15,000, representing the original investment. The net assets at month's end were $16,000 (total assets of $16,500 minus liabilities of $500). The net assets for the month thus increased by $1,000. However, there was a withdrawal of $100 by the owner during the month. Hence, Zinnia must have made a net income of $1,100, computed as the increase of $1,000 in net assets for the period plus the $100 withdrawal by the owner.

Ending balance of owners' equity	$16,000
Less: Beginning balance of owners' equity	15,000
Less: Investments by owners	0
Add: Distributions to owners	100
Net income	$1,100

2.2 CASH BASIS VERSUS ACCRUAL BASIS OF ACCOUNTING

The income statement reports the operating performance of a business entity over a specified period. Thus, it must reflect revenue and expense items applicable to that period. Under the cash-basis accounting(현금주의회계), revenues and expenses are recognized when the related cash is received and disbursed. Thus, income statement recognition of transactions is tied to cash flows. Individuals and professionals like doctors or lawyers generally use the cash basis to measure what they earned for a given period. However, the cash basis accounting is inappropriate when considerable incongruence exists between cash inflows or outflows and the time the company sells or purchases the related items.

Under the accrual-basis accounting(발생주의회계), revenue is recognized when earned(가득되었을 때), and expenses are recognized when incurred(발생하였을 때). Most companies use the accrual-basis accounting in accordance with generally accepted accounting principles(일반적으로 인정된 회계원칙). Accrual-basis accounting means that transactions affecting a company's financial statements are recognized in the periods they occur rather than when the company receives or pays cash.

The revenue and expense recognition principles are based on the accrual-basis accounting. The revenue recognition principle(수익인식원칙) dictates that revenue be recognized in the accounting period it is earned. In a service company(용역회사), revenue is considered earned at the time the service is rendered. For example, assume a laundry business provided cleaning services to a client on October 30, but the client did not pay for the services until the end of November. Under the revenue recognition principle, revenue is earned in October when the service is rendered, not in November when cash is received. The expense recognition principle(비용인식원칙), also known as the matching principle(대응원칙), states that expenses should be deducted from the revenue to which they are directly related. Thus, expense recognition is tied to revenue recognition. For example, salary expenses incurred in rendering services to a client should be matched against the revenue earned from the services rendered. The accrual concept also requires the adjustment(수정) of income statement accounts at the end of a period to appropriately reflect revenues earned and expenses incurred for that period. The alignment of revenues and expenses with the period in which they were earned or incurred under the accrual-basis accounting is called adjusting entries(수정분개) or simply adjustments. Adjusting entries will be explained in more detail in Chapter 4.

EXAMPLE 2-2 *Accrual-basis Accounting*

For the month of January, employees who are paid bi-weekly were last paid on January 28. They have since worked three additional days (January 29~January 31) but will not be paid until the next payday, which is in early February. Assuming that the wage for the three days totals $200, what should be done to reflect the wage expense for the month of January properly?

According to accrual accounting, the company should accrue an additional wage expense of $200 for January to properly reflect the total wage expense for that month.

2.3 INCOME STATEMENT

The income statement(손익계산서) shows the *revenue*, *expenses*, and *profit or loss for a period of time*. A definition of each element follows.

Income(수익, *revenue*) is the increase in owners' equity arising from the sale of goods (as by a retail business) or the rendering of services (as by a doctor). When revenue is earned, it results in an increase in either Cash(현금) or Accounts Receivable(외상매출금) depending on whether it is a cash sale(현금판매) or credit sale(신용판매).

Expenses(비용), resulting from performing those functions necessary to generate revenue, decrease owners' equity. The amount of an expense is either the cost of goods sold, the value of services rendered (e.g., salary expense), or the expenditures for running business operations (e.g., rent expense) during the period.

Profit or loss(당기순손익) is the amount by which total revenues exceed total expenses or vice versa for the reporting period. Profit or net income(당기순이익) increases the owners' equity. However, if total expenses are greater than total revenues, a net loss(당기순손실) results, decreasing the owners' equity.

Revenue does not necessarily mean a cash receipt, and expense does not automatically imply a cash payment. Net income and net cash flows (cash receipts minus cash payments) are different. For example, borrowing from a bank will generate cash inflows. However, this is not revenue since goods have not been sold, nor have services been provided. Further, the owners' equity has not been altered because of the loan. Profit or loss results from revenue and expense transactions as they are recognized in the income statement. Some transactions affect assets, liabilities, and owners' equity but may not affect profit or loss if they are not revenue or expense transactions like taking out a bank loan. Other examples not affecting revenues or expenses include purchasing assets, paying dividends, and issuing shares. More specifically, operating activities(영업활동) affect revenues and expenses. However, investing activities(투자활동) or financing activities(재무활동) do not affect revenues or expenses by themselves. In other words, the results of operating activities are summarized in the income statement, while the results of operating, investing, and financing activities collectively affect the statement of financial position.

EXAMPLE 2-3 *Income Statement*

During October 20×1, Alyssum Company earned $10,000 from services rendered. Expenses incurred during the period were: salary $2,300, rent $2,000, utilities (telephone and electricity) $1,500, and office supplies used $400.

Then, the income statement for the period is as follows:

Alyssum Company
Income Statement
For the Month Ended October 31, 20×1

Service Revenue		$10,000
Less: Operating Expenses		
Salary Expense	$2,300	
Rent Expense	2,000	
Utility Expense	1,500	
Office Supplies Expense	400	
Total Operating Expenses		6,200
Net Income		$3,800

Note that each revenue and expense item has its own account. This specificity enables users to evaluate and control revenue and expense sources and examine relationships among account categories. For instance, the ratio of utility expense(공공요금) to revenue is 15 percent ($1,500/$10,000). If in the previous month the relationship was 5 percent, the manager of the company would, no doubt, attempt to determine the cause for this significant increase.

At the end of the accounting period, net income is transferred (added) to the owners' equity account. In the above example, the net income of $3,800 would be added to the owners' equity on October 31, 20×1.

2.4 STATEMENT OF FINANCIAL POSITION

The statement of financial position(재무상태표) portrays the financial position of a business entity by listing the balances of assets, liabilities, and owners' equity at the *end* of the reporting period. For the case presented in Example 2-3, the end of the reporting period is October 31, 20×1. The statement of financial position is subject to the accounting equation.

$$\text{Assets} = \text{Liabilities} + \text{Equity}$$

The statement of financial position provides a "snapshot" picture of a company's financial position at a point in time. In contrast, the income statement provides a "video" picture of a company's operating activities which are summarized as profit earned over a period of time (for example, for the month of October, 20×1). In addition, the statement of financial position provides "stock(잔액, 저량)" information which is a cumulative amount. The income statement, in contrast, provides "flow(흐름, 유량)" information so that it can partially explain changes in retained earnings which is a statement of financial position item. The statement of financial position is useful for decision-making because it indicates what kind of resources the entity has and what kind of obligations it owes.

The statement of financial position may be prepared either in *report form*(보

고식) or *account form*(계정식). In the report form, assets, liabilities, and owners' equity are listed vertically. In the account form, assets are reported on the left side, and liabilities and owners' equity are reported on the right side.

EXAMPLE 2-4 *The Statement of Financial Position*

In addition to the information given in Example 2-3, Alyssum Company has the following additional accounts as of October 31:

Cash \$10,000; Accounts receivable \$50,500; Office supplies \$10,500; Office equipment \$30,000; Accounts payable \$30,000; owners' equity (before including net income of \$3,800 for the month of October) \$67,600; withdrawal made by the owner of the company, Caroline Alyssum, for her personal use during the month \$400.

Prepare the statement of financial position for Alyssum Company on October 31, 20×1 using the report form.

Alyssum Company
Statement of Financial Position
October 31, 20×1

Assets			
Cash			\$10,000
Accounts Receivable			50,500
Office Supplies			10,500
Office Equipment			30,000
Total Assets			\$101,000
Liabilities and Equity			
Liabilities			
Accounts Payable			\$30,000
Owners' Equity			
Balance, October 1, 20×1		\$67,600	
Net Income for October	\$3,800		
Less: Withdrawals	400	3,400	
Total Owners' Equity			71,000
Total Liabilities & Equity			\$101,000

From the examples given, it is evident that a tie exists between the income statement and the statement of financial position. Net income of \$3,800 (the last item in the income statement from Example 2-3) is added to owners' equity in the statement of financial position in Example 2-4. In effect, the income statement serves as a bridge between two consecutive statements of financial position.

2.5 CLASSIFIED FINANCIAL STATEMENTS

Businesses differ in nature. Therefore, specific transactions differ from business to business. Hence, to facilitate financial analysis and understanding, it is helpful to classify the elements of financial statements into major categories. Financial statements organized in such a fashion are called classified financial statements(분류형재무제표).

(1) Classified Income Statement

In a classified income statement(분류형손익계산서), the amounts for each major revenue and expense group are listed to facilitate the analysis of the statement by financial statement users. The elements in classified income statements covering different periods are easily compared. A comparison over several periods (called trend analysis) of revenue sources, expense items, and the relationship between them might reveal areas requiring attention and corrective action. For example, if revenue from services has been sharply declining over the past several months, management will want to take action to reverse this negative trend.

The elements in an income statement can be classified following the 'function of expense method(기능별비용법)' or the 'nature of expense method(성격별비용법).'

Under the function of expense method, the income statement elements can be classified into four primary functions: revenue, cost of goods sold, operating expenses, and other revenues and expenses.

Revenue(수익) comprises the gross income generated by selling goods (sales revenue) or rendering services (service revenue). Revenue typically results in an inflow of assets, settlement of liabilities, or a combination of both.

Cost of goods sold(매출원가) is the cost of goods sold or services rendered. For example, in a retail business(소매업), it is the cost of buying goods from the manufacturer (e.g., the cost of a toy). In a service business(서비스업, 용역업), it is the cost of services rendered.

Operating expenses(영업비) consist of all expenses incurred or resources used in generating revenues. Operating expenses typically consist of selling expenses and administrative expenses. *Selling expenses*(판매비) are those incurred in selling goods or services (e.g., advertising and promotion, salespeople's salaries) and in distributing goods to the customers (e.g., shipping and handling expenses). They relate solely to the selling function. For example, a sales manager is usually responsible for generating sales in a large business. And the manager's performance is judged on the relationship between promotion costs incurred and sales made. *Administrative expenses*(관리비) apply to the costs of running the business as a whole and do not relate to the selling function. Examples are the salaries of office clerical staff, administrative executive salaries, and general business liability insurance.

Other revenues and expenses(기타수익, 기타비용) apply to incidental sources of revenues and expenses that are of a *nonoperating*(비영업) nature. Other revenues and expenses do not relate to the major activities of the business. Examples are interest income(이자수익), dividend income(배당수익), and interest expense(이자비용).

Under the nature of expense method, the elements of the income statement can be classified into revenue(수익), other income(기타수익), changes in inventory (재고자산변동), raw materials and consumables used(원재료 및 소모품 사용액), employee benefits expense(종업원급여비용), depreciation and amortization expense (감가상각 및 상각비), and other expenses(기타비용).

Example 2-5 shows a classified income statement following the function of expense method.

Example 2-5 *Classified Income Statement*

Clematis Company
Income Statement
For the Year Ended December 31, 20×1

Net Sales			$38,500
Cost of Goods Sold			
Inventory, January 1		$1,000	
Add: Purchases		15,000	
Cost of Goods Available for Sale		16,000	
Less: Inventory, December 31		5,000	11,000
Gross Profit			27,500
Operating Expenses			
Selling Expenses			
Advertising and Promotion Expenses	$3,000		
Salespeople's Salaries Expense	2,000		
Distribution Expense	1,000		
Depreciation Expense	500	6,500	
Administrative Expenses			
Office Salaries Expense	5,000		
Rent Expense	2,000		
Insurance Expense	1,000	8,000	
Total Operating Expenses			14,500
Operating Income			13,000
Other Expenses			
Interest Expense			500
Net Income			$12,500

(2) Statement of Changes in Owners' Equity

The statement of changes in owners' equity(소유주지분변동표, 자본변동표) acts as a bridge connecting the income statement and the statement of financial position. If the statement of changes in owners' equity is prepared, the statement of financial position will show only the ending balance of owners' equity. Therefore, the ending balance of owners' equity is updated as follows:

Beginning balance
+Investments by owners(소유주에 의한 투자)
+Net income(당기순이익) or −Net loss(당기순손실)
−Dividends(배당)

It should be noted that when the statement of owners' equity is prepared for a corporation(주식회사), the owners' equity section in the statement of financial position is shown as shareholders' equity, which typically consists of contributed capital(납입자본) and retained earnings(이익잉여금). Contributed capital is equal to share capital(자본금, capital stock) plus share premium(자본잉여금, additional paid-in capital). Net income earned during the period is added to the retained earnings, while net loss incurred is subtracted from it. Dividends to shareholders are paid out of retained earnings. Drawing(인출금) is not an expense but a withdrawal by owners for personal use in the case of a proprietorship(개인기업). Dividends are a corporation's distribution of assets (typically cash) to its shareholders. Therefore, the payment of dividends is a reduction in shareholders' equity but not an expense.

EXAMPLE 2-6 *Statement of Changes in Owners' Equity*

Let's suppose that Clematis Company is a corporation and has the following information for the year ended December 31, 20×1.

Share Capital, January 1, 20×1	$15,000
Retained earnings, January 1, 20×1	$15,500
Net Income earned during 20×1	$12,500 (See Example 2-5)
Dividends paid during 20×1	$4,000

Suppose that there are no other items affecting the owners' equity.

Then, we can prepare the statement of changes in owners' equity for Clematis Company for the year ended December 31, 20×1 as follows:

Clematis Company
Statement of Changes in Owners' Equity
For the Year Ended December 31, 20×1

Share Capital, January 1		$15,000
Retained Earnings, January 1	$15,500	
Add: Net Income for the year	12,500	
Less: Dividends	(4,000)	24,000
Owners' Equity, December 31		$39,000

(3) Classified Statement of Financial Position

The statement of financial position is classified into major groups of assets and liabilities in order to facilitate analysis of the entity's financial health. For example, a company's liquidity(유동성), which shows its short-term ability to meet current debts with current assets, can be evaluated by comparing current assets(유동자산) with current liabilities(유동부채). Another valuable analysis to check the financial health of a company is to compare total liabilities(총부채) with owners' equity(소유주지분).

A classified statement of financial position(분류형재무상태표) generally breaks down assets into four categories: current assets; long-term investments; property, plant, and equipment; and intangible assets.

Current assets(유동자산) are those assets that are expected to be converted into cash or used up within one year or the normal operating cycle(영업주기) of the business, whichever is longer. The operating cycle is a cash-to-cash cycle that goes through the process of using cash to purchase inventory, selling the inventory, holding the accounts receivable, and collecting the receivables. In effect, the process begins with paying cash and ends with receiving cash in the operating cycle. In most cases, the asset classification is based on one year. Examples of current assets are cash, accounts receivable(외상매출금), inventory(재고자산), and prepaid expenses. Prepaid expenses(선급비용) are expenditures whose benefits will expire within one year from the statement of financial position date. A prepaid expense represents a prepayment for an expense that has not yet been incurred or consumed. For instance, if there is a Prepaid Insurance(선급보험료) of $1,000 as of December 31, 20×1 on an insurance policy(보험증권), which has eight months until expiry, the account would be listed under current assets.

Long-term investments(장기투자자산) refer to investments in other company stocks(주식) or bonds(사채) where the intent is to hold them for a period greater than one year (which is often the case). Investments in securities(투자증권) are reported in the statement of financial position at the original purchase cost or current market values, depending on their nature. Purchase cost includes the market price of the securities and brokerage fees. Note that if the intent is to hold the securities for one year or less, they would be included in the current asset category and reported as short-term financial assets(단기금융자산).

Property, plant, and equipment(유형자산, PP&E) are assets employed in the production of goods or services with an economic useful life(경제적 내용연수) greater than one year. Furthermore, they are *tangible* in nature, which means that they have physical substance(물리적 실질). In other words, PP&E can be physically identified. Examples of PP&E include land, buildings, machinery, and automobiles. Unlike inventory, PP&E is not held for sale in the ordinary course of business.

Intangible assets(무형자산) are assets with a long-term life that lack physical substance. The value of some intangible assets originates from legal rights(법적 권리) granted by the government, such as patents(특허권), copyrights (저작권), and trademarks(상표권). The value of other intangible assets originates from contractual rights(계약상 권리) granted by other companies, such as licenses and franchises. McDonald's, KFC, Pizza Hut, and BBQ Chicken are typical examples of franchises.

When one or more asset categories are immaterial relative to total assets, such categories can be listed under one caption called other assets.

Liabilities(부채) are also classified as either current or noncurrent. As noted above, one year is the demarcation line most often used in classifying them into current or noncurrent. *Current liabilities*(유동부채) will usually be satisfied out of current assets. Examples of current liabilities are accounts payable(외상매입금), short-term notes payable(단기지급어음), and accrued liabilities. Accounts payable are promises to pay when goods or services are purchased on account. In contrast, notes payable are promissory notes that may originate from credit purchases or borrowings. *Accrued liabilities*(발생부채 또는 미지급부채) are liabilities resulting from expenses incurred but not paid at the end of the reporting period. Therefore, accrued liabilities are also called accrued expenses(발생비용, 미지급비용).

Examples of *long-term liabilities*(장기부채), which have a maturity of longer than a year, are long-term notes payable(장기지급어음), long-term debts(장기차입금), bonds payable(사채), and mortgages payable(담보부채). Long-term liabilities are usually interest-bearing liabilities(이자부부채), whereas short-term liabilities are usually non-interest-bearing liabilities(무이자부부채).

Current maturities of long-term liabilities(유동성장기부채), which are to be paid within one year, are to be shown under current liabilities. In other words, the portion due within one year must be reclassified to current liabilities out of noncurrent liabilities. For example, if $1,000 of a $10,000 mortgage payable(담보부채) is to be paid within the following year, that $1,000 would be reclassified as a current liability; the remaining $9,000 would be shown under noncurrent liabilities.

EXAMPLE 2-7 ***Classified Statement of Financial Position***

Clematis Company
Statement of Financial Position
December 31, 20×1

Assets		
Current Assets		
Cash	$3,000	
Accounts Receivable	6,000	
Inventory	5,000	
Office Supplies	1,000	
Total Current Assets		$15,000
Long-Term Investments		
Investments in Other Company Shares		2,000
Property, Plant, and Equipment		
Land	20,000	
Building	30,000	
Machinery	7,000	
Equipment	5,000	
Total Property, Plant, and Equipment		62,000
Intangible Assets		
Patents		4,000
Total Assets		$83,000
Liabilities and Equity		
Current Liabilities		
Accounts Payable	8,000	
Notes Payable	4,000	
Accrued Liabilities	2,000	
Total Current Liabilities		14,000
Noncurrent Liabilities		
Mortgage Payable		30,000
Total Liabilities		44,000
Owners' Equity, December 31 (see Example 2-6)		39,000
Total Liabilities and Equity		$83,000

CHAPTER 2

Multiple Choice Questions

2.1 The primary difference between accrual-basis and cash-basis accounting is:

ⓐ The timing of when revenues and expenses are recorded.
ⓑ Cash-basis accounting is allowed for financial reporting purposes but not accrual-basis accounting.
ⓒ Accrual-basis accounting violates both the revenue recognition and matching principles.
ⓓ Adjusting entries are only a necessary part of cash-basis accounting.

2.2 Edelweiss had the following final balances after the first year of operations: assets, $55,000; shareholders' equity, $25,000; dividends, $3,000; and net income, $10,000. What is the amount of Edelweiss's liabilities?

ⓐ $55,000
ⓑ $30,000
ⓒ $13,000
ⓓ $7,000

2.3 Use the following appropriate amounts to calculate net income: Revenues, $12,000; Liabilities, $5,000; Expenses, $4,000; Assets, $19,000; Dividends, $4,000.

ⓐ $6,000
ⓑ $8,000
ⓒ $4,000
ⓓ $14,000

2.4 Colonial Company has had a net income of $8,000, $5,000, $12,000, and $10,000 over the first four years of the company's existence. What is the ending balance of retained earnings if the annual dividends paid over the last four years average $3,000?

- a $47,000
- b $35,000
- c $23,000
- d $7,000

2.5 Which of the following items would not appear in an income statement?

- a Salaries expense
- b Advertising expense
- c Service revenue
- d Cash

2.6 Which of the following statements regarding financial reports is not correct?

- a A statement of financial position contains assets, liabilities, and shareholders' equity information.
- b An income statement shows revenues and expenses.
- c A statement of shareholders' equity reports revenues, net income, and dividend information.
- d A statement of cash flows shows cash inflows and outflows from operating, investing, and financing activities.

2.7 Expenses are shown in which of the following statements?

- a Income statement
- b Statement of cash flows
- c Statement of financial position
- d Statement of shareholders' equity

2.8 The ending balance of retained earnings is calculated using:

- ⓐ Beginning retained earnings, net income, and dividends.
- ⓑ Ordinary share and dividends.
- ⓒ Shareholders' equity, net income, and dividends.
- ⓓ Net income and dividends.

2.9 Liabilities are shown in which of the following statements?

- ⓐ Income statement
- ⓑ Statement of cash flows
- ⓒ Statement of financial position
- ⓓ Statement of shareholders' equity

2.10 The owners' interest in a corporation is called:

- ⓐ Dividends.
- ⓑ Assets.
- ⓒ Liabilities.
- ⓓ Shareholders' equity.

CHAPTER 2

Exercises

2.1 Elements of financial statements

Match each element of financial statements with its definition.

Elements

ⓐ Assets
ⓑ Liabilities
ⓒ Equity
ⓓ Revenue
ⓔ Expenses

Definitions

1. _____ Increase in economic benefits during the accounting period other than those relating to contributions from equity participants
2. _____ Present obligations which are expected to result in outflows of resources
3. _____ Resources controlled by the entity from which future economic benefits are expected to flow to the entity
4. _____ Decrease in economic benefits during the accounting period other than those relating to distributions to equity participants
5. _____ Residual interests in the assets of the entity after deducting all its liabilities

2.2 Change in capital (1)

Basil Company's capital as of January 1, 20×1 was $10,000. During the year, the net income was $18,000, and the owner withdrew $5,000.

Required:

How much is the capital as of December 31, 20×1?

2.3 Change in capital (2)

Income statement data for Rosemary Company is as follows: Service revenue of $20,000; advertising expense of $4,000; salaries expense of $6,000; utility expense of $2,000.

Required:

If the owner withdrew $3,000 from the business, what was the increase or decrease in the capital?

2.4 Cash basis vs. accrual basis accounting

On July 1, 20×1, Sumac Inc. paid $72,000 for 36 months of advance rent on its warehouse. What would be the amount of rent expense in the 20×2 financial statements for Sumac under both cash-basis and accrual-basis accounting?

2.5 Income statement

Prepare an income statement from the following data: Service revenue of $50,000; utility expense of $5,000; salaries expense of $10,000; rent expense of $12,000.

2.6 Retained earnings

Burdock has an ending Retained Earnings balance of $50,000. If Burdock paid dividends of $4,300 and had a net income of $22,500 during the year, then what was the beginning balance of Retained Earnings?

2.7 Statement of financial position

The following are accounts of Mint Company's business as of September 30, 20×1: Notes payable $5,000; accounts receivable $1,500; cash $2,500; land $11,000; accounts payable $400; building $7,500; equipment $3,100; truck $2,800; mortgage payable $_________; Capital $18,000.

Required:

Prepare a statement of financial position as of September 30, 20×1.

2.8 Classified statement of financial position (1)

On April 1, 20×1, Holly Johnson started a new business. She invested $10,000 in cash and $500 in office equipment during the month. She also bought a small building and a lot with a note payable for $8,500 and $10,000, respectively. Holly Johnson then purchased a used truck for $1,000 cash.

Required:

Prepare a classified statement of financial position for Holly Johnson as of April 30, 20×1.

2.9 Classified statement of financial position (2)

Xiaochen Corporation has the following financial information before preparing the statement of financial position on December 31, 20×1.

Accounts	$	Accounts	$
Cash	10,000	Accounts Payable	13,000
Accounts Receivable	14,000	Other Current Liabilities	11,000
Merchandise Inventory	30,000	Long-term Debt	30,000
PP&E	66,000	Share Capital	50,000
Intangible Assets	12,000	Retained Earnings, January 1	12,000
Expenses	78,000	Revenues	98,000
Dividends	4,000		

Required:

Prepare a classified statement of financial position for Xiaochen Corporation as of December 31, 20×1.

2.10 Financial statements (1)

Mantaray Company provides personal healthcare consulting services to individuals. On December 31, 20×1, the end of the current fiscal year, the balances of selected accounts from the accounting records of Mantaray Company are as follows:

Accounts	$	Accounts	$
Cash	6,350	Accounts Payable	8,650
Accounts Receivable	21,050	Salaries Payable	3,500
Supplies	1,100	Unearned Service Revenue	2,700
Prepaid Rent	7,800	Accumulated Depreciation	25,900
Equipment	65,300	Capital	57,710
Salaries Expense	16,300	Service Revenue	44,500
Advertising Expense	2,200		
Rent Expense	3,200		
Utility Expense	5,890		
Depreciation Expense	1,690		
Supplies Expense	2,880		
Income Tax Expense	1,450		
Other Expenses	7,750		

Required:

Prepare an income statement for the year ended December 31, 20×1 and a statement of financial position as of December 31, 20×1 for Mantaray Company.

2.11 Financial statements (2)

Account balances for Willow Company on December 31, 20×1 are presented below:

	Debit	Credit
Cash	$18,000	
Prepaid Rent	15,000	
Buildings and Equipment	601,000	
Accumulated Depreciation		$193,000
Accounts Payable		10,000
Salaries Payable		14,000
Income Taxes Payable		47,400
Share Capital - Ordinary		250,000
Retained Earnings		64,000
Dividends	10,000	
Service Revenue		350,000
Salaries Expense	180,000	
Rent Expense	31,000	
Utility Expense	26,000	
Income Tax Expense	47,400	
Totals	$928,400	$928,400

Required:

Prepare the income statement and the statement of financial position for the year ended December 31, 20×1.

2.12 Financial statements (3)

Account balances for Woodruff Company on December 31, 20×1 are presented below:

	Debit	Credit
Cash	$15,000	
Accounts Receivable	146,000	
Prepaid Rent	5,000	
Supplies	24,000	
Equipment	300,000	
Accumulated Depreciation		$135,000
Accounts Payable		18,000
Salaries Payable		6,000
Interest Payable		1,000
Notes Payable - due in two years		30,000
Share Capital - Ordinary		200,000
Retained Earnings		50,000
Dividends	20,000	
Sales Revenue		400,000
Salaries Expense	180,000	
Advertising Expense	70,000	
Rent Expense	15,000	
Depreciation Expense	30,000	
Interest Expense	2,000	
Utility Expense	33,000	
Totals	$840,000	$840,000

Required:

Prepare Income Statement and Statement of Financial Position for the year ended December 31, 20×1.

ACCOUNTING TERMINOLOGY IN CHAPTER 2

account form 계정식
accounts payable 외상매입금
accounts receivable 외상매출금
accrual-basis 발생주의
accrual-basis accounting 발생주의회계
accrued expenses 발생비용, 미지급비용
accrued liabilities 발생부채, 미지급부채
accumulated other comprehensive income 기타포괄손익누계액
additional paid-in capital 주식할증발행차금, 자본잉여금
adjusting entries 수정분개
adjustments 수정
administrative expenses 관리비
amortization expense 상각비
balance sheet 대차대조표
bonds 사채
bonds payable 사채
capital adjustments 자본조정
capital stock 자본금
capital transactions 자본거래
cash-basis 현금주의
cash-basis accounting 현금주의회계
cash sales 현금판매
changes in inventory 재고자산변동
circumstances 상황
classified financial statements 분류형재무제표
classified income statement 분류형손익계산서
classified statement of financial position 분류형재무상태표
consumables 소모품
contractual rights 계약상 권리
contributed capital 납입자본
copyrights 저작권
corporation 주식회사
cost of goods sold 매출원가
credit sales 신용판매
current assets 유동자산
current liabilities 유동부채
current maturities of long-term liabilities 유동성장기부채
depreciation expense 감가상각비
distributions to owners 소유주에 대한 분배
dividend income 배당수익
dividends 배당
drawing 인출금
economic useful life 경제적 내용연수
employee benefits expense 종업원급여비용
events 사건
expense recognition principle 비용인식원칙
expenses 비용
financing activities 재무활동
flow 흐름, 유량
function of expense method 기능별비용법
generally accepted accounting principles 일반적으로 인정된 회계원칙
income 수익
income statement 손익계산서

insurance policy 보험증권
intangible assets 무형자산
interest-bearing liabilities 이자부부채
interest expense 이자비용
interest income 이자수익
inventory 재고자산
investing activities 투자활동
investments by owners 소유주에 의한 투자
investments in securities 투자증권
legal rights 법적 권리
liabilities 부채
liquidity 유동성
long-term debts 장기차입금
long-term investments 장기투자자산
long-term liabilities 장기부채
long-term notes payable 장기지급어음
matching principle 대응원칙
mortgage payable 담보부채
nature of expense method 성격별비용법
net assets 순자산, 소유주지분
net income 당기순이익
net loss 당기순손실
net sales 순매출액
non-interest-bearing liabilities 무이자부부채
nonoperating 비영업
operating activities 영업활동
operating cycle 영업주기
operating expenses 영업비
other expense 기타비용
other revenue 기타수익
owners' equity 소유주지분
patents 특허권
physical substance 물리적 실질
prepaid expenses 선급비용
prepaid insurance 선급보험료
profit or loss 당기순손익
property, plant, and equipment (PP&E) 유형자산
proprietorship 개인기업
raw materials 원재료
report form 보고식
retail business 소매업
retained earnings 이익잉여금, 유보이익
revenue 수익
revenue recognition principle 수익인식원칙
selling expenses 판매비
service business 서비스업, 용역업
service company 용역회사
shares 주식
share capital 자본금
share premium 주식할증발행차금
short-term financial assets 단기금융자산
short-term notes payable 단기지급어음
statement of changes in owners' equity 자본변동표, 소유주지분변동표
statement of financial performance 손익계산서, 재무성과표
statement of financial position 재무상태표
stock 잔액, 저량
stocks 주식
total liabilities 총부채
total revenues 총수익
trademarks 상표권
transactions 거래
utility expense 공공요금
when earned 가득되었을 때
when incurred 발생하였을 때

CHAPTER

3

RECORDING TRANSACTIONS

CHAPTER 3

RECORDING TRANSACTIONS

3.1 INTRODUCTION

Recording each transaction in the frame of the accounting equation of 'Assets = Liabilities + Equity' would be highly time-consuming. Also, information about a specific item (e.g., collection of accounts receivable) would be lost through this process. Therefore, an account(계정) should be established to record each type of item in the accounting books. An account in bookkeeping (부기) refers to individual items of assets, liabilities, revenues, expenses, and equity to which changes in value are chronologically recorded with debit and credit entries (to be explained later). Then, at the end of the reporting period, the financial statements can be prepared based on the balances in these accounts.

3.2 ACCOUNTING CYCLE

Firms need to follow specific steps in processing accounting transactions and other events into financial statements. This process is known as the accounting cycle. The accounting cycle(회계순환과정) consists of the steps as presented in Table 3-1.

Table 3-1 The Accounting Cycle

The accounting cycle consists of six necessary steps and some optional steps. (Businesses enter into transactions, signaling the beginning of the accounting cycle)	
Step One	**Analyze the transactions**(거래의 분석).
Step Two	Record the effects of transactions in a journal (**Journal entry**, 분개).
Step Three	Summarize the effects of transactions by **posting**(전기) journal entries to ledger accounts.
Optional	Prepare a **trial balance**(시산표) to check the correctness of journal entries and the posting process and to help prepare financial statements.
Step Four	Prepare the **adjusting entries**(수정분개).
Optional	Prepare a **worksheet**(정산표) as a tool for the preparation of financial statements.
Step Five	Prepare the **financial statements**(재무제표의 작성).
Step Six	**Close** the temporary accounts(임시계정마감).
Optional	Prepare the **reversing entries**(역분개).

We will address each step in the accounting cycle one by one below.

3.3 ACCOUNTS

An account(계정) is an individual unit of accounting record in which increases and decreases in a specific asset, liability, owners' equity, revenue, or expense item are recorded. For example, each company has separate accounts for cash (현금), accounts receivable(매출채권), supplies(소모품), building(건물), machinery (기계장치), accounts payable(매입채무), service revenue(용역수익), salaries expense

(급여), and so on. A separate account exists for each item shown on the financial statements. Thus, the statement of financial position accounts consists of assets, liabilities, and owners' equity. The income statement accounts are either expenses or revenues. Each account shows increases, decreases, and the current balance of the item. For example, an increase in the cash account arises from receiving cash, while a decrease results when a cash payment occurs.

The account can be easily understood using the simplest version, called a 'T account.' T account (T계정), shown in Figure 3-1, consists of a name, a debit side, and a credit side. The term debit(차변) indicates left, and credit(대변) indicates right. They are commonly abbreviated as Dr. for debit and Cr. for credit. These terms come from Latin words that originally meant 'debtor' and 'creditor.' Now, they are merely directional signals. They do not mean increase or decrease, as is commonly thought. The terms debit and credit are used repeatedly in the recording process to describe where entries are recorded. For example, recording an amount on the left side of an account is called 'debiting.' Recording an entry on the right side is 'crediting.' When the totals of the two sides are compared, an account will have a debit balance if the total of the debit amounts exceeds the total of the credit amounts. Conversely, an account will have a credit balance if the credit amounts exceed the debit amounts.

Account Title	
Debit	Credit

Figure 3-1 T Account

Increases and decreases are entered into the account. The side in which the increase or decrease is entered depends upon the nature of the item. For example, being an asset, cash is debited when a transaction increases cash, while cash will be credited when cash decreases as a result of a transaction. Recording journal entries will be discussed further in Section 3.6. The account balance(계정잔액) at the end of the period appears on the side having the greater amount.

Although the "T" account form is usually the most convenient to use, an account form that permits the listing of more detailed information, including a running balance(현시점잔액), is used in practice. Such an account form is shown in Figure 3-2.

		Cash			*Account No. 101*
Date	Explanation	Reference	Debit	Credit	Balance

Figure 3-2 Account – An Example

The *Date* column is for transaction dates. Although seldom used, the *Explanation* column describes any necessary transaction particulars. The *Reference* column indicates the journal(분개장) page number in which the transaction was initially recorded (the journal is explained in Section 3.4). Finally, the *Balance* column shows the new balance after each debit or credit entry.

3.4 TWO ACCOUNTING BOOKS: JOURNAL AND LEDGER

There are two accounting books. The first one is the *journal*(분개장), and the second one is the *ledger*(원장). In accounting practice, business transactions are first recorded in the journal from information in the source documents (e.g., telephone bills). The data are then transferred from the journal to the ledger by debiting and crediting the particular accounts involved. This process is called *posting*(전기). The journal is a book of original entries in which transactions are usually entered daily in chronological order. This process is called journalizing or *journal entry*(분개). Debits and credits are listed along with the appropriate explanations. Thus, the journal reflects all information about a transaction in one place.

Different types of journals exist, which may be grouped into the categories of (1) general journals(일반분개장) and (2) special journals(특수분개장). The latter is used when there are many repetitive transactions (e.g., sales). A typical form of a general journal is shown in Figure 3-3.

		General Journal		*Page No.*
Date	Accounts	Posting Reference	Debit	Credit

Figure 3-3 General Journal

The *Date* column contains the year, month, and day of transactions. The year and month are not repeated for later transactions unless there is a new page or month. The *Accounts* column shows the account debited, the name of which is entered close to the left margin. The dollar amount of the debit is listed in the *Debit* column. The account credited is indented and entered directly underneath the account debited in the *Accounts* column, with the amount entered in the *Credit* column. Directly beneath the credit entry, an explanation for the transaction is given in the Accounts column. If there is a compound entry (an entry with three or more accounts), all debits are listed before the credits. The *Posting Reference* (P.R., 전기조회) column is used for the ledger account number after posting the journal information to the ledger. The posting reference provides a cross-reference between the journal and the ledger. A blank line is left after each journal entry.

All accounts of an entity are kept in a separate book called the '*ledger*(원장).' The ledger classifies and summarizes all the transactions to provide information for preparing the income statement and the statement of financial position. The ledger is also helpful for decision-making because it provides information on the balance in a given account at a particular time. For example, if the business seems poor, managers can adjust the sales plan upward for the reporting period. Similarly, managers may want to know the cash balance at the end of the reporting period to determine whether adequate funds are available to meet operating requirements.

3.5 CHART OF ACCOUNTS

The sequence and numbering of ledger accounts are customarily in the order in which they appear in the financial statements. First, the statement of financial position accounts like assets, liabilities, and owners' equity are listed. Then the income statement accounts like revenues and expenses follow. Of course, the more complex the organization, the greater the number of accounts required. Therefore, each account has its unique number. A listing of the account names and numbers is called the '*chart of accounts*(계정과목표).' The order in which the accounts are listed in the chart of accounts is referred to as the *chart of accounts order*. The chart helps locate a given account within the ledger.

The numbering system for the chart of accounts must leave room for new accounts. Therefore, a range of numbers is assigned to each financial statement category. For example, suppose a company uses a three-digit chart of the accounts system. In that case, it may assign 101-199 to asset accounts, 201-299 to liability accounts, 301-399 to owners' equity accounts, 401-499

Chart of Accounts (partial) – An Illustration

Account Title	Account Number
ASSETS	
Current Assets	
Cash	101
Accounts Receivable	111
Inventory	121
Property, Plant, and Equipment	
Land	141
Building	142
Equipment	143
LIABILITIES	
Current Liabilities	
Accounts Payable	201

Figure 3-4 Chart of Accounts

to revenue accounts, and 501-599 to expense accounts. An illustrative partial chart of accounts is shown in Figure 3-4.

For large businesses, a wider range of numbers would be required for each financial statement grouping. In practice, some companies employ a three-digit numbering system for each account. In such a case, the first digit identifies the financial statement category, and the remaining digits apply to the position of that account within that category. For example, 1 may be the first digit for assets, and cash, the first asset account, would be assigned 101.

3.6 ENTERING DEBITS AND CREDITS IN THE ACCOUNTS

As previously mentioned, a debit (Dr.) is entered on the left side of an account, and a credit (Cr.) on the right side. Debits are sometimes called charges. By convention, increases in assets and expenses are debited. Hence, decreases in these accounts are credited. On the other hand, increases in liabilities, owners' equity, and revenue are credited. Thus, decreases in these accounts are debited. This rule is illustrated in Figure 3-5.

Each transaction involves two or more accounts. In recording a transaction, the debit amount must always equal the credit amount. The

Assets	
Dr. Increase	Cr. Decrease

Liabilities	
Dr. Decrease	Cr. Increase

Equity	
Dr. Decrease	Cr. Increase

Expenses	
Dr. Increase	Cr. Decrease

Revenues	
Dr. Decrease	Cr. Increase

Figure 3-5 Entering Debits and Credits

system of recording the same amount of debit and credit entry is referred to as the double-entry bookkeeping system(복식부기제도). Double-entry bookkeeping is based on the fact that each transaction has a dual effect, called the duality of the transaction(거래의 이중성).

For example, purchasing a car for cash, say $20,000, is an exchange of two different assets with equivalent values. Therefore, we need to record an increase in an asset (car) and a decrease in another asset (cash). Since an increase in an asset is debited, Car is debited. Likewise, Cash is credited since a decrease in an asset is credited. The double-entry bookkeeping system differs from descriptive recording or memorandum entry. Entering transactions in the first accounting book (journal) follows a standardized formal process called a 'journal entry(분개).' The journal entry for the purchase of a car for $20,000 should be entered in the journal as follows:

Dr. Car 20,000 ← Increase in Car (an asset) is debited
    Cr. Cash 20,000 ← Decrease in Cash (an asset) is credited

The process we record a transaction or event in a journal is as follows:

① Journal entries are made in chronological order. In other words, transactions and events are recorded in the journal in the order in which they occurred.
② Debit item(s) precede(s) credit item(s).
③ Account titles and amounts should be recorded for debit and credit entries.
④ Total debit amounts should be equal to total credit amounts.
⑤ The account title for the debited item is recorded in the first column. However, the credit account title should be indented. In other words, when recording credit items, there should be some blank spaces left before entering the credit account titles and amounts.

When there is more than one debit or credit item, it is called a compound entry. Suppose you paid $8,000 and promised to pay the remaining $12,000 (a liability) one month later when you purchased the car. Then, the journal entry should be a compound entry as follows:

Dr. Car	20,000	
Cr. Cash		8,000
Accounts Payable		12,000

Notice that total debit amounts ($20,000) should equal total credit amounts ($20,000), whether a single or compound journal entry.

Once transactions and events are recorded in the first accounting book (journal), the journal entry information is posted to the second accounting book (ledger). This step is called 'posting.'

Posting(전기) is a process of transferring information from the journal to the ledger. Posting involves the following steps:

① The date and amount of the debits and credits are entered in the ledger accounts.
② The journal page numbers of the accounts are listed.
③ The account number, which serves as a cross reference, is transferred from the ledger to the P.R. (posting reference) column of the journal.

An account has a debit balance when the sum of its debits exceeds the sum of its credits. An account has a credit balance when the total credit amount exceeds the total debit amount. Dollar signs are not shown in ledger accounts.

Example 3-1 illustrates an example of recording transactions in the journal and then posting the journal entry information to the ledger accounts.

EXAMPLE 3-1 *Journal Entry and Posting*

Transaction 1 On March 1, Daisy Corporation received $50,000 in cash from selling 5,000 ordinary shares(보통주).

❶ Analysis: The asset Cash is increased. An increase in an asset is debited and is therefore listed on the left side of the account. Share Capital(자본금) - a shareholders' equity account - is increased. An increase in shareholders' equity is credited and is listed on the right side.

❷ Journal entry: The transaction is recorded in the journal as follows:

March 1	Dr. Cash	50,000	
	Cr. Share Capital		50,000
	(Issued 5,000 ordinary shares)		

❸ Posting: The journal entry information is posted to the accounts affected by the transaction as follows:

Cash

Debit		Credit	
3/01	50,000		

Share Capital

Debit		Credit	
		3/01	50,000

Transaction 2 On March 5, the company acquired a car for $6,000 in cash.

❶ Analysis: Two asset accounts are involved. The asset Car is increased and hence debited, while the asset Cash is decreased and thus credited.

❷ Journal entry:

March 5	Dr. Car	6,000	
	Cr. Cash		6,000
	(Bought a car)		

❸ Posting:

Cash

Debit		Credit	
3/01	50,000	3/05	6,000

Car

Debit		Credit	
3/05	6,000		

Transaction 3 On March 8, a piece of equipment(비품) was purchased on account(외상) for $1,000.

❶ Analysis: The purchase of the asset Equipment requires a debit entry. The increase in the liability Accounts Payable(매입채무) requires a credit entry.

❷ Journal entry:

March 8	Dr. Equipment	1,000	
	Cr. Accounts Payable		1,000
	(Acquired equipment on account)		

❸ Posting:

Equipment

3/08	1,000		

Accounts Payable

		3/08	1,000

Transaction 4 On March 10, the company paid the monthly rent of $1,500.

❶ Analysis: An expense is recorded as a debit. Thus, Rent Expense(임차료) is debited. The decrease in the asset Cash is credited.

❷ Journal entry:

March 10	Dr. Rent Expense	1,500	
	Cr. Cash		1,500
	(Paid monthly rent)		

❸ Posting:

Cash

3/01	50,000	3/05	6,000
		3/10	1,500

Rent Expense

3/10	1,500		

Transaction 5 On March 15, the company paid $300 of accounts payable.

❶ Analysis: A reduction in the liability Accounts Payable is debited. A decrease in Cash is credited.

❷ Journal entry:

March 15	Dr. Accounts Payable	300	
	Cr. Cash		300
	(Partial payment of accounts payable)		

❸ Posting:

Cash

3/01	50,000	3/05	6,000
		3/10	1,500
		3/15	300

Accounts Payable

3/15	300	3/08	1,000

Transaction 6 On March 20, the company rendered professional services to clients on account for $15,000.

❶ Analysis: This represents an increase in receivables from clients due to rendering services. Thus, the asset Accounts Receivable increases and is therefore debited. The professional services rendered involve fees that represent revenue to the company. Revenue is credited.

❷ Journal entry:

March 20	Dr. Accounts Receivable	15,000	
	Cr. Service Revenue		15,000
	(Rendered service on account)		

❸ Posting:

Accounts Receivable			
3/20	15,000		

Service Revenue			
		3/20	15,000

Transaction 7 On March 26, the company paid $2,000 in salaries to employees.

❶ Analysis: Since the incurrence of expense is debited, Salaries Expense(급여) is debited. A reduction in Cash due to salary payment is credited.

❷ Journal entry:

March 26	Dr. Salaries Expense	2,000	
	Cr. Cash		2,000
	(Paid employee salaries)		

❸ Posting:

Cash			
3/01	50,000	3/05	6,000
		3/10	1,500
		3/15	300
		3/26	2,000

Salaries Expense			
3/26	2,000		

Transaction 8 On March 29, land was purchased for $8,000 with a down payment(착수금) of $2,000 cash and the balance to be paid later.

❶ Analysis: The asset Land is increased and must be debited. The cash decrease needs to be credited. The balance represents an Accounts Payable. The liability Accounts Payable increases and thus must be credited for $6,000. The transaction involves three accounts, thus needing a compound entry. Of course, the total debits still equal the total credits.

❷ Journal entry:

March 29	Dr. Land	8,000	
	Cr. Cash		2,000
	Accounts Payable		6,000
	(Acquired land with a down payment)		

❸ Posting:

Cash					Land			
3/01	50,000	3/05	6,000		3/29	8,000		
		3/10	1,500					

Cash (cont.)					Accounts Payable			
		3/15	300					
		3/26	2,000		3/15	300	3/08	1,000
		3/29	2,000				3/29	6,000

Transaction 9 On March 31, the company collected $5,000 from customers.

❶ Analysis: Since the asset Cash is increased, it is debited. The reduction in the asset Accounts Receivable requires a credit entry.

❷ Journal entry:

March 31	Dr. Cash	5,000	
	Cr. Accounts Receivable		5,000
	(Partial collection of receivables)		

❸ Posting:

Cash					Accounts Receivable			
3/01	50,000	3/05	6,000		3/20	15,000	3/31	5,000
3/31	5,000	3/10	1,500					
		3/15	300					
		3/26	2,000					
		3/29	2,000					

The journalized transactions of Daisy Corporation for the month of March 20×1 are shown below in the journal. Note that dollar signs are not usually used in journals and ledgers. The account numbers assigned in the P.R. (posting reference) column are based upon the chart of accounts numbering system as explained in Section 3.5. For example, for the March 1 transaction, 101 in the P.R. column indicates that the transaction is posted to the account with a chart of accounts No.101, which is the Cash account. Likewise, 301 in the P.R. column indicates that the transaction is also posted to the account with a chart of accounts No.301, which is the Share Capital account.

Date	Accounts	P.R.	Debit	Credit
March 1	Cash	101	50,000	
	Share Capital	301		50,000
	(Issued 5,000 ordinary shares)			
5	Car	145	6,000	
	Cash	101		6,000
	(Bought a car)			
8	Equipment	143	1,000	
	Accounts Payable	201		1,000
	(Acquired equipment on account)			
10	Rent Expense	512	1,500	
	Cash	101		1,500
	(Paid monthly rent)			
15	Accounts Payable	201	300	
	Cash	101		300
	(Partial payment to creditors)			
20	Accounts Receivable	111	15,000	
	Service Revenue	401		15,000
	(Rendered services on account)			
26	Salaries Expense	501	2,000	
	Cash	101		2,000
	(Paid employee salaries)			
29	Land	141	8,000	
	Cash	101		2,000
	Accounts Payable	201		6,000
	(Acquired land with down payment)			
31	Cash	101	5,000	
	Accounts Receivable	111		5,000
	(Partial collection of receivables)			

A company's entire group of accounts is referred to as the ledger(원장). The ledger keeps, in one place, all the information about changes in specific account balances. Companies may use various kinds of ledgers, but every company has a general ledger(총계정원장). A general ledger contains all the assets, liabilities, equity, revenues, and expenses accounts.

An account has a normal balance(정상잔액) on the side where increases are recorded. Accordingly, assets and expenses have debit normal balances, whereas liabilities, owners' equity, and revenues have credit normal balances.

The posting of Daisy Corporation's March transactions from the journal to the ledger is shown below. The accounts are arranged in the chart of accounts order (assets, liabilities, equity, revenues, and expenses).

The General Ledger of Daisy Corporation as of March 20×1

Cash 101

3/01	50,000	3/05	6,000
3/31	5,000	3/10	1,500
		3/15	300
		3/26	2,000
		3/29	2,000

Accounts Receivable 111

3/20	15,000	3/31	5,000

Land 141

3/29	8,000		

Equipment 143

3/08	1,000		

Car 145

3/05	6,000		

Accounts Payable 401

3/15	300	3/08	1,000
		3/29	6,000

Share Capital 301

		3/01	50,000

Service Revenue 401

		3/20	15,000

Salaries Expense 501

3/26	2,000		

Rent Expense 512

3/10	1,500		

3.7 TRIAL BALANCE

When we prepare journal entries, we are careful to ensure that total debits equal total credits. Similarly, in the process of posting to the ledger accounts, total debits must equal total credits. A trial balance(시산표) is prepared to show this equality in a schedule(표) containing two columns of debit and credit. Then, all accounts are listed in the order they appear in the ledger (chart of accounts order), and their balances are placed under the appropriate columns. When all accounts have been listed, the total in the debit column must be equal to the total in the credit column. If so, there is an equality of debits and credits for the transactions entered into the ledger. If not, an error must have occurred.

Even though the trial balance provides arithmetical proof that total debits equal total credits, it does not guard against all errors. A posting to the wrong accounts may occur. For example, if a debit was incorrectly entered into the Rent Expense account rather than the Car account, the totals in the trial balance columns would agree. But incorrect balances would exist in Rent Expense and Car. Also, if a transaction were erroneously omitted from the ledger, the accounts involved would be misstated, but the debit total will still be the same as the credit total.

The trial balance is a worksheet and not a formal financial statement. Instead, it serves as a tool for preparing the income statement and the statement of financial position.

The trial balance of Daisy Corporation prepared as of March 31, 20×1 is shown below:

Daisy Corporation
Trial Balance
March 31, 20×1

	Debit	Credit
Cash	$43,200	
Accounts Receivable	10,000	
Land	8,000	
Car	6,000	
Equipment	1,000	
Accounts Payable		$6,700
Share Capital		50,000
Service Revenue		15,000
Rent Expense	1,500	
Salaries Expense	2,000	
	$71,700	$71,700

3.8 PREPARATION OF FINANCIAL STATEMENTS

Using the trial balance, we can now prepare the income statement and statement of financial position for Daisy Corporation as follows:

Daisy Corporation
Income Statement
For the Month Ended March 31, 20×1

Service Revenue		$15,000
Less: Expenses		
Rent Expense	$1,500	
Salaries Expense	2,000	
Total Expenses		3,500
Net Income		$11,500

Daisy Corporation Statement of Financial Position March 31, 20×1		
Assets		
Current Assets		
Cash	$43,200	
Accounts Receivable	10,000	
Total Current Assets		$53,200
Noncurrent Assets		
Land	8,000	
Car	6,000	
Equipment	1,000	
Total Noncurrent Assets		15,000
Total Assets		$68,200
Liabilities and Shareholders' Equity		
Current Liabilities		
Accounts Payable		$6,700
Shareholders' Equity		
Share Capital	$50,000	
Retained Earnings	11,500	
Total Shareholders' Equity		61,500
Total Liabilities and Shareholders' Equity		$68,200

CHAPTER 3 Multiple Choice Questions

3.1 Which of the following transactions causes a decrease in shareholders' equity?

ⓐ Pay dividends to shareholders.
ⓑ Obtain cash by borrowing from a local bank.
ⓒ Provide services to customers on account.
ⓓ Purchase office equipment for cash.

3.2 On September 30, Narwhal Co. paid employee salaries $7,000, including $1,000 it owed to its employees last month. What are the effects of this transaction on the accounting equation?

ⓐ Expenses increased, liabilities increased, and assets increased.
ⓑ Assets decreased, liabilities decreased, and expenses increased.
ⓒ Assets decreased, expenses decreased, and liabilities increased.
ⓓ Expenses decreased, liabilities decreased, and assets decreased.

3.3 Which of the following transactions would cause a decrease in both assets and shareholders' equity?

ⓐ Paying insurance premiums for the next two years.
ⓑ Purchasing office equipment on account.
ⓒ Paying advertising for the current month.
ⓓ Providing installation services to customers.

3.4 If the liabilities of a company increased by $55,000 during a month and the shareholders' equity decreased by $21,000 during that same month, did assets increase or decrease, and by how much?

ⓐ $34,000 increase
ⓑ $55,000 increase
ⓒ $34,000 decrease
ⓓ $76,000 increase

3.5 Which accounts are decreased on the debit side and increased on the credit side?

ⓐ Liabilities, shareholders' equity, and revenues
ⓑ Dividends, liabilities, and assets
ⓒ Expenses, dividends, and shareholders' equity
ⓓ Assets, dividends, and expenses

3.6 Which of the following accounts would normally have a credit balance?

ⓐ Accounts Payable, Service Revenue, Ordinary share
ⓑ Salaries Payable, Unearned Revenue, Delivery Expense
ⓒ Income Tax Payable, Service Revenue, Dividends
ⓓ Cash, Repairs and Maintenance Expense, Dividends

3.7 Which of the following is not a possible journal entry?

ⓐ Credit assets, Debit expenses
ⓑ Debit assets, Debit shareholders' equity
ⓒ Credit revenues, Debit assets
ⓓ Debit expenses, Credit liabilities

3.8 Manatee Service Company provides services to customers totaling $3,000, for which it billed the customers. How would the transaction be recorded?

ⓐ Debit Cash $3,000, Credit Service Revenue $3,000
ⓑ Debit Accounts Receivable $3,000, Credit Service Revenue $3,000
ⓒ Debit Accounts Receivable $3,000, Credit Cash $3,000
ⓓ Debit Service Revenue $3,000, Credit Accounts Receivable $3,000

3.9 Milkweed Company received a bill for advertising services received of $400. The bill will be paid in 10 days. How would the transaction be recorded today?

ⓐ Debit Advertising Expense $400, Credit Accounts Payable $400
ⓑ Debit Accounts Payable $400, Credit Advertising Expense $400
ⓒ Debit Accounts Payable $400, Credit Cash $400
ⓓ Debit Advertising Expense $400, Credit Cash $400

3.10 When a company pays utilities of $1,800 in cash, the transaction is recorded as:

ⓐ Debit Utilities Expense $1,800, Credit Utilities Payable $1,800.
ⓑ Debit Utilities Payable $1,800, Credit Cash $1,800.
ⓒ Debit Cash $1,800, Credit Utilities Expense $1,800.
ⓓ Debit Utilities Expense $1,800, Credit Cash $1,800.

CHAPTER 3 Exercises

3.1 Accounting transactions

Answer in the spaces provided whether each of the following represents a recordable transaction.

	Yes or No
ⓐ Collected cash for services	______
ⓑ Paid salaries	______
ⓒ Paid a note payable plus interest	______
ⓓ Hired an employee who will start working next month	______
ⓔ Consumed some supplies	______
ⓕ Purchased a delivery truck, payment to be made next year	______
ⓖ Withdrawal of cash by owner for personal use	______
ⓗ Agreed to supply a company with products over the next few years	______

3.2 Analysis of transactions (1)

The following transactions occur for the Hedgehog Company.

ⓐ Provide services to customers on account for $5,000.
ⓑ Purchase equipment by signing a note with the bank for $10,000.
ⓒ Pay advertising of $2,000 for the current month.

Required:

Analyze each transaction and indicate the amount of increases and decreases in the accounting equation.

3.3 Analysis of transactions (2)

Suppose a company has the following statement of financial position accounts:

Accounts	Balances
Cash	$5,000
Supplies	3,500
Land	9,000
Buildings	?
Equipment	4,500
Accounts payable	3,600
Salaries payable	2,700
Share Capital - Ordinary	?
Retained earnings	11,600

Required:

Calculate the missing amounts assuming the company has total assets of $40,000.

3.4 T-accounts

For "T" accounts listed below, state which side represents an increase and which represents a decrease.

Assets and Expenses	
Dr.	Cr.

Liabilities, Equity, and Revenues	
Dr.	Cr.

3.5 Normal balance of accounts

For the accounts listed below, indicate whether the account's normal balance is a debit or credit. A normal balance is the side of the account where increases are recorded.

Accounts	Normal Balance (Debit or Credit)
ⓐ Service Revenue	______
ⓑ Rent Expense	______
ⓒ Accounts Receivable	______
ⓓ Accounts Payable	______
ⓔ Share Capital	______
ⓕ Office Supplies	______
ⓖ Insurance Expense	______
ⓗ Trademark	______
ⓘ Office Building	______
ⓙ Notes Payable	______

3.6 Accounts (1)

For each transaction below, write the titles of the accounts to be debited and credited in the appropriate column.

Description of the transaction	Debit	Credit
ⓐ Issued ordinary shares for cash	______	______
ⓑ Paid salaries expense	______	______
ⓒ Purchased a truck on credit	______	______
ⓓ Received cash for professional services rendered	______	______
ⓔ Paid accounts payable	______	______
ⓕ Borrowed money from a bank by issuing a note	______	______

3.7 Accounts (2)

For each of the following accounts, indicate whether we use a debit or a credit to increase the balance of the account.

- a Accounts Receivable
- b Accounts Payable
- c Salaries Expense
- d Service Revenue
- e Supplies
- f Share Capital - Ordinary
- g Advertising Expense
- h Dividends

3.8 Journal entries (1)

Journalize the following business transactions in general journal form. Identify each transaction by number.

- a Shareholders invest $25,000 in cash to start a business as a corporation.
- b Purchased $500 of office supplies on credit.
- c Purchased office equipment for $6,000, paid $3,500 in cash, and issued a 30-day, $2,500 note payable.
- d Billed clients for $4,000 service revenue (not received yet).
- e Paid $700 in cash for the current month's rent.
- f Paid $250 cash for office supplies purchased on account in transaction b.
- g Received a bill for $500 for advertising for the current month (not paid yet).
- h Paid $2,500 cash for office salaries.
- i Paid $1,200 cash dividends to shareholders.
- j Received a check for $3,000 from a client in payment of an account receivable for services billed in transaction d.

3.9 Journal entries (2)

Transactions for the Peony Company for the month of July are presented below.

ⓐ Shareholders invested an additional $36,000 cash in the business.
ⓑ Purchased land costing $18,000 in cash.
ⓒ Purchased equipment costing $9,000 for $4,000 cash and the remainder on credit.
ⓓ Purchased supplies on account for $800.
ⓔ Paid $3,000 for a one-year insurance policy.
ⓕ Received $2,000 for services performed.
ⓖ Received $4,000 for services previously performed on account.
ⓗ Paid wages to employees for $2,500.

Required:

Journalize each transaction and identify each transaction by number.

3.10 Journal entries (3)

Record the following transactions for the Magnolia Music Store:

ⓐ Provide music lessons to students for $10,000 on account.
ⓑ Purchase music supplies on account, $1,000.
ⓒ Pay rent for the current month, $2,000.
ⓓ Receive $10,000 cash from students in ⓐ above.

3.11 Journal entries (4)

Record the following transactions. If an entry is not required, state "No Entry."

ⓐ Started business by issuing 10,000 ordinary shares for $20,000.
ⓑ Hired Rebecca as an administrative assistant, promising to pay her $2,000 every two weeks.
ⓒ Rented a building for three years at $500 per month and paid six months' rent in advance.
ⓓ Purchased equipment for $8,000 cash.
ⓔ Purchased $1,500 of supplies on account.
ⓕ Provided services to customers for $7,800 cash.
ⓖ Paid employee salaries, $5,000.

ⓗ Paid for supplies purchased in item ⓔ.
ⓘ Paid $1,000 for current advertising in a local newspaper.
ⓙ Paid utility bill of $1,200 for the current month.

3.12 Compound journal entries

A company purchases a building for $100,000, paying $50,000 cash and signing a three-month note payable for the remainder. Record the transaction.

3.13 Posting (1)

Record the following transactions in the 'T' accounts listed below.

ⓐ Received $2,500 for professional services rendered.
ⓑ Purchased equipment for $1,000, making a down payment of 30%.
ⓒ Incurred utility expense of $100 (not paid yet).
ⓓ Paid $400 to creditors.

Cash	

Accounts Payable	

Equipment	

Service Revenue	

Utility Expense	

3.14 Posting (2)

Consider the following transactions for Lemming Corporation:

ⓐ Sell ordinary shares for $10,000.
ⓑ Purchase equipment for $11,000 cash.
ⓒ Pay employee salaries of $3,500.
ⓓ Provide services to customers for $6,000 cash.

Required:

1. Post these transactions to the Cash T-account. Assume the balance of Cash before these transactions is $4,000.
2. Calculate the ending balance of the Cash account.

3.15 Posting and cash balance

Consider the following transactions for a company:

- ⓐ Sell ordinary shares for $10,000.
- ⓑ Purchase equipment for $8,500 cash.
- ⓒ Provide services to customers for $6,000.
- ⓓ Pay employee salaries of $3,500.

Required:

1. Post these transactions to the Cash T-account. Assume the balance of Cash before these transactions is $3,000.
2. How much is the ending balance of cash?

3.16 Trial balance (1)

Arrange the following accounts in proper order and prepare a trial balance.

Accounts Receivable	$10,000
Postage Expense	6,000
Rent Expense	8,000
Service Revenue	30,000
Retained Earnings	12,000
Share Capital	20,000
Notes Payable	7,000
Equipment	25,000
Copyright	9,000
Cash	11,000

3.17 Trial balance (2)

The following trial balance for Redbud Company was prepared by the owner, who has little accounting knowledge. Therefore, it does not balance.

Trial Balance		
Accounts Payable	$10,000	
Accounts Receivable		$5,000
Building	65,000	
Cash	50,000	
Notes Payable		50,000
Notes Receivable	10,000	
Share Capital		70,000
	$135,000	$125,000

Required:

Prepare a correct trial balance.

3.18 Trial balance (3)

Use the following information to prepare a trial balance.

Cash	$6,000	Dividends	$1,200
Unearned revenue	1,200	Salaries expense	3,200
Prepaid insurance	1,200	Accounts receivable	3,600
Accounts payable	1,900	Share Capital - Ordinary	6,000
Retained earnings	1,800	Service revenue	7,100
Utility expense	2,000	Advertising expense	800

3.19 Accounting terms

Listed below are five terms, followed by a list of phrases that describe or characterize five of the terms. Match each phrase with the best term by placing the letter designating the term in the space provided.

(a) Assets
(b) Journal entry
(c) Revenues
(d) Credit
(e) Trial balance

1. ______ Refers to the right side of an account
2. ______ Convention used to record transactions of a company
3. ______ Resources earned by providing goods and services to customers
4. ______ Resources controlled by a company
5. ______ List of all accounts and their balances after external transactions are recorded

Accounting Terminology in Chapter 3

account 계정
account balance 계정잔액
accounting cycle 회계순환과정
accounts payable 매입채무
accounts receivable 매출채권
adjusting entries 수정분개
analysis of transaction 거래의 분석
bookkeeping 부기
buildings 건물
cash 현금
chart of accounts 계정과목표
credit 대변
debit 차변
double-entry bookkeeping system 복식부기제도
down payment 착수금
duality of the transactions 거래의 이중성
equipment 비품
general journal 일반분개장
general ledger 총계정원장
journal 분개장
journal entry 분개
ledger 원장
machinery 기계장치
normal balance 정상잔액
on account 외상
ordinary shares 보통주
posting 전기
posting reference 전기조회
rent expense 임차료
retained earnings 이익잉여금
reversing entries 역분개
running balance 현시점잔액
salaries expense 급여
service revenue 용역수익
share capital 자본금
special journals 특수분개장
supplies 소모품
T-account T계정
temporary accounts 임시계정
transaction 거래
trial balance 시산표
worksheet 정산표

CHAPTER

4

ADJUSTING AND CLOSING ENTRIES

CHAPTER 4

ADJUSTING AND CLOSING ENTRIES

4.1 INTRODUCTION

As discussed in Chapter 2, companies use the accrual-basis accounting(발생주의회계) in recording their business transactions. Under the accrual-basis accounting, revenue is recognized when earned(수익은 가득되었을 때 인식한다) irrespective of when cash is received, and expenses are recognized when incurred(비용은 발생하였을 때 인식한다) regardless of when cash is paid. As a result, revenue is typically earned when goods or services have been provided since the company has performed what it has to do to earn revenue. In contrast, some revenues are recognized over time, such as interest income on a bank deposit(은행예금) that is earned when the reporting period elapses.

When a transaction is initiated in one accounting period and concluded in a later period, adjusting journal entries(수정분개) are necessary. Adjusting entries are entered at the end of the reporting period to record revenues and expenses applicable to that period. An adjusting entry always involves an income statement account (revenue or expense) and a statement of financial position account (asset or liability). In other words, adjusting entries are made to prepare the income statement and the statement of financial position by correctly recognizing assets, liabilities, revenues, and expenses. As a result, financial statement items will be either overstated or understated without proper adjusting entries.

There are four basic types of adjusting entries. They are ① prepaid (unexpired) expenses, ② unearned (deferred) revenues, ③ accrued expenses, and ④ accrued revenues. Some items involve cash receipt or payment before duly recognized as revenues or expenses. Other items must be included in the financial statements before cash payment or receipt. That is, the need for the adjustments arises because of differences in the timing of cash payments or receipts and recognition of expenses or revenues in the accounting books(회계장부). Therefore, adjusting items can be classified into two major categories of deferrals(이연항목) which include prepaid expenses(선급비용) and unearned revenues(선수수익) and accruals(발생항목) which include accrued expenses(발생비용) and accrued revenues(발생수익).

Table 4-1 shows how adjusting entries can be classified according to their relationship to the cash flows.

Table 4-1 Types of Adjustments

		Cash Receipts or Cash Payments	
		Cash First	Cash Later
Book Recognition	Expenses	Prepaid Expenses =Assets e.g.) Prepaid Insurance Prepaid Rent Office Supplies	Accrued Expenses =Accrued Liabilities e.g.) Salaries Payable Income Taxes Payable Advertising Payable
	Revenues	Unearned Revenues =Liabilities e.g.) Unearned Service Fees Unearned Sales Revenues	Accrued Revenues =Accrued Assets e.g.) Interest Receivable Rent Receivable

The characteristics of adjusting entries are summerized in Table 4-2.

Table 4-2 Characteristics of Adjusting Entries

For what?	To prepare financial statements properly. That is, to correctly recognize assets, liabilities, revenues, and expenses.
Why?	There is a discrepancy between book recognition of revenues or expenses and cash receipts or payments because financial accounting follows the accrual-basis accounting.
When?	At the end of each accounting period when financial statements are prepared.
What types?	Prepaid expenses, unearned revenues, accrued expenses, and accrued revenues.

Now, we will learn the four different types of adjusting entries one by one.

4.2 PREPAID EXPENSES(선급비용)

Prepaid expenses are assets because they relate to expenditures that have future economic benefits. Examples are prepaid insurance(선급보험료), prepaid rent(선급임차료), office supplies(사무용소모품) and so forth. When a prepayment expires (or is used up or consumed) in a given accounting period, it is required to record the expired portion as an expense. Thus, prepaid expenses are items that have been prepaid but not incurred yet.

Prepaid expenses are initially recorded as an asset when paid and need to be adjusted at the end of an accounting period. Therefore, two journal entries are involved: one at the time when paid and one at the end of an accounting period.

The journal entry at the time of payment would be as follows:

Prepaid Expense (asset)	×××	
Cash		×××

The journal entry to adjust a prepaid expense to an expense for the period takes the following form:

Expense	×××	
Prepaid Expense (asset)		×××

EXAMPLE 4-1 ***Prepaid Rent(선급임차료)***

On April 1, Dogwood Company, which prepares semi-annual financial statements on June 30 and December 31, respectively, paid $1,200 to the landlord for one year's rent at the start of the rental agreement. The April 1 transaction resulted in an increase in Prepaid Rent (asset) and a decrease in Cash. The journal entry is:

April 1	Prepaid Rent	1,200	
	Cash		1,200

On June 30, a quarter of the prepaid annual rent or $300 ($1,200×3/12) has expired, and three quarters ($900) are yet to expire. Therefore, we need to reflect the expired portion ($300) as an expense and the unexpired portion ($900) as an asset. Note that the company recorded Prepaid Rent of $1,200 on April 1, when the annual rent was paid in advance. Therefore, we must decrease the asset by $300 to reflect the expired portion as an expense during the period consumed or expired under the accrual-basis accounting. The adjusting entry requires a decrease in the account Prepaid Rent, which thus must be credited, and the recognition of Rent Expense which must be debited. This journal entry is:

June 30	Rent Expense	300	
	Prepaid Rent		300

Rent Expense(임차료) of $300 would be adequately reflected in the semi-annual income statement(반기손익계산서) for the period. Therefore, the semi-annual statement of financial position(반기재무상태표) as of June 30 would show Prepaid Rent of $900 as an asset.

As you might have noticed, the adjusting entry for a prepaid expense is to adjust the already recorded asset (prepaid expense) so that you can adequately measure related expenses (expired portion) and assets (unexpired portion). That is why we sometimes call the adjusting entry for a prepaid expense an alignment of a recorded item.

4.3 UNEARNED REVENUES(선수수익)

Unearned revenue refers to cash received in advance before recognizing revenue. Since a future obligation exists for the company to perform the services for which the advance payment was received, unearned revenue constitutes a liability. (Although liability is usually considered an obligation requiring a future cash payment, it can also relate to rendering future services.)

Like prepaid expenses, unearned revenues are recorded when received and adjusted at the end of an accounting period. Therefore, when received, unearned revenue is recorded as follows as a liability:

	Debit	Credit
Cash	×××	
Unearned Revenue (liability)		×××

Later, when the services are performed or time elapses, revenue is then earned, and the following adjusting entry is required:

	Debit	Credit
Unearned Revenue (liability)	×××	
Revenue		×××

Example 4-2 Unearned Rent Income(선수임대수익)

Refer to Example 4-1, where the tenant, Dogwood Company, paid $1,200 to the landlord for a one-year rent at the start of the rental agreement. Now, let's learn how the landlord should account for the rent at the time of receipt on April 1 and June 30, assuming that the landlord also prepares semi-annual financial statements on June 30.

On April 1, the landlord would record $1,200 as a liability since the landlord has an obligation to provide the rental space to the tenant for one year. Therefore, even though the landlord received cash on April 1, it is too early to recognize rent income since the landlord has not completed providing the tenant with the rental space. That is why the landlord should record the cash receipt as a liability on April 1 and will record rent income as time passes.

Therefore, the following journal entry will be made by the landlord on April 1:

Date	Account	Debit	Credit
April 1	Cash	1,200	
	Unearned Rent Income		1,200

Then on June 30, when the landlord prepares the semi-annual financial statements, the landlord has earned three months' rent income of \$300 (\$1,200×3/12), and the remaining \$900 indicates the obligation that the landlord should provide in the remaining rental period of nine months. Therefore, the following adjusting entry should be made to correctly measure revenue (rent income) and liability (unearned rent income):

June 30	Unearned Rent Income	300	
	Rent Income		300

The adjusting entry is to adjust the already recorded liability (unearned rent income) so that you can adequately measure related revenue (earned portion) and liability (unearned portion). Therefore, the adjusting entry for an unearned revenue is also considered an alignment of a recorded item, similar to the adjusting entry for prepaid expenses.

4.4 ACCRUED EXPENSES(발생비용)

An accrued (unrecorded) expense is an expense that has been incurred by the end of the reporting period but has not been paid. An example would be unpaid interest expense incurred on loans payable. An accrued expense requires an adjusting entry in the journal as follows:

Accrued Expense	×××	
Accrued Payable		×××

Example 4-3 *Accrued Rent Expense(발생임차료)*

Let's use the same example of rent expense as in Example 4-1 with a slight modification. On April 1, 20×1, Dogwood Company, which prepares the semi-annual financial statements on June 30 and December 31, respectively, entered into a rental agreement with the landlord under which Dogwood Company would pay \$1,200 for one year's rent at the end of the rental agreement on March 31, 20×2.

On June 30, when Dogwood Company prepares the semi-annual financial statements, it has used the rented space for three months without paying the rent yet. Dogwood Company should accrue rent expense and rent payable of $300 so that related expense and liability would be measured appropriately and reflected in the semi-annual financial statements. This adjusting entry is:

June 30	Rent Expense	300	
	Rent Payable		300

With the above adjusting entry, Rent Expense(임차료) of $300 would be properly reflected in the semi-annual income statement. As a result, the semi-annual statement of financial position as of June 30 would show Rent Payable(미지급임차료) of $300 as an accrued liability(미지급부채). On the other hand, rent expense and payable would be understated without adjusting entry.

4.5 ACCRUED REVENUES(발생수익)

Accrued or unrecorded revenue represents revenue that has been earned but has not been received by the end of the reporting period. An example is an interest earned on notes receivable. The appropriate adjusting entry is:

Accrued Receivable	×××	
Accrued Income		×××

Example 4-4 Accrued Rent Income(발생임대수익)

Let's use the same example of rent income as in Example 4-2 with a slight modification. On April 1, 20×1, the landlord, who prepares the semi-annual financial statements on June 30 and December 31, respectively, entered into a rental agreement with a tenant under which the tenant would pay one year's rent of $1,200 at the end of the rental agreement on March 31, 20×2.

On June 30, when the landlord prepares the semi-annual financial statements, it has earned rent income for three months even though it has not received the rent yet. Therefore, the landlord should accrue rent income and rent receivable of $300 so that the related revenue and asset would be appropriately measured and reflected in the semi-annual financial statements. This adjusting entry is:

June 30	Rent Receivable	300	
	Rent Income		300

With this adjusting entry, Rent Income(임대수익) of $300 would be properly reflected in the semi-annual income statement. As a result, the semi-annual statement of financial position as of June 30 would show Rent Receivable(미수임대료) of $300 as an asset. On the other hand, rent income and receivable would be understated without this adjusting entry.

Since we have used the same rent example to illustrate the four different types of adjustments, it should have been easy to understand. A clear understanding of adjusting entries is the key to understanding the accrual basis of accounting.

4.6 DEPRECIATION(감가상각)

Even though not as clear-cut as the four types of adjustments, recording periodic depreciation is an adjusting entry made at the end of each accounting period. Some assets (e.g., a car) decline in usefulness over time due to use and obsolescence. The depreciation expense, as well as the decline in the usefulness of the asset for each period, requires adjusting entries. An offset (contra) account is used to record depreciation and update the carrying amount of depreciable assets(감가상각대상자산). Thus, the asset's cost less related accumulated depreciation(감가상각누계액), a contra account(차감계정), gives us the carrying amount (book value, 장부금액) of the asset at a given point in time. As time goes on, the carrying amount of the asset diminishes. Depreciation expense is, of course, an income statement account. Therefore, the carrying amount of the asset is shown in the statement of financial position.

Methods for determining the depreciation expense for a period are numerous. The method we will use in this chapter is the simplest one. It is called straight-line depreciation(정액법감가상각) and provides for equal depreciation charges for each period. For example, suppose a car having a five-year life expectancy was acquired on January 1 for $12,000. Each year the depreciation would be $2,400 ($12,000÷5 years). The depreciation expense for the first six-month period is $1,200 ($2,400×6/12). If the semi-annual financial statements are prepared on June 30, the appropriate adjusting entry would be as follows:

June 30	Depreciation Expense	1,200	
	Accumulated Depreciation		1,200

The carrying amount(장부금액) of the car on June 30 is $10,800 ($12,000 −$1,200). The car would be shown in the statement of financial position as follows:

Car	$12,000
Less: Accumulated Depreciation	1,200
Carrying amount	$10,800

As you might have noticed, the accounting for depreciation is a case of prepaid expense. Car is recorded as an asset when acquired, and the related expenses are reflected in the income statement when its economic benefits are consumed or expired.

4.7 CLOSING ENTRIES(마감분개)

After the financial statements have been prepared from a worksheet (to be fully discussed in the next chapter) at the end of an accounting period, an income summary account(집합손익계정) is established to close out temporary accounts(임시계정). All income statement accounts, such as revenues and expenses, are temporary accounts.

The income statement and statement of financial position are interrelated. The net results of operations (net income or net loss) either increase or decrease the statement of financial position. In other words, a change in the statement of financial position is equal to the net results of operations excluding capital transactions(자본거래).[1] At the end of each accounting period, the net results of operations are transferred to the statement of financial position. Income statement accounts are maintained only for an accounting period, and the net results of operations are transferred (added) to the Retained Earnings(이익잉여금) account in the statement of financial position. Closing entries are then made in which all revenue accounts are debited so that zero balances are left in them, and the total is credited to the Income Summary account. The closing entry for revenue is:

December 31	Revenue	×××	
	Income Summary		×××

Similarly, all expense accounts are credited to bring their balances to zero, and the total is debited to the Income Summary account. The closing entry for expenses is:

December 31	Income Summary	×××	
	Expenses		×××

After the closing entries have been made, all the revenue and expense accounts will have zero balances. Hence, we will start fresh with zero income statement account balances for the new accounting period. Thus, revenue and expenses applicable to the new accounting period can be recorded.

The Income Summary itself is a temporary account(임시계정). It reflects net income or net loss for the period since total revenues and total expenses have been transferred to it. The net income or net loss representing the difference between the debit balance and the credit balance of the Income Summary account is then transferred to Retained Earnings. Retained

1 Capital transactions refer to transactions with owners such as investments by owners (equity issues to shareholders) or distributions to owners (dividends to owners).

Earnings(이익잉여금, 유보이익) is the accumulated earnings of the company since its inception after subtracting cumulative dividends paid out. Retained Earnings customarily has a credit balance since, in most cases, a company is profitable over the years. It is possible, however, for Retained Earnings to have a debit balance (deficit) when the company has been operating at net losses. The closing entry to transfer profit from Income Summary to Retained Earnings is:

December 31	Income Summary	×××	
	Retained Earnings		×××

The closing entry to transfer a net loss from Income Summary to Retained Earnings is:

December 31	Retained Earnings	×××	
	Income Summary		×××

Since the purpose of closing entries is to determine and transfer the net income or net loss to shareholders' equity, they affect only income statement accounts. Statement of financial position accounts (except for dividends or drawing accounts) are not closed out. They remain intact because assets, liabilities, and equity continue to exist into the next accounting period. For this reason, balance sheet accounts are called permanent accounts(영구계정). Dividends account for a corporation (or Drawing account(인출계정) for a sole proprietorship or partnership) is a temporary account that needs to be closed, just like income statement accounts.

Alternatively, revenues and expenses can be directly closed to Retained Earnings instead of using the Income Summary account. The result is the same whether the Income Summary account is used or not.

Now, look at Example 4-5 to see how income statement accounts are closed out to Retained Earnings account.

Example 4-5 *Closing Entries*

Willow Corporation has the following trial balance as of December 31, 20×1.

Willow Corporation Trial Balance December 31, 20×1		
Cash	$4,000	
Accounts Receivable	5,000	
Equipment	12,000	
Accounts Payable		$5,000
Share Capital		10,000
Retained Earnings		2,000
Service Revenue		12,000
Salary Expense	3,000	
Rent Expense	4,000	
Utility Expense	1,000	
	$29,000	$29,000

The closing entries in the journal as of December 31, 20×1 are as follows:

Service Revenue	12,000	
Income Summary		12,000
(To close revenues)		
Income Summary	8,000	
Salary Expense		3,000
Rent Expense		4,000
Utility Expense		1,000
(To close expenses)		

The balance in Income Summary is now $4,000 ($12,000 less $8,000), which represents the net income for the period since revenue exceeds expenses. The profit must now be transferred to Retained Earnings as follows:

Income Summary	4,000	
Retained Earnings		4,000

After this entry, Income Summary is closed out with a zero balance. Therefore, after the closing entries, no income statement account balances exist. The net effect has been to increase the Retained Earnings account by $4,000, the profit for the year. Hence, the Retained Earnings account has an ending balance of $6,000 ($2,000 + $4,000).

While the Income Summary account balance is closed to Retained Earnings in a corporation, a sole proprietor uses a different account. In place of Retained Earnings, the proprietor's Income Summary is closed to the owner's Capital account(자본계정).

4.8 POST-CLOSING TRIAL BALANCE(마감후시산표)

After the closing entries have been prepared, a post-closing trial balance may be prepared to ensure that the statement of financial position accounts (the income statement accounts have all been closed) are in balance. If the accounts are not balanced, an error in recording or posting the closing entries is indicated. The post-closing trial balance shows only assets, liabilities, and owners' equity accounts.

The post-closing trial balance for Willow Corporation would look like the following:

Willow Corporation
Post-closing Trial Balance
December 31, 20×1

Cash	$4,000	
Accounts Receivable	5,000	
Equipment	12,000	
Accounts Payable		$5,000
Share Capital		10,000
Retained Earnings		6,000
	$21,000	$21,000

CHAPTER 4 Multiple Choice Questions

4.1 Adjusting entries are primarily needed for:

ⓐ Cash-basis accounting.
ⓑ Accrual-basis accounting.
ⓒ Current value accounting.
ⓓ Manual accounting systems.

4.2 Making insurance payments in advance is an example of:

ⓐ An accrued revenue.
ⓑ An accrued expense.
ⓒ An unearned revenue.
ⓓ A prepaid expense.

4.3 When a magazine sells subscriptions to customers, it is an example of:

ⓐ An accrued expense.
ⓑ An accrued revenue.
ⓒ A prepaid expense.
ⓓ An unearned revenue.

4.4 When a company makes an end-of-period adjusting entry which includes a credit to Prepaid Rent, the debit is usually made to:

ⓐ Cash.
ⓑ Rent Expense.
ⓒ Rent Payable.
ⓓ Rent Receivable.

4.5 Prepayments occur when:

ⓐ Cash payment occurs before the expense recognition.
ⓑ Sales are delayed pending credit approval.
ⓒ Customers are unable to pay the full amount due when goods are delivered.
ⓓ Cash payment occurs after the expense is incurred and liability is recorded.

4.6 Adjusting entries:

ⓐ Often include the Cash account.
ⓑ Usually are recorded at the beginning of the accounting period.
ⓒ Always involve at least one income statement account and one statement of financial position account.
ⓓ Adjust the balance of revenue and expense accounts to zero.

4.7 On April 1, a $4,800 premium on a one-year insurance policy on equipment was paid and charged to Prepaid Insurance. At the end of the year, the financial statements would report the following:

ⓐ Insurance Expense $4,800; Prepaid Insurance $0.
ⓑ Insurance Expense $3,600; Prepaid Insurance $1,200.
ⓒ Insurance Expense $3,650; Prepaid Insurance $4,800.
ⓓ Insurance Expense $1,200; Prepaid Insurance $3,600.

4.8 An adjusted trial balance is:

- ⓐ a list of all accounts and their balances after adjusting entries.
- ⓑ a list of all accounts and their balances before adjusting entries.
- ⓒ a list of all accounts and their balances after closing entries.
- ⓓ a trial balance adjusted for cash-basis accounting.

4.9 The primary purpose of closing entries is to:

- ⓐ prove the equality of the debit and credit entries in the general journal.
- ⓑ ensure that all assets and liabilities are recognized in the appropriate period.
- ⓒ update the Retained Earnings balance and prepare revenue, expense, and dividend accounts for the next period's transactions.
- ⓓ assure that adjusting entries balance.

4.10 The closing process includes which of the following?

- ⓐ Closing the balance of the retained earnings account to zero.
- ⓑ Closing the balance of only the dividends account to zero.
- ⓒ Closing the balances of only revenue and expense accounts to zero.
- ⓓ Closing the balances of revenue, expense, and dividend accounts to zero.

CHAPTER 4 Exercises

4.1 Adjusting entries (1)

For each of the following transactions, make the necessary adjusting entries for Hickory Corporation on December 31, 20×1.

a. Received $9,000 on September 1, 20×1 for a half-year's rent in advance. On this date, the unearned rent income account was credited for the amount received.
b. On November 1, 20×1, Hickory Corporation loaned another party $4,000 on an 8 percent, six-month note.
c. The company holds a large amount of supplies in the administrative department. The supplies account showed a balance of $2,000. At year's end, the supplies on hand amounted to $500.
d. On July 1, 20×1, the company paid $850 for a five-year insurance policy. The transaction was initially recorded as a debit to Prepaid Insurance.
e. Interest income accrued on bonds owned by the company as of the end of the year was $200.
f. On December 1, the company signed a lease to rent a car for six months at $0.20 per kilometer. During December, 1,000 kilometers were driven. No recognition has been made yet to the rental charge on the car.
g. On December 18, the company signed an agreement to buy a new car on March 2, 20×2, from a car dealer. No down payment was made.

4.2 Adjusting entries (2)

The following information for Aspen Company is available on July 31, 20×4, the end of a monthly accounting period.

- ⓐ Aspen Company purchased a 2-year insurance policy on April 1, 20×4, and debited Prepaid Insurance for $3,600.
- ⓑ On February 1, 20×4, a tenant in an apartment building owned by Aspen Company paid $4,800, which represents six months' rent in advance. The amount received was credited to the Unearned Rent account.
- ⓒ On July 1, 20×4, the balance in the Office Supplies account was $200. During July, office supplies costing $630 were purchased. A physical count of office supplies on July 31 revealed that $240 was still on hand.
- ⓓ On March 31, 20×4, Aspen Company purchased a delivery van for $33,000. It is estimated that the annual depreciation will be $7,800.
- ⓔ Aspen Company has two office employees who earn $75 and $100 per day, respectively. They are paid each Friday for a five-day workweek that begins each Monday. July 31 is a Thursday in 20×4.

Required:

Prepare adjusting entries for Aspen Company for the month of July for each situation given. Appropriate adjusting entries had been recorded in previous months.

4.3 Adjusting entries (3)

Presented below are the Unadjusted Trial Balance and Adjusted Trial Balance for Spruce Company on December 31.

Spruce Company
Trial Balance
December 31

	Before Adjustment		After Adjustment	
	Dr.	**Cr.**	**Dr.**	**Cr.**
Cash	$3,000		$3,000	
Accounts Receivable	2,800		3,700	
Prepaid Rent	2,100		1,500	
Supplies	1,200		500	
Equipment	18,000		18,000	
Accumulated Depreciation		$1,300		$1,600
Accounts Payable		2,700		3,000
Notes Payable		10,000		10,000
Interest Payable				120
Salaries Payable				600
Unearned Service Revenue		4,460		4,360
Share Capital		8,200		8,200
Dividends	3,200		3,200	
Service Revenue		8,000		9,000
Salaries Expense	2,060		2,660	
Utility Expense	1,800		2,100	
Rent Expense	500		1,100	
Supplies Expense			700	
Depreciation Expense			300	
Interest Expense			120	
Totals	$34,660	$34,660	$36,880	$36,880

Required:

Prepare, in journal form, the adjusting entries that explain the changes in the balances from the unadjusted trial balance to the adjusted trial balance.

4.4 Adjusting entries (4)

Prepare adjusting entries, as needed, for the following items.

ⓐ The Supplies account shows a balance of $500, but a count of supplies reveals only $200 on hand at year-end.

ⓑ The company initially records the payments of all insurance premiums as Prepaid Insurance. The unadjusted trial balance at year-end shows a balance of $500 in Prepaid Insurance. A review of insurance policies reveals that $100 insurance is unexpired.

ⓒ Employees work Monday through Friday, and salaries of $2,500 per week are paid each Friday. The company's year-end falls on Tuesday.

ⓓ At year-end, the company received a utility bill for December's electricity usage of $200 that will be paid in early January.

4.5 Adjusting entries (5)

Prepare necessary adjusting entries for each of the following cases.

ⓐ On January 1, office supplies of $700 were acquired on credit. On January 31, a count of office supplies revealed that $600 was on hand. Prepare proper entries on January 1 and January 31.

ⓑ On January 1, a landlord receives $600 from a tenant as an advance for three months' rent. Prepare proper entries on January 1 and January 31.

ⓒ On January 1, the company borrowed $10,000 from a bank for one year at a 15 percent interest rate. The interest for one year is $1,500 ($10,000×15%). For January, accrued interest expense is $125 ($1,500/12). Prepare the appropriate adjusting entry on January 31.

ⓓ The last payroll date was January 28. The next payroll date is February 11. For the last few days of the month (January 29~January 31), the company owes its employees $500 in salaries. Prepare the appropriate journal entry for accrued salaries.

ⓔ A landlord has not received a tenant's January rent of $300. Prepare the proper adjusting entry at the end of January.

4.6 Adjusting entries (6)

Prepare adjusting entries for the following independent situations.

a Halibut Foods purchased a one-year hazard insurance policy on August 1 and recorded the $4,200 premium to prepaid insurance. Prepare the adjusting entries for Halibut Foods at its December 31 year-end.

b During the year, Peony Company paid salaries of $24,000. In addition, $5,000 in salaries has accrued by the end of the year but has not been paid. What is the adjusting entry to record accrued salaries at the end of the year?

c The employees of Woodpecker Inc. work Monday through Friday. Every other Friday, the company issues payroll checks totaling $32,000. The current pay period ends on Friday, January 3. Woodpecker Inc. is now preparing the financial statements for the year ending on December 31. What is the adjusting entry to record accrued salaries at the end of the year?

d On September 1, 20×1, Goldilocks sold 400 one-year subscriptions for $120 each. The total amount received was credited to Unearned Revenue. What would be the required adjusting entry on December 31, 20×1?

e At the beginning of the period, a company reports a balance in office supplies of $500. The company purchases an additional $3,500 of office supplies for cash during the period. By the end of the period, only $800 of office supplies remains. Record the period-end adjusting entry.

f A company purchased new equipment for $24,000 cash on August 1, 20×1. At the time of purchase, the equipment was expected to be used in operations for four years (48 months) and have no resale or scrap value at the end. The company depreciates the equipment evenly over the 48 months ($500/month). Record the adjusting entry for depreciation on December 31, 20×1.

g A company borrowed $20,000 with 8% interest on October 1, 20×1. This amount plus interest is due on September 30, 20×2. Record the adjusting entry on December 31, 20×1.

4.7 Closing entries (1)

Columbine Company's adjusted trial balance shows the following accounts:

Professional Service Revenue \$10,000; Rental Income \$2,000; Promotion and Entertainment Expense \$3,000; Interest Expense \$1,000; Contribution Expense \$500; Retained Earnings \$5,000.

Required:

Prepare closing entries for ⓐ revenues, ⓑ expenses, and ⓒ transfer of profit or loss to retained earnings.

4.8 Closing entries (2)

The adjusted trial balance for Wicker Company on December 31, 20×2 is presented below:

	Debit	Credit
Cash	\$11,000	
Accounts Receivable	150,000	
Prepaid Rent	5,000	
Supplies	25,000	
Equipment	300,000	
Accumulated Depreciation		\$135,000
Accounts Payable		20,000
Salaries Payable		4,000
Interest Payable		1,000
Notes Payable - due in two years		30,000
Ordinary Shares		200,000
Retained Earnings		50,000
Dividends	20,000	
Service Revenue		400,000
Salaries Expense	180,000	
Advertising Expense	70,000	
Rent Expense	15,000	
Depreciation Expense	30,000	
Interest Expense	2,000	
Utility Expense	32,000	
Totals	\$840,000	\$840,000

Required:

Prepare the closing entries for Wicker Company for the year ended December 31, 20×2.

4.9 Closing entries (3)

The adjusted trial balance for Willow Company on December 31, 20×1 is presented below:

	Debit	Credit
Cash	$18,000	
Prepaid Rent	15,000	
Buildings, Net of Accumulated Depreciation	408,000	
Account Payable		$10,000
Salaries Payable		14,000
Share Capital - Ordinary		250,000
Retained Earnings		64,000
Dividends	10,000	
Service Revenue		350,000
Salaries Expense	180,000	
Rent Expense	31,000	
Utility Expense	26,000	
Totals	$688,000	$688,000

Required:

Prepare the closing entries for Willow Company for the year ended December 31, 20×1.

4.10 Closing entries and capital at the end of a period

After all revenue and expense accounts have been closed at the end of the fiscal year, Income Summary has a debit of $19,300 and a credit of $25,800. On the same date, Katherine Linden—Capital has a credit balance of $52,000, and Katherine Linden—Drawing has a balance of $1,800.

Required:

ⓐ Journalize the entries required to complete the closing of the accounts.

ⓑ Determine the amount of Katherine Linden—Capital at the end of the period.

4.11 Effect of closing entries on retained earnings

Snow Leopard Inc. has the following balances on December 31 before closing entries:

Revenues	$40,000
Retained Earnings, January 1	10,000
Cash	8,000
Expenses	25,000
Accounts Payable	7,000
Dividends	2,000
Supplies	15,000

Required:

Based upon the balances above, what net adjustment would be made to Retained Earnings due to closing entries?

4.12 Accounting terms

Listed below are five terms, followed by a list of phrases that describe or characterize five of the terms. Match each phrase with the correct term by placing the letter designating the term in the space provided.

- a Adjusted trial balance
- b Statement of financial position
- c Prepaid expenses
- d Post-closing trial balance
- e Income statement

1. _____ Financial statement showing that assets equal liabilities plus shareholders' equity.
2. _____ Assets created before the expense is recognized.
3. _____ A list of accounts and their balances used as the source data to prepare the financial statements.
4. _____ Financial statement that provides a measure of net income.
5. _____ A list of only permanent accounts and their balances prepared to prove that total debits equal total credits.

ACCOUNTING TERMINOLOGY IN CHAPTER 4

accounting books 회계장부
accrual-basis accounting 발생주의회계
accruals 발생항목
accrued expense 발생비용
accrued liabilities 미지급부채
accrued rent expense 발생임차료
accrued rent income 발생임대수익
accrued revenues 발생수익
accumulated depreciation 감가상각누계액
adjusting entries 수정분개
bank deposit 은행예금
book value 장부금액
capital account 자본계정
capital transactions 자본거래
carrying amount 장부금액
closing entries 마감분개
contra account 차감계정
deferrals 이연항목
depreciable assets 감가상각대상자산
depreciation 감가상각
drawing account 인출계정
income summary account 집합손익계정
office supplies 사무용소모품
permanent accounts 영구계정
post-closing trial balance 마감후시산표
prepaid expenses 선급비용
prepaid insurance 선급보험료
prepaid rent 선급임차료
rent expense 임차료
rent income 임대수익
rent payable 미지급임차료
rent receivable 미수임대료
retained earnings 이익잉여금, 유보이익
semi-annual income statement 반기손익계산서
semi-annual statement of financial position 반기재무상태표
straight-line depreciation 정액법감가상각
temporary accounts 임시계정
unearned rent income 선수임대수익
unearned revenues 선수수익

CHAPTER

5

PREPARATION OF FINANCIAL STATEMENTS

CHAPTER 5

PREPARATION OF FINANCIAL STATEMENTS

5.1 INTRODUCTION

Chapters 3 and 4 taught us to record transactions, prepare adjusting entries, and close temporary accounts to retained earnings. Errors in the accounting process, such as posting a wrong amount from the journal to the ledger, may happen. A critical means of avoiding errors is the preparation of an informal schedule called a *worksheet*(정산표) at the end of a reporting period. The worksheet is not a permanent accounting record but instead is used to put the detailed accounting data in one place, and hence to save time and effort in correcting errors. Of course, it is easier to make corrections in an informal schedule than in formal accounting records. Errors are reduced because the worksheet helps identify discrepancies that may result from errors made in journal entries, errors made in posting, or miscalculations made in determining account balances.

5.2 WORKSHEET FOR A SERVICE FIRM

A service firm derives service revenues from rendering services. For example, medical doctors, accountants, or lawyers generate service revenues by rendering professional services to patients or clients.

The worksheet is customarily prepared on a multi-column sheet called analysis paper. The columns of a typical worksheet appear in the following order: trial balance, adjustments, income statement, and statement of financial position.

After the trial balance(시산표) is copied onto the worksheet, adjusting entries(수정분개) are reflected so that adjusted account balances(수정후계정잔액) may then be derived. Adjusted balances are then divided into the income statement and statement of financial position items. The income statement can be easily prepared using the income statement columns of the worksheet with minor modifications to fit the standard income statement format. Likewise, the statement of financial position can also be easily prepared using the worksheet's statement of financial position columns.

Preparation of the worksheet provides a quick review of ledger account balances and the adjusting entries affecting the accounts. A worksheet also serves as a source for preparing the adjusting and closing entries. Further, it facilitates the preparation of the financial statements since it can be proven in the worksheet that the income statement and statement of financial position accounts reconcile.

In preparing a worksheet, the following steps are necessary:

① Copy the Trial Balance data and paste them to the first two columns of the worksheet. Make sure that the debit totals equal the credit totals.

② Fill in the adjusting entry data in the Adjustments columns. For cross-references(상호조회), the debit and credit for each entry should be keyed (starting with entry ⓐ). If an adjusting entry is for an account not listed on the trial balance, it should be added on the next available line below the trial balance totals. The debits and credits in the Adjustments columns must be proven before proceeding further.

③ Copy adjusted account amounts (ledger balances after adjusting entries) and paste them to the appropriate Income Statement or Statement of Financial Position columns.

④ Total the debit and credit columns for the income statement and statement of financial position.

⑤ Determine net income or net loss, the balancing figure in the Income Statement and Statement of Financial Position columns. Write Net Income or Net Loss under the Income Statement and Statement of Financial Position columns. For example, suppose there is a net income (the credit total exceeds the debit total in the Income Statement columns). In that case, net income will be shown in the debit of the Income Statement columns and, on the same line, in the credit of the Statement of Financial Position columns (representing an increase in owners' equity) to balance it. Of course, total assets must be equal to the sum of liabilities and equity. An error is indicated if the Statement of Financial Position columns do not agree.

EXAMPLE 5-1 *Worksheet for a Service Company*

The trial balance and additional information for adjusting entries for Chickadee Service Corporation are as follows:

Chickadee Service Corporation
Trial Balance
December 31, 20×4

Cash	$6,000	
Accounts Receivable	12,000	
Supplies	500	
Prepaid Insurance	2,000	
Equipment	10,000	
Accumulated Depreciation		$3,000
Accounts Payable		4,000
Notes Payable		2,000
Unearned Service Revenue		1,000
Share Capital		10,000
Retained Earnings		3,000
Service Revenue		15,000
Salaries Expense	5,000	
Utility Expense	2,500	
	$38,000	$38,000

Additional Information for Adjusting Entries:

The following six items require adjusting entries. Why and how adjusting entries are prepared for them are explained here. Adjusting entries are indicated in the worksheet, as ⓐ through ⓕ in this example.

ⓐ ***Supplies.*** A count of supplies at year's end revealed that $200 was on hand. Since the beginning balance was $500, $300 must have been used and thus represents the supplies expense for the period. Because no Supplies Expense account exists, one must be established on the next available line of the worksheet. The adjusting entry is:

Supplies Expense	300	
Supplies		300

ⓑ ***Insurance.*** Prepaid insurance of $2,000 at the beginning of the year was for a two-year policy commencing January 1, 20×4. Thus, the insurance expense for 20×4 is $1,000 ($2,000/2 years). Since no account for insurance expense exists, one must be set up. The adjusting entry is:

Insurance Expense	1,000	
Prepaid Insurance		1,000

ⓒ ***Depreciation.*** Equipment was acquired on January 1, 20×1, and has a 10-year life. Hence, the depreciation expense for 20×4, using the straight-line method(정액법), would be $1,000 ($10,000/10 years). The account Depreciation Expense must be entered at the bottom of the worksheet. The entry is:

Depreciation Expense	1,000	
Accumulated Depreciation		1,000

ⓓ ***Service Revenue.*** At the beginning of the year, there was a liability for unearned service revenue of $1,000. The advance cash receipt for future two-year services was made on January 1, 20×4. Therefore, $500 of the unearned service revenue had been earned by December 31, 20×4. The appropriate adjusting entry is:

Unearned Service Revenue	500	
Service Revenue		500

ⓔ ***Interest.*** A note payable of $2,000 was issued on October 1, 20×4. It bears an annual interest rate of 10 percent. The note is for one year. The accrued interest expense for three months (October 1, 20×4 to December 31, 20×4) is $50 ($2,000 × 10% × 3/12). The accrual entry is:

Interest Expense	50	
Interest Payable		50

ⓕ ***Salaries.*** The salaries expense shown in the trial balance constitutes payroll expense(급여비용) paid during the year. Not included is $150 for salaries incurred in the later part of December to be paid in the next payroll period, which is the first week of January 20×5. The following entry reflects the accrual:

Salaries Expense	150	
Salaries Payable		150

After the adjusting entries have been reflected on the worksheet, the debit totals must equal the credit totals.

Let's now prepare a worksheet for Chickadee Service Corporation on December 31, 20×4, following the abovementioned steps.

STEP 1 ***Copy the trial balance data and paste them to the first two columns of the worksheet***

Note that the amount of each ledger account is reflected in the appropriate Trial Balance column. The account balances reflect all transactions for the accounting period before preparing any necessary adjusting entries. The debit totals and credit totals in the Trial Balance columns must agree.

STEP 2 ***Reflect the adjusting entries in the Adjustments columns***

Chickadee Service Corporation
Worksheet
For the Year Ended December 31, 20×4

Account	Trial Balance		Adjustments		Income Statement		Statement of Financial Position	
	Dr.	Cr.	Dr.	Cr.	Dr.	Cr.	Dr.	Cr.
Cash(현금)	6,000						6,000	
Accounts Receivable(매출채권)	12,000						12,000	
Supplies(소모품)	500			ⓐ 300			200	
Prepaid Insurance(선급보험료)	2,000			ⓑ1,000			1,000	
Equipment(비품)	10,000						10,000	
Accumulated Depreciation (감가상각누계액)		3,000		ⓒ1,000				4,000
Accounts Payable(매입채무)		4,000						4,000
Notes Payable(어음채무)		2,000						2,000
Unearned Service Revenue(선수수익)		1,000	ⓓ 500					500
Share Capital(자본금)		10,000						10,000
Retained Earnings(이익잉여금)		3,000						3,000
Service Revenue(용역수익)		15,000		ⓓ 500		15,500		
Salaries Expense(급여비용)	5,000		ⓕ 150		5,150			
Utility Expense(공공요금)	2,500				2,500			
	38,000	38,000						
Supplies Expense(소모품비용)			ⓐ 300		300			
Insurance Expense(보험비용)			ⓑ1,000		1,000			
Depreciation Expense(감가상각비)			ⓒ1,000		1,000			
Interest Expense(이자비용)			ⓔ 50		50			
Interest Payable(미지급이자)				ⓔ 50				50
Salaries Payable(미지급급여)				ⓕ 150				150
			3,000	3,000				
Net Income(당기순이익)					5,500			5,500
					15,500	15,500	29,200	29,200

STEP 3 ***Copy the adjusted account balances and paste them to the Income Statement or Statement of Financial Position columns***

Revenues and expenses are copied to the appropriate Income Statement columns, while assets, liabilities, and equity are copied to the Statement of Financial Position columns.

STEP 4 ***Total Income Statement and Statement of Financial Position columns***

The difference between the debit and credit totals in the Income Statement *must* be the same as the difference between the corresponding totals in the Statement of Financial Position. This difference represents either net income or net loss for the period. In this case, there is a net income of $5,500.

STEP 5 ***Enter net income or net loss to balance the columns***

Because net income increases retained earnings(이익잉여금), net income is entered in the credit column of the Statement of Financial Position. As a result, the debit and credit totals of the Statement of Financial Position columns must be the same. They are $29,200 in the example. In case of a net loss, the income statement's debit totals (expenses) exceed the credit totals (revenues). Net loss would then be entered in the credit column of the income statement columns. On the other hand, the net loss would be entered in the debit column of the statement of financial position columns because a net loss decreases retained earnings. Now that the Income Statement and Statement of Financial Position columns agree, we can prepare the financial statements.

5.3 PREPARATION OF FINANCIAL STATEMENTS

We can prepare the financial statements for Chickadee Service Corporation using the worksheet. The worksheet provides all data needed for the income statement and statement of financial position.

EXAMPLE 5-2 *Preparation of Financial Statements for a Service Company*

Chickadee Service Corporation
Income Statement
For the Year Ended December 31, 20×4

Service Revenue		$15,500
Less: Expenses		
Salaries Expense	$5,150	
Utility Expense	2,500	
Supplies Expense	300	
Insurance Expense	1,000	
Depreciation Expense	1,000	
Interest Expense	50	
Total Expenses		10,000
Net Income		$5,500

Chickadee Service Corporation
Statement of Changes in Shareholders' Equity
For the Year Ended December 31, 20×4

Share Capital - January 1, 20×4		$10,000
Retained Earnings - January 1, 20×4	$3,000	
Add: Net Income for the year	5,500	8,500
Shareholders' Equity - December 31, 20×4		$18,500

Chickadee Service Corporation
Statement of Financial Position
December 31, 20×4

Assets		
Current Assets		
Cash	$6,000	
Accounts Receivable	12,000	
Supplies	200	
Prepaid Insurance	1,000	
Total Current Assets		$19,200
Noncurrent Assets		
Equipment	$10,000	
Less: Accumulated Depreciation	4,000	6,000
Total Assets		$25,200

Liabilities and Shareholders' Equity

Current Liabilities		
Accounts Payable	$4,000	
Notes Payable	2,000	
Interest Payable	50	
Salaries Payable	150	
Unearned Service Revenue	500	
Total Current Liabilities		$6,700
Shareholders' Equity		
Share Capital	$10,000	
Retained Earnings	8,500	
Total Shareholders' Equity		18,500
Total Liabilities and Shareholders' Equity		$25,200

5.4 AFTER THE FINANCIAL STATEMENTS ARE PREPARED

After we prepare the financial statements, we need to transfer the net income or loss via closing entries of revenues and expenses to the retained earnings in the statement of financial position. The closing entries for the income statement accounts are as follows:

Service Revenue	15,500	
Income Summary		15,500
Income Summary	10,000	
Salaries Expense		5,150
Utility Expense		2,500
Supplies Expense		300
Insurance Expense		1,000
Depreciation Expense		1,000
Interest Expense		50
Income Summary	5,500	
Retained Earnings		5,500

The income statement accounts will have zero balances after the closing entries at the end of an accounting period. Then, we may prepare a post-closing trial balance(마감후시산표) to ensure that the statement of financial position's debit and credit totals agree. However, trial balances (unadjusted, adjusted, and post-closing trial balances) are prepared to help accountants prepare the financial statements. Hence, they are not required parts of the financial reporting.

Chickadee Service Corporation
Post-closing Trial Balance
December 31, 20×4

	Dr.	Cr.
Cash	$6,000	
Accounts Receivable	12,000	
Supplies	200	
Prepaid Insurance	1,000	
Equipment	10,000	
Accumulated Depreciation		$4,000
Accounts Payable		4,000
Notes Payable		2,000
Interest Payable		50
Salaries Payable		150
Unearned Service Revenue		500
Share Capital		10,000
Retained Earnings		8,500
	$29,200	$29,200

CHAPTER 5 Multiple Choice Questions

5.1 When a company issues ordinary shares for cash, what is the effect on the accounting equation for the company?

ⓐ Assets increase, and liabilities increase.
ⓑ Assets increase, and shareholders' equity increases.
ⓒ Assets decrease, and liabilities decrease.
ⓓ Liabilities decrease, and shareholders' equity increases.

5.2 Which of the following accounts would normally have a debit balance and appear in the statement of financial position?

ⓐ Accounts Receivable
ⓑ Unearned Revenue
ⓒ Salaries Expense
ⓓ Dividends

5.3 Accounts Receivable account has a beginning balance of $10,000, and the company provides services of $50,000 on account during the month. The ending balance was $12,000. How much did the company receive from customers during the month?

ⓐ $50,000
ⓑ $52,000
ⓒ $48,000
ⓓ $62,000

5.4 A trial balance represents the:

- a Source documents used to determine the effects of transactions on the company's accounts.
- b List of all accounts and their balances at a particular date to ensure that debits equal credits.
- c Chronological record of all transactions affecting the company.
- d Process of transferring debit and credit information from the journal to the accounts in the general ledger.

5.5 Of the following six accounts, which ones are income statement accounts?

(1) Service Revenue	(2) Dividends
(3) Salaries Expense	(4) Ordinary share
(5) Retained Earnings	(6) Cash

- a (1) and (3)
- b (4), (5), and (6)
- c (2), (4), and (5)
- d (1), (3), and (5)

5.6 Statement of financial position accounts would not include:

- a Interest Expense.
- b Salaries Payable.
- c Prepaid Rent.
- d Unearned Revenues.

5.7 Income statement accounts would not include:

- a Salaries Payable.
- b Advertising Expense.
- c Supplies Expense.
- d Service Revenue.

5.8 At the beginning of the year, Gloria Inc. had $12,000 in retained earnings. During the year, Gloria earned a net income of $3,000 and paid cash dividends of $2,000. What is the year-end retained earnings?

ⓐ $15,000
ⓑ $12,000
ⓒ $13,000
ⓓ $11,000

5.9 Which of the following is not considered a primary financial statement?

ⓐ Statement of financial position
ⓑ Statement of cash flows
ⓒ Adjusted trial balance
ⓓ Income statement

5.10 Which of the following is the accrual-basis performance measure?

ⓐ Dividends
ⓑ Net income
ⓒ Cash flows from operating activities
ⓓ Change in cash

CHAPTER 5

Exercises

5.1 Worksheet for a service firm

Complete the worksheet below after making adjusting entries for the following data:

ⓐ Insurance expired, $50
ⓑ Depreciation, $2,000
ⓒ Earned $250 of unearned service revenue
ⓓ Accrued salaries, $100
ⓔ Accrued interest expense on the note payable, $20
ⓕ Service revenue earned but not received, $150
ⓖ Supplies on hand at year's end, $1,500

Grebe Corporation
Worksheet
For the Year Ended December 31, 20×1

Account	Trial Balance		Adjustments		Income Statement		Statement of Financial Position	
	Dr.	Cr.	Dr.	Cr.	Dr.	Cr.	Dr.	Cr.
Cash	12,900							
Accounts Receivable	8,000							
Prepaid Insurance	750							
Supplies	2,200							
Equipment	52,700							
Accumulated Depreciation		10,000						
Notes Payable		2,000						
Unearned Service Revenue		1,750						
Share Capital		40,000						
Retained Earnings		20,000						
Service Revenue		5,000						
Salaries Expense	1,000							
Utility Expense	1,200							
	78,750	78,750						

5.2 Financial statements for a service firm (1)

The adjusted trial balance of Loon Company appears below.

Loon Company
Adjusted Trial Balance
December 31, 20×1

	Debit	Credit
Cash	$7,400	
Accounts Receivable	3,200	
Office Supplies	1,800	
Office Equipment	17,500	
Accumulated Depreciation		$4,000
Accounts Payable		4,000
Unearned Service Revenue		5,000
Share Capital		12,000
Retained Earnings		4,400
Service Revenue		4,500
Office Supplies Expense	600	
Depreciation Expense	1,500	
Salaries Expense	1,900	
	$33,900	$33,900

Required:

Prepare ⓐ the income statement and ⓑ the statement of financial position in good form for the month ended December 31, 20×1.

5.3 Financial statements for a service firm (2)

The adjusted trial balance of Orchid Corporation appears below.

Orchid Corporation
Worksheet
For the Year Ended December 31, 20×1

Account	Trial Balance		Adjustments		Income Statement		Statement of Financial Position	
	Dr.	Cr.	Dr.	Cr.	Dr.	Cr.	Dr.	Cr.
Cash	7,000							
Accounts Receivable	23,000							
Supplies	1,000			ⓐ 700				
Prepaid Insurance	3,000			ⓑ 1,500				
Building	15,000							
Accumulated Depreciation		3,000		ⓒ 1,000				
Accounts Payable		6,000						
Share Capital		15,000						
Retained Earnings		14,000						
Service Revenue		36,000						
Salaries Expense	25,000		ⓓ 500					
	74,000	74,000						
Supplies Expense			ⓐ 700					
Insurance Expense			ⓑ 1,500					
Depreciation Expense			ⓒ 1,000					
Salaries Payable				ⓒ 500				
			3,700	3,700				

Required:

Prepare ⓐ the income statement and ⓑ the statement of financial position in good form for the year ended December 31, 20×1 on a separate page (Do not just fill out the Income Statement and Statement of Financial Position Columns of the worksheet).

5.4 Financial statements for a service firm (3)

The following is the adjusted trial balance for Crane Company.

Crane Company
Adjusted Trial Balance
For the Year Ended December 31, 20×1

Cash	$6,130	
Accounts Receivable	2,300	
Prepaid Rent	750	
Equipment	13,400	
Accumulated Depreciation		$1,200
Accounts Payable		1,700
Notes Payable - Due on June 30, 20×2		5,000
Bob Stellar, Capital		12,000
Bob Stellar, Drawing	870	
Service Revenue		6,600
Wages Expense	1,450	
Rent Expense	900	
Utility Expense	475	
Depreciation Expense	150	
Miscellaneous Expenses	75	
Totals	$26,500	$26,500

Required:

Prepare an Income Statement for the year ended December 31, 20×1 and a Statement of Financial Position as of December 31, 20×1 for Crane Company.

5.5 Financial statements for a service firm (4)

These items are taken from the financial statements of Toucan Corporation for 20×1.

Accumulated depreciation	$17,500
Accounts payable	13,200
Accounts receivable	14,200
Advertising expense	1,800
Cash	17,500
Depreciation expense	3,400
Dividends	12,000
Equipment	65,000
Miscellaneous expense	8,000
Ordinary shares	13,000
Prepaid rent	3,500
Retained earnings (beginning of the year)	32,000
Salaries expense	36,000
Salaries payable	3,200
Service revenue	85,000
Utility expense	2,500

Required:

Prepare an income statement for 20×1 and a statement of financial position as of December 31, 20×1 for Toucan Corporation.

5.6 Financial statements for a service firm (5)

The adjusted trial balance for Hornbill Company on December 31, 20×2 is presented below:

	Debit	Credit
Cash	$11,000	
Accounts Receivable	150,000	
Prepaid Rent	5,000	
Supplies	25,000	
Equipment	300,000	
Accumulated Depreciation		$135,000
Accounts Payable		20,000
Salaries Payable		4,000
Interest Payable		1,000
Notes Payable - due in two years		30,000
Ordinary Shares		200,000
Retained Earnings		50,000
Dividends	20,000	
Service Revenue		400,000
Salaries Expense	180,000	
Advertising Expense	70,000	
Rent Expense	15,000	
Depreciation Expense	30,000	
Interest Expense	2,000	
Utility Expense	32,000	
Totals	$840,000	$840,000

Required:

Prepare the Income Statement for the year ended December 31, 20×2 and the Statement of Financial Position on December 31, 20×2 for Hornbill Company.

5.7 Financial statements for a service firm (6)

The adjusted trial balance for Woodpecker Company on December 31, 20×1 is presented below:

	Debit	Credit
Cash	$22,000	
Prepaid Rent	13,000	
Buildings and Equipment	668,000	
Accumulated Depreciation - Buildings and Equipment		$260,000
Account Payable		37,000
Salaries Payable		13,000
Income Taxes Payable		22,000
Share Capital - Ordinary		200,000
Retained Earnings		100,000
Dividends	10,000	
Service Revenue		400,000
Salaries Expense	220,000	
Supplies Expense	20,000	
Rent Expense	30,000	
Advertising Expense	12,000	
Utility Expense	15,000	
Income Tax Expense	22,000	
Totals	$1,032,000	$1,032,000

Required:

Prepare the income statement and statement of financial position for Woodpecker Company for the year ended December 31, 20×1.

Accounting Terminology in Chapter 5

accounts payable 매입채무
accounts receivable 매출채권
accumulated depreciation 감가상각누계액
adjusted account balance 수정후계정잔액
adjusting entries 수정분개
cash 현금
cross-reference 상호조회
depreciation expense 감가상각비
equipment 비품
insurance expense 보험비용
interest expense 이자비용
interest payable 미지급이자
net income 당기순이익
notes payable 어음채무
post-closing trial balance 마감후시산표
prepaid insurance 선급보험료
retained earnings 이익잉여금
salaries expense 급여비용
salaries payable 미지급급여
service revenue 용역수익
share capital 자본금
straight-line method 정액법
supplies 소모품
supplies expense 소모품비용
trial balance 시산표
unearned service revenue 선수수익
utility expense 공공요금
worksheet 정산표

CHAPTER

6

ACCOUNTING FOR MERCHANDISING FIRMS

6.1 INTRODUCTION

6.2 ACCOUNTING FOR MERCHANDISE SALES

6.3 ACCOUNTING FOR MERCHANDISE PURCHASES

6.4 COST OF GOODS SOLD

6.5 CONDENSED INCOME STATEMENT

6.6 WORKSHEET FOR MERCHANDISING FIRMS

6.7 FINANCIAL STATEMENTS FOR MERCHANDISING FIRMS

CHAPTER 6

ACCOUNTING FOR MERCHANDISING FIRMS

6.1 INTRODUCTION

A merchandising firm(도소매업) buys goods for resale to customers. An example is a department store. The same accounting procedures apply to a service business except that additional accounts are needed to reflect the purchase and sale of merchandise. Merchandise(상품) (also called inventory) is goods purchased and held for resale purposes.

Every merchandising firm has inventories. Inventory(재고자산) is the dollar value of the merchandise on hand at either the beginning or end of the reporting period. Ending inventory consists of unsold merchandise as of the end of the period.

There are two alternative inventory recording systems: perpetual and periodic. Under the perpetual inventory system(계속기록법), daily records are maintained for each inventory item. The perpetual method is typically used for high dollar-value items such as automobiles. Under the periodic inventory system(실지재고조사법), the inventory at the end of the reporting period is determined by taking a physical count of the merchandise on hand. The periodic system is typically used for low dollar-value items such as candies since it is impractical to keep track of changes in such items. Due to its simplicity, this textbook uses the periodic inventory system.

6.2 ACCOUNTING FOR MERCHANDISE SALES

Firms may sell goods for cash or on credit. An asset is debited at the time of sale, and sales revenue is credited.

The journal entry for a cash sale is:

Cash	×××	
Sales(매출액)		×××

The entry for a credit sale is:

Accounts Receivable(매출채권)	×××	
Sales		×××

Firms recognize sales revenue when firms deliver goods to customers under accrual-basis accounting. Sales returns and allowances(매출환입및에누리) reduce the gross sales(총매출액) of the firm. Sales returns(매출환입) mean that the goods sold are returned to the seller because of defects or unsatisfactory conditions. Sales allowances(매출에누리) mean that the seller allows buyers a reduction of the selling price of the goods sold because of quality problems, but the buyers agree to keep the purchased goods. The appropriate journal entry in these situations is:

Sales Returns and Allowances	×××	
Cash (or Accounts Receivable)		×××

Sales discounts(매출할인) represent cash discounts given by the seller to the purchaser for early payment of the accounts payable due. For example, suppose that the credit terms(신용조건) of a sale are 1/10, n/30. Here, 1 represents the cash discount percentage, 10 represents the cash discount period in days, n stands for the net amount (after subtracting sales returns and allowances from the sale), and 30 represents the credit period in days. The credit terms indicate that if the customer pays in 10 days, the customer gets 1 percent off the invoice(송장) price; otherwise, the customer must pay the net amount of sales after subtracting sales returns and allowances no later than 30 days. Note that if the customer remits after 10 days (but before 30 days), the customer will not get any cash discount.

The journal entry for a sales discount is:

Cash	×××	
Sales Discount	×××	
Accounts Receivable		×××

Example 6-1 Sales Discounts

Shoebill Company sold $10,000 of merchandise to a customer on terms of 1/10, n/30. The payment was made within 10 days. The amount of the discount is, therefore, $100 ($10,000 × 1%). Thus, the seller will receive $9,900 ($10,000 − $100). Appropriate journal entries for the original credit sale and the payment from the customer, respectively, are:

[At the time of sale]

Accounts Receivable	10,000	
Sales		10,000

[At the time of collection within the cash discount period]

Cash	9,900	
Sales Discounts	100	
Accounts Receivable		10,000

A trade discount(거래할인) is different from a cash discount. A trade discount represents a reduction from the list price for substantial quantity sales or a customary price reduction allowed to customers. Trade discount is not considered a recordable transaction and is not recognized in the seller's or purchaser's accounting records.

For example, if the list price of an item is $5,000 and a trade discount of 20 percent is given, the recorded sale would be $4,000 ($5,000 − $1,000). The journal entry is:

Accounts Receivable	4,000	
Sales		4,000

Figure 6-1 illustrates how different price structures are treated for accounting purposes. A list price(표시가격), also called a catalog price(목록가격), is not recognized for accounting purposes. Customers usually get a trade discount(거래할인) which represents the difference between the list price and invoice price. Trade discount is not recognized as mentioned above. The invoice price(송장가격) is the transaction price agreed upon between the seller and purchaser. Therefore, the invoice price becomes the basis of recording sales by the seller and purchases by the purchaser. When the purchaser takes advantage of a cash discount(현금할인), the seller records a sales discount(매출할인), and the purchaser records a purchase discount(매입할인). A cash price(현금가격) is the actual cash received by the seller or paid by the purchaser after taking into account the cash discount. Figure 6-1 shows the different prices and accounting treatments for them with an example.

Price			Accounting treatments
$5,000		**List price**	Not recognized
↓	$1,000	*Trade discount*	Not recognized
$4,000		**Invoice price**	Recognized
↓	$40	*Cash discount*	Recognized
$3,960		**Cash price**	Recognized

Figure 6-1 Accounting treatments of prices

Example 6-2 shows a partial income statement, highlighting a presentation of the sales revenue for a merchandising business. Here, sales returns and allowances, and discounts are contra accounts to sales revenue, meaning they are reported as a reduction of gross sales revenue to report net sales revenue.

EXAMPLE 6-2 ***Reporting Sales***

Flamingo Company
A partial Income Statement

Gross Sales Revenue		$300,000
Less: Sales Returns and Allowances	$15,000	
Sales Discounts	8,000	(23,000)
Net Sales Revenue		$277,000

6.3 ACCOUNTING FOR MERCHANDISE PURCHASES

The inventory account represents the amount of goods in stock at a given point in time. In the periodic inventory recording system, this is the amount on hand at the end of the reporting period. Purchases of merchandise from suppliers are entered into a separate account called Purchases(매입) at the cost of buying the goods. The Purchases account is for merchandise intended for resale. The journal entry for a merchandise purchase is:

Purchases	×××	
Cash (or Accounts Payable)		×××

The Purchases account is reported in the Cost of Goods Sold(매출원가) section of the income statement. At the end of the reporting period, it is closed out to the income summary account(집합손익계정) since it is a temporary account.

Purchase returns and allowances(매입환출및에누리) reduce the cost of gross purchases(총매입액). Purchase returns represent goods returned to the supplier. In contrast, purchase allowances represent a price reduction given to customers on the condition that the customers keep the goods at a reduced price. Purchase returns and purchase allowances are combined as a single account since they typically result from unsatisfactory conditions of the goods purchased by the customers. The journal entry for purchase returns and allowances is:

Cash (or Accounts Payable)	×××	
Purchase Returns and Allowances		×××

Purchase discounts are cash discounts given by the supplier to the purchaser for early payment of accounts payable. The entry for a purchase discount when the purchaser pays the accounts payable within the cash discount period is:

Accounts Payable	×××	
Purchase Discounts		×××
Cash		×××

Example 6-3 *Recording Purchases*

Flamingo Company purchased merchandise for $6,000 from a supplier on terms of 2/15, n/30. If Flamingo remits cash for the purchase within 15 days, the purchase discount is $120 ($6,000×2%). The payment to the supplier is $5,880 ($6,000−$120). Flamingo's journal entries for the purchase and the payment are:

[At the time of purchase]

Purchases	6,000	
Accounts Payable		6,000

[At the time of payment within the cash discount period]

Accounts Payable	6,000	
Purchase Discounts		120
Cash		5,880

Freight-in(매입운임, transportation-in) is an account to reflect the transportation charges paid by the purchaser for goods delivered. The journal entry to record freight-in is:

Freight-in	×××	
Cash (or Accounts Payable)		×××

Freight-in is added to the purchases account because it is an element of the delivered cost of the goods.

Example 6-4 shows a partial income statement highlighting the presentation of purchases.

EXAMPLE 6-4 *Reporting Purchases*

Flamingo Company A Partial Income Statement		
Purchases		$150,000
Freight-in		3,000
Delivered Cost of Purchases		153,000
Less: Purchase Returns and Allowances	$25,000	
Purchase Discounts	13,000	(38,000)
Net Purchases		$115,000

6.4 COST OF GOODS SOLD

Under the periodic inventory system, merchandising businesses do not record inventory decreases due to sales made during the year. As a result, the beginning inventory is not updated until the end of an accounting period. Hence, firms must determine the ending inventory(기말재고) by a physical count at the end of an accounting period.

The ending inventory amount is an asset(자산) to be reported in the statement of financial position. In other words, the updated ending inventory replaces the beginning inventory. The cost of goods sold(매출원가) must be measured and reported in the income statement. Reporting the ending inventory in the statement of financial position and the cost of goods sold in the income statement are interrelated and done formally by the closing entries (to be discussed in 6.6) under the periodic inventory system. More specifically, they can be expressed as follows:

Beginning Inventory+Net Purchases=Cost of Goods Available for Sale
=Cost of Goods Sold+Ending Inventory

The cost of goods available for sale(판매가능원가) can be expressed as a two-way equation, as can be seen above. The lefthand side of the above equation shows that the sum of beginning inventory and net purchases equals the cost of goods available for sale. Net purchases(순매입) are determined as follows:

	Purchases
+	Freight-in
−	Purchase Returns and Allowances
−	Purchase Discounts
=	Net Purchases

The righthand side of the equation shows that the cost of goods available for sale can be divided into the cost of goods sold (sold part) and ending inventory (remaining part). The sold part is reported in the income statement as the cost of goods sold. In contrast, the remaining part is reported in the statement of financial position as the ending inventory.

Example 6-5 shows a partial income statement highlighting the cost of goods sold section in the income statement.

EXAMPLE 6-5 *Cost of Goods Sold*

Flamingo Company
A Partial Income Statement

Inventory, January 1, 20×1 (beginning inventory)	$75,000
Net Purchases (Example 6-4)	115,000
Cost of Goods Available for Sale	190,000
Less: Inventory, December 31, 20×1 (ending inventory)	60,000
Cost of Goods Sold	$130,000

6.5 CONDENSED INCOME STATEMENT

We can prepare a condensed income statement(요약손익계산서) for a merchandising firm. A condensed income statement may comprise four major categories: sales(매출액), cost of goods sold(매출원가), operating expenses(영업비용), and income tax expense(법인세비용). In addition, a condensed income statement may also show several profit subtotals, such as gross profit(매출총이익), operating profit(영업이익), income before income taxes(법인세차감전이익) as well as net income(당기순이익).

Example 6-6 illustrates a condensed income statement for a merchandising firm.

EXAMPLE 6-6 *Condensed Income Statement*

Flamingo Company
Income Statement
For the Year Ended December 31, 20×1

Net Sales (Example 6-2)	$277,000
Cost of Goods Sold (Example 6-5)	130,000
Gross Profit	147,000
Operating Expenses	52,000
Income before Income Taxes (Operating Income)	95,000
Income Tax Expense*	19,000
Net Income	$76,000

* Income Tax Expense is the tax the company incurs based on its operating income. We assumed a tax rate of 20 percent here, so the income tax expense for the year is $19,000 ($95,000 × 20%).

6.6 WORKSHEET FOR MERCHANDISING FIRMS

We learned the worksheet for a service firm in Chapter 5. In addition to the accounts mentioned there, the worksheet for a merchandising business will have some new accounts, such as sales(매출액), inventory(재고자산), purchases (매입), and cost of goods sold(매출원가). Just like service business, we prepare adjusting entries before preparing financial statements for merchandising firms. However, we have one more process at the end of an accounting period in case of merchandising firms. It is to compute cost of goods sold for merchandising firms. We compute the cost of goods sold for an accounting period under the periodic inventory system by the following equation:

Cost of Goods Sold = Beginning Inventory + Net Purchases − Ending Inventory

Under the periodic inventory system, we use closing entries to (1) update inventory by replacing the beginning inventory with the ending inventory in the statement of financial position and (2) compute the cost of goods sold for the period to be reported in the income statement. The closing entry for merchandising firms under the periodic inventory system is as follows:

Cost of Goods Sold	×××	
Inventory - Ending	×××	
Inventory - Beginning		×××
Purchases		×××

EXAMPLE 6-7 Worksheet for a Merchandising Firm

The unadjusted trial balance for Macaw Corporation is as follows:

	Dr.	Cr.
Cash	6,000	
Accounts Receivable	12,000	
Merchandise Inventory	15,000	
Supplies	500	
Prepaid Insurance	2,000	
Equipment	10,000	
Accumulated Depreciation		3,000
Accounts Payable		4,000
Notes Payable		2,000
Share Capital		10,000
Retained Earnings		16,000
Sales		38,000
Purchases	20,000	
Salaries Expense	5,000	
Utility Expense	2,500	
	73,000	73,000

Additional information on December 31, 20×1:

ⓐ The ending balance of supplies is $200.
ⓑ The ending balance of prepaid insurance is $1,000.
ⓒ The depreciation expense for the period is $1,000.
ⓓ Interest expense incurred but not paid yet is $50.
ⓔ Salaries expense incurred but not paid amount to $150.
ⓕ A physical count of merchandise inventory revealed that the ending inventory is $17,000.

Required:

Prepare necessary adjusting and closing entries on December 31, 20×1.
Prepare a worksheet for Macaw Corporation for the year ended on December 31, 20×1.

(1) Adjusting and closing entries

Adjusting entries:

ⓐ Consumption of supplies on hand

Supplies Expense	300	
Supplies		300

ⓑ Expiration of Prepaid Insurance

Insurance Expense	1,000	
Prepaid Insurance		1,000

ⓒ Depreciation expense for the year

Depreciation Expense	1,000	
Accumulated Depreciation		1,000

ⓓ Accrued interest expense

Interest Expense	50	
Interest Payable		50

ⓔ Accrued salaries expense

Salaries Expense	150	
Salaries Payable		150

ⓕ Closing entry for computing Cost of Goods Sold and updating inventory:

Cost of Goods Sold	18,000	
Inventory - Ending	17,000	
Inventory - Beginning		15,000
Purchases		20,000

(2) Worksheet

Macaw Corporation
Worksheet
For the Year Ended December 31, 20×1

Account	Trial Balance		Adjustments/ Closing		Income Statement		Statement of Financial Position	
	Dr.	Cr.	Dr.	Cr.	Dr.	Cr.	Dr.	Cr.
Cash	6,000						6,000	
Accounts Receivable	12,000						12,000	
Inventory	15,000		ⓕ 17,000	ⓕ 15,000			17,000	
Supplies	500			ⓐ 300			200	
Prepaid Insurance	2,000			ⓑ 1,000			1,000	
Equipment	10,000						10,000	
Accumulated Depreciation		3,000		ⓒ 1,000				4,000
Accounts Payable		4,000						4,000
Notes Payable		2,000						2,000
Share Capital		10,000						10,000
Retained Earnings		16,000						16,000
Sales		38,000				38,000		
Purchases	20,000			ⓕ 20,000				
Salaries Expense	5,000		ⓔ 150		5,150			
Utility Expense	2,500				2,500			
	73,000	73,000						

Cost of Goods Sold			ⓕ 15,000	ⓕ 17,000	18,000			
			ⓕ 20,000					
Supplies Expense			ⓐ 300		300			
Insurance Expense			ⓑ 1,000		1,000			
Depreciation Expense			ⓒ 1,000		1,000			
Interest Expense			ⓓ 50		50			
Interest Payable				ⓓ 50				50
Salaries Payable				ⓔ 150				150
			54,500	54,500	28,000	38,000	46,200	36,200
Net Income					10,000			10,000
					38,000	38,000	46,200	46,200

6.7 FINANCIAL STATEMENTS FOR MERCHANDISING FIRMS

Using the worksheet, let's prepare the income statement and statement of financial position for the merchandiser. First, make sure you follow the standard forms of financial statements in preparing them. You must include proper headings(표제) for them, including the company name, the statement's title, a period for the income statement, and a specific date for the statement of financial position. Then, you are supposed to prepare classified financial statements with proper classifications of the items to be included in the statements and arrange them in the proper order.

In the income statement, report revenue(수익) first, followed by the cost of goods sold to match the direct cost with the revenue. As a result of the direct matching(직접대응) of the cost of goods sold with sales, the gross profit(매출총이익) is reported. Then, report operating expenses(영업비용) other than the cost of goods sold. Operating expenses can further be classified into selling expenses(판매비) and general administrative expenses(일반관리비). The difference between the gross profit and operating expenses is reported as operating profit or operating income(영업이익).

Other revenues(기타수익) and other expenses(기타비용) are usually separately reported below operating profit. Then, income before income taxes is reported, from which income tax expense(법인세비용) is subtracted to arrive at net income. Net Income(당기순이익) is often called the bottom line number because it is the final number on the income statement. Double underline the net income amount to indicate that Net Income is the last item in the income statement.

For the statement of financial position, classify assets into current assets (유동자산) and noncurrent assets(비유동자산). Likewise, classify liabilities into current liabilities(유동부채) and noncurrent liabilities(비유동부채). You need to report contra accounts(차감계정), such as accumulated depreciation(감가상각누계액), right below the related account in such a way to subtract the contra account from the related account to report the item at its carrying amount(장부금액). Also important is to make sure that the accounting equation(회계등식) always holds, i.e., Assets = Liabilities + Owners' Equity. Do not forget to double underline total assets(자산총계) and total liabilities and owners' equity(부채와 자본총계) to indicate that they are the last items in each side of the statement of financial position.

We now prepare Macaw Corporation's financial statements—the income statement and statement of financial position—using the worksheet in Example 6-7.

EXAMPLE 6-8 ***Financial Statements for a Merchandising Firm***

Macaw Corporation
Income Statement
For the Year Ended December 31, 20×1

Sales		$38,000
Cost of Goods Sold		
Merchandise Inventory, January 1, 20×1	$15,000	
Purchases	20,000	
Cost of Goods Available for Sale	35,000	
Less: Merchandise Inventory, December 31, 20×1	17,000	18,000
Gross Profit		20,000
Operating Expenses		
Salaries Expense	5,150	
Utility Expense	2,500	
Supplies Expense	300	
Insurance Expense	1,000	
Depreciation Expense	1,000	
Interest Expense	50	
Total Operating Expenses		10,000
Net Income		$10,000

Macaw Corporation
Statement of Financial Position
December 31, 20×1

Assets		
Current Assets		
Cash	$6,000	
Accounts Receivable	12,000	
Inventory	17,000	
Supplies	200	
Prepaid Insurance	1,000	
Total Current Assets		$36,200
Property, Plant, and Equipment		
Equipment	10,000	
Less: Accumulated Depreciation	(4,000)	
Net Property, Plant, and Equipment		6,000
Total Assets		$42,200
Liabilities and Owners' Equity		
Current Liabilities		
Accounts Payable	4,000	
Notes Payable	2,000	
Interest Payable	50	
Salaries Payable	150	
Total Current Liabilities		6,200
Total Liabilities		6,200
Owners' Equity		
Share Capital	10,000	
Retained Earnings	26,000	
Total Owners' Equity		36,000
Total Liabilities and Owners' Equity		$42,200

CHAPTER 6

Multiple Choice Questions

6.1 Which of the following best describes credit sales?

a Cash sales to customers that are new to the company
b Sales to customers using credit cards
c Sales to customers on account
d Sales with a high risk that the customer will return the product

6.2 Credits sales are recorded as:

a Debit Cash, Credit Unearned Revenue.
b Debit Service Revenue, Credit Accounts Receivable.
c Debit Cash, Credit Service Revenue.
d Debit Accounts Receivable, Credit Service Revenue.

6.3 Orca Inc. shipped the wrong shade of paint to a customer. The customer agreed to keep the paint upon being offered a 10% price reduction. Orca would record this reduction by crediting Accounts Receivable and debiting:

a Sales Revenue.
b Sales Discounts.
c Sales Returns.
d Sales Allowances.

6.4 When customers purchase products on account, Narwhal Company offers them a 2% reduction in the amount owed if they pay within 10 days. This is an example of a:

ⓐ Bad debt.
ⓑ Sales discount.
ⓒ Sales return.
ⓓ Sales allowances.

6.5 Titmouse Inc. shipped the wrong material to a customer, who refused to accept the order. This is an example of a:

ⓐ Sales Revenue.
ⓑ Sales discount.
ⓒ Sales return.
ⓓ Sales allowance.

6.6 Warbler Company offers a 20% trade discount when providing $2,000 or more of plumbing services to its customers. In March 20×1, Warbler provided $4,000 of plumbing services to Cypress Inc. and $1,500 of services to Pine Inc. Each of these customers was granted credit terms of 2/10, net 30. If both customers paid for the plumbing services within the discount period, what was the net sales figure for these two transactions?

ⓐ $5,500
ⓑ $4,312
ⓒ $4,486
ⓓ $4,606

6.7 Cost of goods sold is:

ⓐ Beginning inventory + Net purchases − Ending inventory.
ⓑ Ending inventory + Net purchases − Beginning inventory.
ⓒ Beginning inventory + Ending inventory − Net purchases.
ⓓ Beginning inventory + Net purchases + Ending inventory.

6.8 Net purchases is determined by:

ⓐ Purchases − Purchase returns and allowances − Purchase discounts.
ⓑ Purchases − Purchase returns and allowances − Purchase discounts + Transportation-in.
ⓒ Purchases − Purchase returns and allowances + Purchase discounts.
ⓓ Purchases − Purchase returns and allowances + Purchase discounts + Transportation-in.

6.9 Cost of goods available for sale is determined by:

ⓐ Beginning inventory + Net purchases − Ending inventory.
ⓑ Beginning inventory + Net purchases.
ⓒ Net purchases − Beginning inventory.
ⓓ Net purchases − Ending inventory.

6.10 Ending inventory includes:

ⓐ Physical count of inventory + Goods shipped on FOB shipping points.
ⓑ Physical count of inventory − Goods shipped on FOB shipping points.
ⓒ Physical count of inventory + Goods shipped on FOB destination.
ⓓ Physical count of inventory − Goods shipped on FOB destination.

CHAPTER 6

Exercises

6.1 Merchandise sales

Prepare journal entries for the following transactions of a seller:

October 3: Sold merchandise to a customer for $800 on terms of 3/20, n/60.
October 6: The customer returned $100 of the goods because of damages.
October 11: Received payment from the customer for the balance due.

6.2 Merchandise purchases

Prepare the appropriate journal entries to be made by a purchaser.

October 3: Purchased merchandise for $800 on terms of 3/20, n/60.
October 6: Returned $100 of the goods because of damages.
October 11: Paid the balance due to the supplier.

6.3 Merchandise transactions - Periodic inventory system (1)

A company had the following inventory transactions during May:

May 3: Purchased inventory on account for $3,500, terms 2/10, n/30.
May 5: Paid freight costs of $200 on inventory purchased on May 3.
May 6: Returned inventory with a cost of $500.
May 12: Paid the full amount due on May 3 purchase.
May 25: Sold all inventory purchased on May 3 (less those returned on May 6) for $5,000 on account.

Required:

Record all transactions, assuming the company uses a periodic inventory system.

6.4 Merchandise transactions - Periodic inventory system (2)

Presented here are selected transactions for Puffin Company during April. Puffin Company uses the periodic inventory system.

April 1: Sold merchandise to Mallard Company for $2,000 on terms of 2/10, n/30. The merchandise sold had a cost of $1,000.

April 2: Purchased merchandise from Plover Corporation for $3,000 on terms of 1/10, n/30.

April 4: Purchased merchandise from Gannet Company for $1,000 on terms of n/30.

April 10: Received payment from Mallard Company for April 1 sale less appropriate discount.

April 11: Paid Plover Corporation for April 2 purchase.

April 13: Paid Gannet Company for April 4 purchase.

Required:

Journalize the April transactions for Puffin Company.

6.5 Net purchases

Information regarding purchases is presented below. Compute the net purchases.

Freight-In	$15,000
Purchase Discounts	12,000
Purchases	210,000
Purchase Returns and Allowances	30,000

6.6 Sales discounts

On April 8, Stingray Inc. sold 100 printers to Oleander Company at $600 each and offered a 2% discount for payment within 10 days. On April 15, Oleander Company paid the full amount in cash. Prepare a journal entry for Stingray Inc. record on April 15.

6.7 Net sales (1)

Armadillo Company reported the following amounts at the end of the year: total sales =$550,000; sales discounts=$12,000; sales returns=$44,000; sales allowances= $17,000. What is the company's net sales for the year?

6.8 Net sales (2)

A company reports the following amounts at the end of the year: total sales=$400,000; cash=$35,000; sales discounts=$10,000; accounts receivable=$20,000; sales returns =$15,000; operating expenses=$70,000; sales allowances=$25,000. Compute net sales.

6.9 Adjusting and closing entries for merchandise transactions

For each item listed below, prepare the appropriate adjusting/closing entries.

- ⓐ Merchandise inventory on January 1 was $40,000; on December 31, $33,000.
- ⓑ As of January 1, there was $6,000 of office supplies. At year's end, the amount of supplies on hand was $1,500.
- ⓒ The last payroll day was December 27, a Tuesday. The weekly payroll (five-day work week) is $20,000.

6.10 Income statement for a merchandising firm

The following information is from the Income Statement columns of a worksheet.

	Dr.	Cr.
Income Summary*	21,000	28,000
Sales		105,000
Purchases	40,000	
Salaries Expense	12,000	
Utility Expense	9,000	
Advertising Expense	6,000	
Rent Expense	14,000	

* $21,000 represents the beginning inventory and $28,000 represents the ending inventory.

Required:

Prepare the income statement.

6.11 Financial statements for a merchandising firm

The adjusted trial balance for Tapir Company on December 31, 20×1 is presented below:

	Debit	Credit
Cash	$26,000	
Accounts Receivable	135,000	
Merchandise Inventory	39,000	
Equipment	400,000	
Accumulated Depreciation - Equipment		$235,000
Accounts Payable		28,000
Accrued Liabilities		7,000
Bonds Payable - due in five years		30,000
Share Capital - Ordinary		120,000
Retained Earnings		130,000
Dividends	20,000	
Sales Revenue		414,000
Cost of Goods Sold	180,000	
Selling Expenses	85,000	
General Administrative Expenses	65,000	
Income Tax Expense	14,000	
Totals	$964,000	$964,000

Required:

Prepare Income Statement and Statement of Financial Position for the year ended December 31, 20×1.

Accounting Terminology in Chapter 6

accounting equation 회계등식
accounts receivable 매출채권
accumulated depreciation 감가상각누계액
carrying amount 장부금액
cash discounts 현금할인
cash price 현금가격
catalog price 목록가격
condensed income statement 요약손익계산서
contra account 차감계정
cost of goods available for sale 판매가능원가
cost of goods sold 매출원가
credit terms 신용조건
current assets 유동자산
current liabilities 유동부채
direct matching 직접대응
ending inventory 기말재고
freight-in 매입운임
general administrative expenses 일반관리비
gross profit 매출총이익
gross purchases 총매입액
gross sales 총매출액
heading 표제
income before income taxes 법인세차감전이익
income summary 집합손익
income tax expense 법인세비용
inventory 재고자산
invoice 송장
invoice price 송장가격
list price 표시가격
merchandise 상품
merchandising firm 도소매업
net income 당기순이익
net purchases 순매입
noncurrent assets 비유동자산
noncurrent liabilities 비유동부채
operating expenses 영업비용
operating income 영업이익
operating profit 영업이익
other expenses 기타비용
other revenues 기타수익
periodic inventory system 실지재고조사법
perpetual inventory system 계속기록법
purchase discounts 매입할인
purchase returns and allowances 매입환출및에누리
purchases 매입
sales 매출액
sales allowances 매출에누리
sales discounts 매출할인
sales returns 매출환입
sales returns and allowances 매출환입및에누리
selling expenses 판매비
total assets 자산총계
total liabilities and owners' equity 부채와 자본총계
trade discount 거래할인
transportation-in 매입운임
trial balance 시산표
worksheet 정산표

CHAPTER

7

CASH AND FINANCIAL ASSETS

CHAPTER 7

CASH AND FINANCIAL ASSETS

7.1 INTRODUCTION

Transactions involving cash occur frequently. Cash is the most liquid asset of a business and is immediately available for paying current obligations. Creditors(채권자) are particularly interested in ratios involving cash—for example, the ratios of cash to total current liabilities—because such ratios represent the funds available to repay them. Since cash is the easiest asset to steal, stringent accounting procedures and record-keeping must be followed for cash transactions.

Financial assets(금융자산) include cash, equity instruments(지분상품) of another company, contractual rights(계약상권리) to receive cash from another company, and others with a similar nature. More specifically, financial assets include the company's cash and its accounts receivable(매출채권), as well as investments in other company's stocks(주식) and bonds(사채). Some of the financial assets are held for trading purposes(단기매매목적) or in anticipation of capital gains(자본이득). Others are held to receive cash flows from them throughout the duration. When the financial assets are held for trading purposes, they are carried at fair values(공정가치) whose changes are reported in the profit or loss of the period. When the financial assets are held to receive cash flows, they are carried at amortized costs(상각후원가). Fair values usually approximate market values(시장가치). Assets that are carried at amortized cost are measured at cost less impairment loss(손상차손). Accounts receivable and investments in the bonds of other companies are usually accounted for at amortized cost. In this chapter, we will learn accounting for cash and financial assets held for trading since both have the common characteristic of being highly liquid assets.

7.2 CASH

Cash takes various kinds of forms. Cash includes currency(통화), coins(주화), demand deposits(요구불예금, checking account), petty cash(소액현금), undeposited customer checks(고객수표), and money orders(우편환). Although other items, such as postage stamps and postdated checks, are controlled by the cashier, they are not cash. Postage represents a prepaid expense(선급비용), while postdated checks(선일자수표) are receivables. Postdated checks cannot be cashed until the date arrives.

Cash equivalents(현금성자산) are short-term, highly liquid investments that are readily convertible to known amounts of cash and which are not subject to a significant risk of changes in value. Therefore, an investment usually qualifies as a cash equivalent only when it has a short maturity of three months or less from the date of acquisition. Equity instruments(지분상품) are excluded from cash equivalents since the issuer does not redeem them; therefore, no maturity exists for equity instruments.

7.3 CONTROL OF CASH

Internal control(내부통제) over cash through the segregation of duties(업무분장) is essential because of its susceptibility to theft. For example, an individual having physical custody over cash should not be responsible for handling the accounting records. Furthermore, there should be frequent surprise counts for cash on hand.

Some controls applicable to cash receipts(현금수취) are:

① Cash sales should have supporting documents such as point-of-sale system register tapes.
② Cash receipts should be deposited at the bank each day.

Some controls dealing with cash disbursements(현금지출) are:

① Cash payments should be made only by an authorized individual.
② Approved supporting documentation should exist prior to payment.
③ The person who approves the expenditure should not be the one who signs the check.
④ Credit cards or pre-numbered checks should be used.
⑤ Spoiled checks should be voided.
⑥ The individual preparing the checks should perform no other function having to do with cash.

Since there are numerous cash transactions with the bank, there should be separate cash controls for cash in banks. Two controls are essential regarding the preparation of the bank reconciliation(은행계정조정):

① The person preparing the bank reconciliation should not be involved in cash receipt or payment functions.
② The envelope containing the bank statement and cleared checks should not be opened by any party other than the preparer of the bank reconciliation.

7.4 BANK RECONCILIATION

Companies or individuals can maintain two types of bank accounts: savings and checking accounts. The savings account(정기예금계정) earns interest income for a fixed period but with some restrictions on withdrawals. The checking account(당좌계정), also called a draft account, facilitates transactions involving cash. Frequent deposits and withdrawals can be made without any restrictions on the checking account. Instead, no or meager interest is paid to the checking account.

The three parties involved in a check are the drawer, drawee, and payee. The drawer is the party issuing the check; the drawee is the bank upon which the check is drawn; and the payee is the party receiving payment (in other words, the party to whom the check is written). When the payee deposits the check, the payee must endorse(배서) the check.

A bank statement(은행명세서) shows a monthly deposit made, checks cleared, various charges and credits (to be mentioned in the next section), and account balances at the beginning and end of the period. A bank reconciliation is prepared based on the information contained in the bank statement. Thereon are deposits made, checks cleared, and charges or credits (deductions or additions) to the account. An example of a deduction to the company's account is a bank service charge or fee, while an example of an addition to the account is the amount collected by the bank on a customer's note.

Rarely does the ending balance in the bank statement agree with the ending balance in the cash account per the company's books. Therefore, a bank reconciliation is required to reflect the reconciling items. After the reconciliation, the adjusted bank balance(수정후은행잔액) must equal the adjusted book balance(수정후장부잔액). When it does, it indicates that both records are correct. Therefore, reconciliation of differences relates to (1) items shown on the company's books but not on the bank statement and (2) items shown on the bank statement but not on the company's books (See Table 7-1 and Table 7-2).

Table 7-1 Reconciling items for the bank statement

The bank balance is adjusted for items reflected on the company's books that are not on the bank statement. They include several types of items.	
Outstanding checks (미인출수표)	The company issued these checks, but the bank has not cleared them yet. As a result, these have not been recorded as withdrawals by the bank yet. Therefore, the outstanding checks are deducted from the bank balance.
Deposits in transit (은행미기록예금)	These refer to deposits recorded by the company, but the bank has not recorded the deposits yet. Such deposits are added to the bank balance.
Errors in recording checks (수표기장오류)	Mistakes, such as transaction errors, can be made in recording checks. For example, an overstatement of the company's payment should be added to the company balance.
Bank errors in charging or crediting the company's account (은행의 기타오류)	The bank balance is understated if a company's account is charged erroneously for another company's cleared check. Then, the mischarged check should be added to the bank balance. Likewise, if a deposit made by the company is incorrectly added to someone else's account, the amount should be added to the bank balance.

Table 7-2 Reconciling items for the books

The book balance (cash account) is adjusted for items shown on the bank statement that are not reflected on the company's books.	
Collections (추심액)	The bank sometimes collects notes receivable with interest on them for the company, which the company has not recorded yet. Also, the company may not have yet recorded electronic money transfers to the company's account. Therefore, the collections must be added to the book balance.
NSF (not sufficient funds) checks (부도수표)	NSF checks refer to checks that have been returned to the company because of insufficient funds in the issuer's checking account. In this case, the company's bank issues a debit memorandum for the dishonored amount, reducing the book balance.
Bank charges (은행수수료)	Bank service fees reduce the company's cash balance. These amounts are not known until the bank statement is received. Examples include the monthly service charge, check printing costs, and dishonored check fees.
Interest earned (이자수익)	Interest income credited by the bank on the checking account increases the company's cash balance.
Errors in the books (회사장부상오류)	Various types of mistakes can be made in the books.

It is important to understand typical clearance procedures of checks or the use of electronic funds transfer (EFT, 온라인자금이체) as a payment for purchases (See Figure 7-1). When goods are traded between the seller and the buyer (Step ①), payment can usually be made by checks or electronic transfer. When a check is drawn by the buyer and sent to the seller (Step ②), the buyer records payment of purchases by recording "Dr. Accounts Payable ××× Cr. Cash ×××." When the seller receives the check from the buyer, the seller endorses it, deposits it with the seller's bank, and records the collection of accounts receivable by recording "Dr. Cash ××× Cr. Accounts Receivable ×××" (Step ③). Then, the seller's bank refers the check to the buyer's bank (Step ④). When the buyer maintains sufficient cash with the buyer's bank, the buyer's bank clears the check, transfers cash to the seller's bank, and records a decrease in the buyer's cash balance (Step ⑤). Finally, the seller's bank records an increase in cash for the seller. However, if the buyer's cash balance is insufficient, the buyer's bank refuses a cash transfer to the seller's bank. In this case, the seller's bank does not record an increase in cash for the seller. When the seller learns of the NSF check, which was not cleared, it must reverse the journal entry made in Step ③.

The issued checks in the process of being cleared are called outstanding checks for the buyer. More specifically, they are checks between Step 2 and Step 5 in Figure 7-1. The same checks become deposits in transit for the seller. They are checks between Step 3 and Step 5 in Figure 7-1.

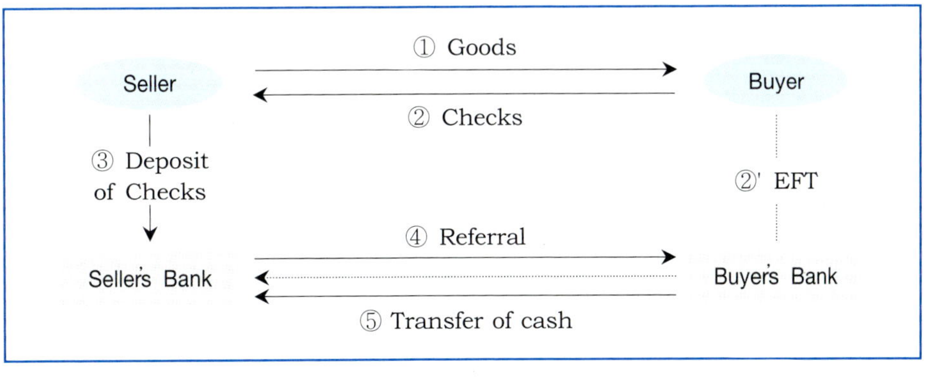

Figure 7-1 Clearance of Checks

Sometimes, the buyer may use an electronic funds transfer to the seller's bank, depicted as Step ②' in Figure 7-1. The dotted line shows the process of electronic funds transfers from the buyer's bank to the seller's account at the seller's bank at the buyer's request. The use of credit cards is another method to collect receivables or pay payables.

After the bank reconciliation has been prepared, journal entries are prepared for the reconciling items affecting the company's book balance only. The reason is that the amounts on the company's books need to be updated for any items reflected on the bank statement that the company has not recorded yet. However, reconciling items to the bank balance are not journalized since they have already been recorded in the books.

EXAMPLE 7-1 *Bank Reconciliation*

Wisteria Corporation provides the following data in connection with the preparation of its bank reconciliation on June 30, 20×1:

Balance per bank $4,889; balance per books $4,400; outstanding checks $700; deposits in transit $300; collection of notes receivable $200 and interest $16; collection fee on notes receivable $12; NSF checks $100; and monthly service charge $15.

Wisteria Corporation
Bank Reconciliation
June 30, 20×1

Balance per bank	$4,889	Balance per books		$4,400
Add: Deposits in transit	300	Add: Collection of notes and interest		216
	$5,189			$4,616
Less: Outstanding checks	(700)	Less: NSF checks	$100	
		Collection fee	12	
		Service charge	15	
				(127)
Adjusted bank balance	$4,489	Adjusted book balance		$4,489

Journal entries on June 30, 20×1:

June 30	Cash	216	
	Notes Receivable		200
	Interest Income		16
	Accounts Receivable	100	
	Cash		100
	Bank Service Charge	27	
	Cash		27

After the journal entries have been posted, the books are up to date. For example, the cash balance per books will now agree with the bank balance, namely $4,489. The cash T-account is shown below for clarification.

Cash

Balance before adjustment	4,400	NSF checks	100
Notes receivable and interest collected	216	Service charges	27
Balance after adjustment	4,489		

7.5 CASH SHORT AND OVER

In a business involving over-the-counter cash receipts, occasional errors may occur in making change. The cash shortage or overage is revealed when the cash count at the end of the day disagrees with the cash receipts record. Assuming that the count is $600 and the cash receipts reading shows $620, the appropriate journal entry is:

Cash	600	
Cash Short and Over	20	
Sales		620

Cash Short and Over(현금과부족) is an income statement account that is grouped with miscellaneous expenses(기타비용) or miscellaneous revenue(기타수익), respectively.

7.6 FINANCIAL ASSETS

Companies have different motivations for investing in securities issued by other companies. One motivation is to earn a return on investment(투자이익). For example, a company can receive interest income(이자수익) from a debt investment(채권투자) or dividend income(배당수익) from an equity investment(주식투자). Another motivation is to exercise control over the investee(피투자회사).

Financial assets or instruments(금융자산) are grouped into three separate categories for accounting purposes. These categories are as follows:

ⓐ ***Amortized cost financial assets***(상각후원가측정금융자산). Only debt securities (채무증권) are eligible for this classification if they meet the business model test(사업모형검증) and the cash flow characteristics test(현금흐름특성검증). Equity securities(지분증권) are not included in this category since they do not have maturities.

ⓑ ***FVPL (fair value through profit and loss) financial assets***(당기손익-공정가치측정금융자산). Securities bought and held primarily for sale in the near future to generate holding gains on price changes. Both equity securities and debt securities can be held for this purpose.

ⓒ ***FVOCI (fair value through other comprehensive income) financial assets***(기타포괄손익-공정가치측정금융자산). Financial assets other than those classified as amortized cost or FVPL.

Fair value(공정가치) is defined as “The price that would be received to sell an asset or paid to transfer a liability in an orderly transaction between market participants at the measurement date.” Market values(시장가치) typically represent fair values.

All three classifications are possible for investments in debt securities since debt securities have to be redeemed or purchased back by the issuing company at the maturity date(만기일). However, only FVPL or FVOCI classifications are possible for investments in equity securities.

A debt instrument that meets both the business model test and cash flow characteristics test[1] must be measured at amortized cost unless the fair value option(공정가치선택권) is elected. A debt security that meets the cash flow characteristics test and is not designated as FVPL security must be measured at FVOCI if it is held to collect contractual cash flows or to sell it if the price is right. All other investments in debt instruments are measured at FVPL.

All investments in equity instruments that lack significant influence(중대한 영향력) or control(통제) over the investee are carried at fair value with changes in fair value recognized in profit or loss unless the FVOCI option is elected.

Fair value option(공정가치선택권). A company can exercise an option to designate, at initial recognition, a financial asset as an FVPL (in case of debt instruments) or FVOCI (in case of equity instruments) asset. The fair value option can be exercised if doing so eliminates or significantly reduces an 'accounting mismatch(회계불일치)' that would otherwise arise from measuring assets or liabilities or recognizing the gains or losses on them on different bases. The fair value option is available at initial recognition(최초인식시점) and irrevocable(취소불능). If the FVPL option is elected, the financial assets must be carried at fair values, and the subsequent changes in fair value must be included in profit and loss. Likewise, if the FVOCI option is chosen, the financial assets must be carried at fair values, and the subsequent changes in fair value (holding gains and losses) must be accounted for as other comprehensive income(기타포괄손익).

As noted above, there are differences in accounting for the holding gains and losses depending on the three classifications of financial assets. For the amortized cost financial assets, holding gains and losses are not recognized in profit and loss since the assets are carried at amortized cost. The FVPL assets are carried at fair value, and the related holding gains and losses are recognized in profit and loss in the period of value changes. The FVOCI assets are carried at fair value, but the related holding gains and losses are not

1 Business model test: The financial asset is held to collect their contractual cash flows (rather than to sell the assets prior to the maturity to realize changes in value); Cash flow characteristics test: The contractual terms of the financial asset give rise to cash flows that are solely payments of principal(원금) and interest(이자) on the principal amount outstanding. Only debt instruments are capable of meeting the contractual cash flow characteristics test.

recognized in profit and loss in the period of value changes; however, they are accounted for as other comprehensive income and accumulated in the shareholders' equity account until realized.

Unlike the differences in accounting for the holding gains and losses across the three classifications of financial assets, interest income on debt instruments and dividend income on equity instruments are recognized in profit or loss.

EXAMPLE 7-2 *FVPL Securities*

On May 1, 20×1, Carnation Inc. purchased 5,000 ordinary shares of Begonia Company for $17 per share plus a 2% brokerage commission. The journal entry is:

	Debit	Credit
FVPL Securities	86,700*	
Cash		86,700

* (5,000 shares × $17) + 2% (5,000 shares × $17) = $86,700

On August 5, 20×1, Carnation received cash dividends of $2 per share. The journal entry is:

	Debit	Credit
Cash	10,000**	
Dividend Income		10,000

** (5,000 shares × $2) = $10,000

On December 31, 20×1, the share price of Begonia was $20 per share. The journal entry to recognize holding gains and losses is:

	Debit	Credit
FVPL Securities	13,300***	
Holding gains - P&L		13,300

*** (5,000 shares × $20) − $86,700 = $13,300

EXAMPLE 7-3 *Investments in debt securities*

Lemur Inc. purchased several investments in debt securities during 20×1. The following information pertains to these securities. The fluctuations in their fair values are not considered permanent.

Classifications	12/31/20×1	12/31/20×2	12/31/20×1	12/31/20×2
Amortized cost:	Fair value	Fair value	Amortized cost	Amortized cost
ABC Bonds	$375,000	$400,000	$367,000	$360,000
FVPL:	Fair value	Fair value	Cost	
DEF Bonds	$139,000	$175,000	$138,000	
FVOCI:	Fair value	Fair value	Cost	
GHI Bonds	$130,000	$150,000	$140,000	

Required:

1. What amount would Lemur report for its total investments in debt securities at 12/31/20×1?
2. What total unrealized holding gain would Lemur report in its 20×2 income statement for its investments in debt securities?
3. What would be the balance in Lemur's accumulated other comprehensive income for these investments in its 12/31/20×2 statement of financial position (ignore taxes)?

Solutions:

1. Amortized cost securities are carried at amortized cost, whereas FVPL and FVOCI securities are carried at fair values. Hence, the carrying amount of the investments in debt securities at 12/31/20×1 is computed as follows:
   Total investments in debt securities = $367,000 (amortized cost for ABC bonds) + $139,000 (fair value for DEF bonds) + $130,000 (fair value for GHI bonds) = $636,000.
2. Change in fair values during the period for the FVPL securities only is included in the current period net income. Hence, the amount of holding gains and losses included in 20×2 net income is computed as follows:
   Holding gains and losses included in net income of the period = $175,000 (12/31/20×2 fair value) − $139,000 (12/31/20×1 fair value) = $36,000 (Holding gains).
3. AOCI (accumulated other comprehensive income) on the FVOCI securities is measured as the difference between year-end fair value and the cost. Hence, the AOCI on the FVOCI securities on 12/31/20×2 is computed as follows:
   AOCI balance on 12/31/20×2 = $150,000 (fair value at 12/31/20×2) − $140,000 (cost) = $10,000.

CHAPTER 7

Multiple Choice Questions

7.1 Which of the following best describes the goal of internal controls?

ⓐ Ensuring the business is profitable.
ⓑ Enhancing the health of employees.
ⓒ Improving the accuracy and reliability of financial information.
ⓓ Ensuring compliance with tax regulations.

7.2 Cash may not include:

ⓐ Foreign currency.
ⓑ Money orders.
ⓒ Accounts receivable.
ⓓ Undeposited customer checks.

7.3 Cash transactions recorded by the bank but not yet recorded by the company include all of the following except:

ⓐ Service fees.
ⓑ Interest earned.
ⓒ Outstanding checks.
ⓓ NSF checks.

7.4 Which of the following is a correct statement?

ⓐ Adjusted bank balance should equal adjusted book balance.
ⓑ Outstanding checks refer to checks recorded by the bank but not by the company as payments yet.
ⓒ Deposits in transit should be added to the book balance in the bank reconciliation.
ⓓ Not sufficient fund checks should be subtracted from the bank balance in the bank reconciliation.

7.5 Baobab Company provides th following data for the preparation of its bank reconciliation:

Balance per book	$31,400
Balance per bank	31,960
Outstanding checks	6,560
Deposits in transit	5,000
Not sufficient fund checks informed by the bank	800
Service charges by the bank	200

Which of the following is the adjusted book balance?

ⓐ $31,400
ⓑ $31,960
ⓒ $30,400
ⓓ $33,520

7.6 Lobster Company purchased equity securities for $100,000 and classified them as fair value through profit and loss (FVPL) securities. At the end of the year, the fair value of the securities was $105,000. How should the investment be reported in the year-end financial statements?

ⓐ The investment in securities would be reported in the statement of financial position at its $100,000 cost.
ⓑ The investment in securities would be reported in the statement of financial position at its $105,000 fair value.
ⓒ An unrealized holding gain would be reported in other comprehensive income.
ⓓ Both ⓑ and ⓒ are correct

7.7 Lobster Company purchased equity securities for $100,000 and classified them as fair value through other comprehensive income (FVOCI) securities. At the end of the year, the fair value of the securities was $105,000. How should the investment be reported in the year-end financial statements?

ⓐ The investment in securities would be reported in the statement of financial position at its $100,000 cost.
ⓑ The investment in securities would be reported in the statement of financial position at its $105,000 market value.
ⓒ An unrealized holding gain would be reported in other comprehensive income.
ⓓ Both ⓑ and ⓒ are correct.

7.8 Oriole Inc. purchased 1,000 shares of stock in Trout Company for $30 per share. The investment is properly classified as fair value through profit and loss (FVPL) security. By the end of the year, the stock price has increased to $32 per share. How would the change in stock price affect Oriole's net income?

ⓐ Increase net income by $32,000
ⓑ Increase net income by $30,000
ⓒ Increase net income by $2,000
ⓓ No effect

7.9 The primary difference between accounting for FVOCI securities and accounting for FVPL securities is:

ⓐ Measuring the fair value of the long-term and short-term share portfolios.
ⓑ Computing the acquisition cost.
ⓒ Determining whether the unrealized holding gain or loss on investments is reported in current net income or comprehensive income.
ⓓ Accounting for dividends received.

7.10 Which investment securities held by Zebra Inc. may be classified as amortized cost securities in its statement of financial position?

ⓐ Debt securities
ⓑ Equity securities
ⓒ Ordinary shares
ⓓ All of these are correct

CHAPTER 7

Exercises

7.1 Bank reconciliation (1)

The records of Camellia Company showed the following for the month of April:

ⓐ Cash balance per books–April 30, $15,000.

ⓑ Cash balance per bank statement–April 30, $12,853.

ⓒ On April 30, outstanding checks amounted to $642.

ⓓ The following two customer checks deposited by Camellia Company were returned to the company and were marked NSF:

Forsythia Shirts	$300
Daffodil Garment	$840

ⓔ A deposit of $3,100 was made on April 30 but was not included in the bank statement.

ⓕ The bank collected a $2,000 note for Camellia Company from the Azalea Company.

ⓖ The bank service charge was $25.

ⓗ The bank charged Camellia Company $524 in error.

Required:

Prepare a statement of bank reconciliation as of April 30.

7.2 Bank reconciliation (2)

Using the following information, prepare a statement of bank reconciliation for Nene Company for November 30, 20×1.

ⓐ The bank statement balance is $9,200.

ⓑ The cash account balance is $7,462.

ⓒ Outstanding checks amount to $1,650.

ⓓ Deposits in transit are $300.

ⓔ The bank service charge is $12.

ⓕ The collection of notes receivable by the bank is $400.

7.3 Bank reconciliation and adjusting entries

Grace Company's general ledger shows a cash balance of $7,850 on May 31, 20×2. May cash receipts of $1,250, included in the general ledger balance, are placed in the night depository at the bank on May 31 and processed by the bank on June 1. The bank statement dated May 31 shows an NSF check for $200 and a service fee of $50. The bank processes all checks written by the company by May 31 and lists them on the bank statement, except for one check totaling $1,640. The bank statement shows a balance of $7,990 on May 31.

Required:

ⓐ Prepare a bank reconciliation to calculate the correct ending balance of cash on May 31.

ⓑ Make necessary journal entries for Grace Company to update its cash balance.

7.4 Accounting terms

Listed below are six terms followed by a list of phrases that describe or characterize the terms. Match each phrase with the best term by placing the letter designating the term in the space provided.

ⓐ Bank service fees
ⓑ Deposits in transit
ⓒ Interest earned
ⓓ NSF checks
ⓔ Company error
ⓕ Checks outstanding

1. ______ Fees imposed by the bank to the company for providing routine services.
2. ______ Checks written to the company that are returned by the bank as having inadequate funds.
3. ______ The company recorded a deposit twice.
4. ______ Checks written by the company but not yet recorded by the bank.
5. ______ Cash receipts received by the company but not yet recorded by the bank.
6. ______ Money earned on the average daily balance of the checking account.

7.5 Financial asset classifications (1)

ⓐ Under IFRS 9, what reporting categories are used to account for debt investments? What about equity investments when the investor cannot significantly influence the operations of the investee?

ⓑ Under IFRS 9, which reporting categories are used to account for equity investments when the investor cannot significantly influence the operations of the investee?

7.6 Financial asset classifications (2)

Sumac Inc. purchased $75,000 of bonds on January 1, 20×1. The bonds pay interest semiannually and mature in 10 years when the $75,000 principal will be paid. The bonds do not pay any amounts other than interest and principal. During 20×1, the fair value of the bonds increased to $80,000. Sumac reports investments under IFRS 9.

Required:

How much unrealized gain or loss will Sumac include in 20×1 net income for the bonds?

ⓐ Sumac intends to collect contractual cash flows and sell the bonds within the next couple of years if the price is right.

ⓑ Sumac intends to hold the bonds until maturity.

7.7 FVPL securities (1)

On January 1, Ravens Corporation had idle funds that it used to purchase 300 shares of Robin Company at $12, plus a brokerage commission of $30. On August 1, a dividend of $0.60 per share was received. On October 1, 200 shares were sold for $14 per share, less a brokerage commission of $20.

Required:

Prepare the appropriate journal entries.

7.8 FVPL securities (2)

On March 1, 20×1, Jaguar Company purchased 5,000 shares of Tapir Corporation ordinary shares for $100,000 and classified them as trading securities. Thus the cost per share is $20. On December 31, 20×1, the market value of the shares was $12 per share. On December 31, 20×2, it was $23 per share.

Required:

Prepare the appropriate journal entries for the trading securities on December 31, 20×1, and December 31, 20×2.

7.9 FVPL securities (3)

The investment in FVPL equity securities of Conifer Corporation on December 31, 20×1 consists of the following. All the FVPL securities were purchased during 20×1.

	Cost	Market Value
X Company Ordinary Shares	$70,000	$75,000
Y Company Ordinary Shares	50,000	43,000
Z Company Preference Shares	100,000	90,000
Total	$220,000	$208,000

Required:

ⓐ Prepare journal entries to record holding gains and losses on the FVPL securities on December 31, 20×1.

ⓑ Suppose the company continues to hold the same investment portfolio until December 31, 20×2 and the market value of the FVPL securities happened to be $230,000. Prepare necessary journal entries on December 31, 20×2 to recognize holding gains and losses.

7.10 Investment in debt securities

Black Eagle Inc. purchased several investments in debt securities during 20×1. The following information pertains to these securities. The fluctuations in their fair values are not considered permanent.

Classifications	12/31/20×1	12/31/20×2	12/31/20×1	12/31/20×2
Amortized cost assets:	Fair value	Fair value	Amortized cost	Amortized cost
Osprey Bonds	$35,000	$40,000	$36,000	$35,000
FVPL assets:	Fair value	Fair value	Cost	
Falcon Bonds	$14,000	$13,000	$13,500	
FVOCI assets:	Fair value	Fair value	Cost	
Macaw Bonds	$15,000	$16,000	$14,000	

Required:

ⓐ What amount would Black Eagle report for the total of its investments in debt securities at 12/31/20×1?

ⓑ What would be the balance in Black Eagle's accumulated other comprehensive income for these investments in its 12/31/20×2 statement of financial position (ignore taxes)?

ⓒ What total unrealized holding gain would Black Eagle report in its 20×2 income statement relative to its investments in debt securities?

7.11 FVOCI securities

Ivy Inc. buys and sells securities expecting to earn profits on short-term differences in price. On December 27, 20×1, Ivy purchased Carrots Inc.'s bonds at par for $87,500. On December 31, the bonds had a fair value of $87,300. Ivy has the intent and ability to hold the bonds until fair value recovers. Ivy sold the bonds on January 3, 20×2, for $88,000. Prepare journal entries for the bond transactions.

ACCOUNTING TERMINOLOGY IN CHAPTER 7

accounting mismatch 회계불일치
accounts receivable 매출채권
adjusted bank balance 수정후은행잔액
adjusted book balance 수정후장부잔액
amortized cost financial assets
상각후원가측정금융자산
amortized costs 상각후원가
at initial recognition 최초인식시점
bank charges 은행수수료
bank reconciliation 은행계정조정
bank statement 은행명세서
bonds 사채
brokerage commission 중개수수료
business model test 사업모형검증
capital gains 자본이득
cash disbursements 현금지출
cash equivalents 현금성자산
cash flow characteristics test
현금흐름특성검증
cash receipts 현금수취
cash short and over 현금과부족
checking account 당좌계정, 요구불예금
coins 주화
collections 추심액
contractual rights 계약상권리
control 통제
creditors 채권자
currency 통화
customer checks 고객수표
debt investments 채권투자
debt securities 채무증권
demand deposits 요구불예금
deposits in transit 은행미기록예금
dividend income 배당수익
draft account 당좌계정, 요구불예금
electronic funds transfer 온라인자금이체
endorse 배서
equity instruments 지분상품
equity investment 주식투자
equity securities 지분증권
fair value 공정가치
fair value option 공정가치선택권
financial assets 금융자산
financial instruments 금융상품
FVOCI (fair value through other comprehensive income) financial assets
기타포괄손익-공정가치측정금융자산
FVPL (fair value through profit and loss) financial assets
당기손익-공정가치측정금융자산
holding gains and losses 보유손익
impairment loss 손상차손
interest earned 이자수익
interest income 이자수익
internal control 내부통제
investee 피투자회사
irrevocable 취소불능
market value 시장가치

maturity date 만기일
miscellaneous expenses 기타비용
miscellaneous revenues 기타수익
money order 우편환
NSF checks 부도수표
other comprehensive income 기타포괄손익
outstanding checks 미인출수표
postdated checks 선일자수표
prepaid expense 선급비
return on investment 투자이익
savings account 정기예금계정
segregation of duties 업무분장
significant influence 중대한 영향력
stocks 주식
trading purpose 매매목적

CHAPTER

8

INVENTORIES

CHAPTER 8

INVENTORIES

8.1 INTRODUCTION

A merchandising business or retail store is mainly involved in selling goods. The merchandise on hand for resale is called inventory(재고자산). Inventory is classified as a current asset(유동자산) since it is typically converted into cash within one year. In contrast, manufacturing firms have three types of inventories consisting of raw materials(원재료), work-in-process(재공품), and finished goods(완제품).

For ordinary merchandising and manufacturing firms, inventory can amount to the material percentage of its assets. Therefore, accounting for inventory significantly affects the statement of financial position and income statement.

8.2 DETERMINING THE OWNERSHIP OF GOODS

When determining inventory quantities, it is essential to determine whether the company owns the inventory. However, determining ownership can be complicated concerning goods in transit(적송품) and consigned goods(위탁품) at the end of the period.

Goods in transit should be included in the inventory of the company that has legal title to the goods. Legal title(법적소유권) is determined by the terms of transactions(거래조건). When the terms of transactions are FOB (free on board) shipping point(선적지인도조건), the ownership of the goods passes to the buyer when the public carrier(운송회사) accepts the goods from the seller. Under an FOB shipping point basis, the buyer bears and incurs transportation-in(매입운임). Included in the transportation-in are freight-in, insurance expense, and other directly related costs incurred in transporting the goods from the seller's place to the buyer's. When the terms are FOB destination(도착지인도조건), the ownership of the goods remains with the seller until the goods reach the buyer's place. As such, the seller incurs transportation-out(판매운임). These concepts are illustrated in Figure 8-1.

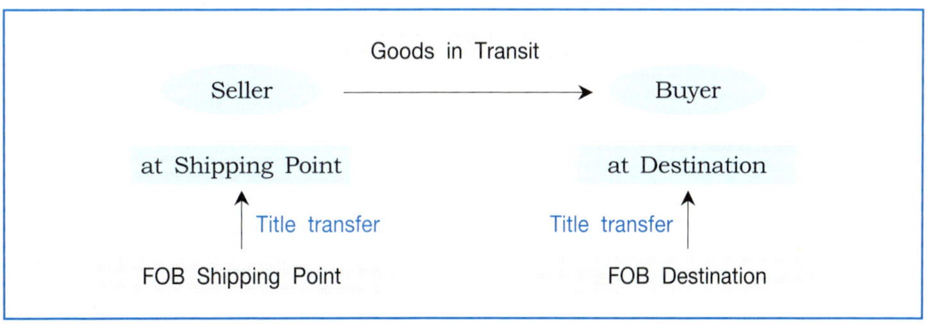

Figure 8-1 Terms of Transactions

In some businesses, it is customary to hold other parties' goods and sell them for a fee, but without taking ownership of the goods. These are called consigned goods(위탁품). Since the consignor(위탁인) has ownership of consigned goods, the consignee(수탁인) should not include the consigned goods in its inventory even though it has custody over them. Figure 8-2 shows this situation.

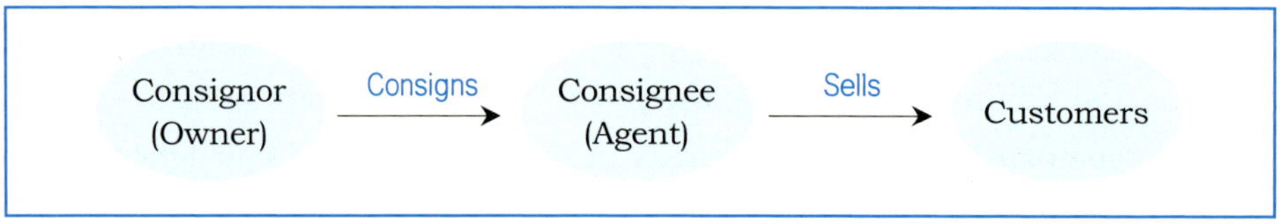

Figure 8-2 Consigned Goods

8.3 PERPETUAL AND PERIODIC INVENTORY SYSTEMS

There are two different systems for recording inventory: perpetual inventory system and periodic inventory system. Firms can use any of the two systems. We briefly described these two systems in Chapter 6. This chapter provides more information about how to account for inventory, with an emphasis on the periodic system of accounting.

In the *perpetual inventory system*(계속기록법), the Inventory(재고자산) account is used to record each purchase and sale of inventory items. In other words, the Inventory account is continuously (perpetually) updated to reflect changes in inventory, which is affected by purchases(매입), sales(판매), purchase returns and allowances(매입환출및에누리), purchase discounts(매입할인) and inventory shrinkage(재고자산감모손실). In addition, under this system, the Cost of Goods Sold(매출원가) is determined each time a sale occurs. The perpetual system had traditionally been used in businesses where units sold are of relatively high value since the expense of maintaining inventory records would be considered prohibitive. However, thanks to bar code and QR code technology, the perpetual system is now widely used even for small unit-value items.

In the *periodic inventory system*(실지재고조사법), inventory is counted physically at regular intervals, at least annually. Therefore, the Inventory account is not continuously updated for each inventory transaction. Firms engaging in the sale of low-priced items typically use the periodic inventory system.

The periodic inventory system is common in the retail business(소매업), where profits on individual units are meager, and the business depends on sales of large quantities of goods, as is the case with hardware stores.

There are some distinct differences between the two inventory recording systems.

① Account names are different. The perpetual system uses the account Inventory(재고자산), while the periodic system uses the account Purchases(매입) for recording purchases of goods.
② The perpetual system keeps track of changes in inventory by recognizing all the items affecting inventory. Therefore, Inventory is debited when goods are purchased, while Inventory is credited when goods are sold. Inventory is also credited when purchase returns, purchase discounts, and inventory shrinkage occur. However, under the periodic system, only Purchases are recorded at cost, while the Cost of Goods Sold is not recognized at the time of sale. Instead, the Cost of Goods Sold is calculated and recognized through the closing process under the periodic system.
③ At the time of sale, two entries are prepared under the perpetual system to record the sale of goods at the selling price and reduce inventory at cost. Under the periodic system, the sale of goods is recorded at the selling price. However, the inventory decrease from the sale is not recorded under the periodic inventory system.
④ Each time goods are sold, the Cost of Goods Sold(매출원가) is recorded under the perpetual system. In contrast, the Cost of Goods Sold is determined only once, at the end of an accounting period, under the periodic system as follows:

Cost of Goods Sold = Beginning Inventory + Net Purchases − Ending Inventory

Suppose there are 1,000 sales transactions during the period. Then, the Cost of Goods Sold is determined 1,000 times under the perpetual system, while it is calculated only once under the periodic system.

⑤ The way the temporary accounts are closed is also very different. As explained above, the Cost of Goods Sold is measured each time goods are sold under the perpetual system. However, the Cost of Goods Sold under the periodic system is recognized through the closing process. The Beginning Inventory(기초재고자산), Purchases(매입), and Transportation-in accounts are credited. The contra-purchase accounts, such as the Purchase Returns and Allowances, and Purchase Discounts, are debited. The Ending Inventory(기말재고자산) account is established by debiting it. Finally, the Cost of Goods Sold, computed as the balancing amount, is debited. Under the perpetual system, there is no need for closing entries to determine the Cost of Goods Sold or to update Inventory at the end of an accounting period since they have been recorded throughout the period.

Table 8-1 shows a comparative summary of the accounting for inventory under the perpetual and periodic systems.

Table 8-1 Perpetual vs. Periodic Inventory Systems

	Perpetual System	Periodic System
Purchases	Inventory ××× Cash ×××	Purchases ××× Cash ×××
Sales	Cash ××× Sales ××× Cost of Goods Sold ××× Inventory ×××	Cash ××× Sales ×××
Closing entries for purchase- and inventory-related accounts	No entry	Cost of Goods Sold ××× Inventory - Ending ××× Purchase Returns ××× Purchase Discounts ××× Inventory - Beginning ××× Purchases ××× Transportation-in ×××
Closing entries for revenues and expenses	Revenue ××× Income Summary ××× Income Summary ××× Cost of Goods Sold ××× Other Expenses ××× Income Summary* ××× Retained Earnings ×××	Revenue ××× Income Summary ××× Income Summary ××× Cost of Goods Sold ××× Other Expenses ××× Income Summary* ××× Retained Earnings ×××

* The closing entry of Income Summary to Retained Earnings is for a profit situation. However, the closing entry will be reversed if a loss occurs.

8.4 COST-BASED INVENTORY VALUATION METHODS

There are various methods of determining inventory value when identical goods are acquired at different times and prices. The method used does not have to conform to the physical flow of the goods. There are four methods generally used in practice. They are the first-in-first-out (FIFO), last-in-first-out (LIFO), average cost, and specific identification methods. FIFO, LIFO, and average cost methods are called cost-flow assumption methods(원가흐름가정법) since we assume that the flows of goods follow the assumed flows for accounting purposes, irrespective of actual flows of goods.

A combination of different inventory costing methods (FIFO, LIFO, or Average Cost method) and inventory recording systems (Periodic or Perpetual Recording System) results in different Ending Inventory and Cost of Goods Sold, except for the FIFO method. In this textbook, we will learn the different cost methods only under the periodic recording system for the sake of convenience and ease of understanding.

The following data relate to Poinsettia Company's merchandise transactions for the year ended December 31, 20×1:

Date/Type		Units	Cost per Unit	Total Cost
January 1	Inventory	150	$8	$1,200
February 20	Purchases	200	9	1,800
April 20	Purchases	250	10	2,500
September 20	Purchases	200	11	2,200
Goods available for sale		800		$7,700

Suppose that the physical inventory on December 31 is 430 units. Accounting for inventory is centered around breaking down the Cost of Goods Available for Sale(판매가능원가) into Cost of Goods Sold and Ending Inventory. Poinsettia Company's cost of goods available for sale in 20×1 is $7,700. Therefore, the sum of the cost of goods sold and inventing inventory will be the same at $7,700, irrespective of the method used.

(1) First-In-First-Out (FIFO) Method(선입선출법)

This method assumes that goods are sold in the order of receipt. In other words, items purchased or manufactured first are assumed to have been sold first, and items remaining unsold at the end of an accounting period are the items purchased or manufactured recently. Hence, the cost of goods sold is based on the older costs, while ending inventory is measured at the latest costs.

EXAMPLE 8-1 ***FIFO Method***

Determine Ending Inventory and Cost of Goods Sold for the period ended December 31, 20×1, assuming that Poinsettia Company uses the FIFO method.

Under the FIFO method, merchandise on hand is considered to be those most recently received. Hence, the year-end inventory of 430 units is measured as follows:

The last purchase (September 20)	200	units @ $11=	$2,200
Next most recent purchase (April 20)	230	units @ $10=	2,300
Total	430		$4,500

Therefore, the cost of goods available for sale of $7,700 is assigned to $4,500 of ending inventory (reported in the statement of financial position) and $3,200 of the cost of goods sold (reported in the income statement).

(2) Last-In-First-Out (LIFO) Method(후입선출법)

This method assumes that goods are sold in the reverse order of their acquisition. In other words, items purchased or manufactured most recently are assumed to have been sold first, and items remaining unsold at the end of an accounting period are the items purchased or manufactured earlier. Hence, the cost of goods sold is based on the latest costs, while ending inventory is reflected at the earlier costs.

EXAMPLE 8-2 LIFO Method

Determine Ending Inventory and Cost of Goods Sold for the period ended December 31, 20×1, assuming that Poinsettia Company uses the LIFO method.

Under the LIFO method, ending inventory is measured at the costs of the earliest purchases. Therefore, the cost of goods sold is based on the most recent costs. The year-end inventory is computed as follows:

Beginning inventory (January 1)	150 units @ $8=	$1,200
The first purchase (February 20)	200 units @ $9=	1,800
Next purchase (April 20)	80 units @ $10=	800
Total	430	$3,800

Therefore, the cost of goods available for sale of $7,700 is assigned to $3,800 of ending inventory (reported in the statement of financial position) and $3,900 of the cost of goods sold (reported in the income statement).

LIFO has some advantages over other methods. Firstly, LIFO matches the most recent costs with current sales. Therefore, net income and income taxes would be reduced in an inflationary period. Secondly, LIFO results in a more accurate measurement of net income in an inflationary period because current costs are matched against current revenue. LIFO results in less "paper" profit. However, LIFO is often criticized as based on unrealistic cost flow assumptions. Therefore, LIFO is not allowed under the IFRS (International Financial Reporting Standards).

(3) Average Cost Method(평균원가법)

The average cost method assumes that beginning inventory and purchases made during the current period are indistinguishable for costing purposes. Therefore, they are combined, and an average cost is computed. The same average cost is used for the computation of both ending inventory and cost of goods sold. The average cost method under the periodic inventory recording system is called the weighted-average cost method(총평균원가법). In contrast, the average cost method under the perpetual inventory recording system is called the moving-average cost method(이동평균원가법). This textbook will use the weighted-average cost method for illustration purposes.

The cost of goods available for sale(판매가능원가) is divided by the units available for sale(판매가능수량) to obtain a weighted-average cost. The weighted-average cost is then used to determine the ending inventory and cost of goods sold. The advantage of this method is that costs are assigned equally to both inventory and goods sold.

Example 8-3 *Weighted-Average Cost Method*

Determine the Ending Inventory and Cost of Goods Sold for the period ended December 31, 20×1, assuming Poinsettia Company uses the weighted-average cost method.

The average unit cost is computed as follows:

$$\text{Cost per unit} = \frac{\text{Cost of goods available}}{\text{Units available}} = \frac{\$7{,}700}{800} = \$9.625$$

The Ending Inventory is:

430 units @ $9.625=$4,139

The Cost of Goods Sold is:

370 units @ $9.625=$3,561

Example 8-4 compares the results of the three methods discussed above regarding the ending inventory and cost of goods sold. As a reminder,

Cost of goods available for sale=Ending inventory+Cost of goods sold, or
Cost of goods sold=Beginning inventory+Purchases−Ending inventory

Example 8-4 *Comparison of Inventory Valuation Methods*

The tabulated results of the three methods reveal the following comparisons:

	FIFO	LIFO	Weighted Average Cost
Cost of Goods Available for Sale	$7,700	$7,700	$7,700
Less: Ending Inventory, Dec. 31	4,500	3,800	4,139
Cost of Goods Sold	$3,200	$3,900	$3,561

It should be noted that if ending inventory is overstated, then the cost of goods sold will be understated, and net income will be overstated. On the other hand, if ending inventory is understated, then the cost of goods sold will be overstated, and net income will be understated. Thus, the selected method can have a material effect on net income and related tax. It also impacts the statement of financial position in terms of inventory valuation.

(4) Specific Identification Method(개별법)

The specific identification method identifies the actual costs of ending inventory by reference to specific invoices. It is often used when the cost per unit is high, like cars, ships, precious metals, and things of that nature.

Example 8-5 *Specific Identification Method*

Suppose a reference to specific invoices for Poinsettia Company reveals that items purchased on February 20, April 20, and September 20 are left unsold. Then, the ending inventory is calculated by individually identifying specific invoices.

Purchase invoice #131 (February 20)	180	units @ $9=	$1,620
Purchase invoice #145 (April 20)	130	units @ $10=	1,300
Purchase invoice #198 (September 20)	120	units @ $11=	1,320
Ending inventory	430		$4,240

8.5 OTHER INVENTORY VALUATION METHODS

In Section 8.4, we have learned diverse cost-based inventory valuation methods. However, inventory valuation at cost can lead to an overstatement of assets when the market value falls below the cost. At other times, inventory valuation at cost is not straightforward since it takes a lot of effort and time to determine inventory costs. Therefore, it is sometimes desirable to use approximation methods to estimate inventory. For example, it is not worthwhile taking physical inventory to prepare interim financial statements (중간재무제표) since doing so will be very costly and time-consuming. Therefore, firms usually use approximation methods to estimate inventory instead of taking a physical inventory. Furthermore, firms and insurance agents use approximation methods to estimate fire loss, theft loss, etc.

In this section, we will learn three non-cost-based inventory valuation methods.

(1) Lower of Cost or Net Realizable Value Method(저가법)

A conservative means of valuing inventory is to use the lower cost or net realizable value (LCNRV) method. Net realizable value(순실현가능가치) refers to the most likely amount the firm will realize by selling the goods. NRV (net realizable value) is measured by selling prices minus directly related costs to sell the goods. As a result, the inventory loss is recognized for the period, even though the inventory has not been sold. Under this method, the cost (as determined under FIFO or weighted average) or NRV, whichever is lower, is used. However, increases in NRV of inventory are not recorded since this would violate accounting conservatism(보수주의).

The application of the LCNRV rule may result in different inventory valuations depending on how the LCNRV rule is applied. The LCNRV rule can be applied on an individual-item basis(개별기준), major category basis(조별기준), or total inventory basis(총계기준). IFRS mandates that the individual item basis must be used in principle in applying the LCNRV rule. The total inventory basis is not allowed. However, the major category basis may be used if it can be justified that the major category basis results in better measurement than the individual item basis.

EXAMPLE 8-6 *Lower of Cost or Net Realizable Value Method*

The following data relate to Hydrangea Company's inventory items on December 31, 20×1.

Lot	Quantity	Unit Cost	Unit NRV	Total Cost	Total NRV	LCNRV
W	200	$7.0	$7.5	$1,400	$1,500	$1,400
X	250	9.0	10.0	2,250	2,500	2,250
Y	300	10.0	9.0	3,000	2,700	2,700
Z	400	11.0	12.0	4,400	4,800	4,400
Total				$11,050	$11,500	$10,750

Determine the ending inventory to be reported on the statement of financial position on December 31, 20×1, and prepare proper journal entries to recognize Loss on Inventory Valuation for Hydrangea Company.

The IFRS requires companies to apply the LCNRV rule on an individual-item basis. Therefore, inventory would be valued at $10,750.

A loss on inventory valuation should be recorded as follows because the NRV is lower than the cost by $300:

	Debit	Credit
Loss on Inventory Valuation	300	
Inventory		300

(2) Gross Profit Method(매출총이익법)

The gross profit method utilizes the fact that gross profit is calculated by subtracting the cost of goods sold from net sales. For example, if the cost of goods sold is 70 percent of net sales, gross profit will be 30 percent of net sales. Recall from Chapter 6 that gross profit plus the cost of goods sold equals net sales.

This method can be used to estimate the inventory at the end of an interim period (e.g., quarter, month). For instance, we can use the method to estimate the inventory loss from fire for insurance reimbursement. We use the expected gross profit rate (gross profit to net sales) for the period under this method. Ending inventory can be computed by preparing a partial income statement starting with sales and ending with gross profit. The amounts for beginning inventory, net purchases, and net sales are entered into the partial income statement.

Example 8-7 Gross Profit Method

The following data relate to Cyclamen Company's transactions during the first half of the accounting period of 20×1.

Beginning inventory:	$15,000
Net purchases:	90,000
Net sales:	200,000

The gross profit rate has been running at 60 percent of net sales.
Estimate the ending inventory on June 30, 20×1 using the gross profit method.

Cyclamen Company
Income Statement (partial)

Net Sales (1/1~6/30)		$200,000
Less: Cost of Goods Sold		
Beginning Inventory, 1/1	$15,000	
Net Purchases (1/1~6/30)	90,000	
Cost of Goods Available for Sale	$105,000	
Less: Ending Inventory, 6/30	?	
Cost of Goods Sold (40%×$200,000)		80,000
Gross Profit (60%×$200,000)		$120,000

Since the cost of goods available for sale minus ending inventory is equal to the cost of goods sold, the ending inventory as of June 30, 20×1 must be $25,000. The proof is:

Cost of Goods Available for Sale	−	Ending Inventory	=	Cost of Goods Sold
$105,000	−	$25,000	=	$80,000

(3) Retail Inventory Method(소매재고법, 매출가격환원법)

Department stores and other retailers mainly use the retail inventory method. The retail inventory method is based on the relationship between the cost of goods available for sale and the retail price of such goods.

The retail inventory method utilizes the following relationship:

Goods Sold = Beginning Inventory + Purchases − Ending Inventory

We can express the above relationship in terms of both cost(원가) and retail price(소매가격). Under the periodic system, the cost of goods sold is not recognized when goods are sold. However, goods sold at the retail price are recognized as Sales. Therefore, we can easily determine the ending inventory at the retail price based on the above relationship, but not at cost. However, what is needed is the ending inventory at cost rather than at retail price. Therefore, the ending inventory at cost(기말재고원가) can be estimated by multiplying the ending inventory at retail price by cost-to-retail ratio(원가 대 소매가격 비율) as follows:

Ending Inventory at Cost = Ending Inventory at Retail Price × Cost-to-Retail Ratio

EXAMPLE 8-8 *Retail Inventory Method*

Merchandise records for the month of December of Petunia Company show the following information.

	Cost	Retail Price
Merchandise Inventory, December 1	$45,000	$60,000
Purchases	50,000	68,000
Sales for December		100,000

Estimate merchandise inventory as of December 31 for Petunia Company using the retail inventory method.

The ending merchandise inventory can be estimated as follows:

	Cost	Retail Price
Merchandise Inventory, December 1	$45,000	$60,000
Purchases	50,000	68,000
Merchandise Available for Sale	$95,000	$128,000
Sales for December		100,000
Merchandise Inventory, December 31, at retail		$28,000
Merchandise Inventory, December 31, at cost	$20,776*	

* Cost-to-retail ratio = Cost/Retail = $95,000/$128,000 = 74.2%
$28,000 × 74.2% = $20,776

The retail inventory method is useful because it provides inventory figures for financial reporting and assists in detecting inventory shortages.

CHAPTER 8

Multiple Choice Questions

8.1 Nuthatch Inc. has a beginning inventory for the year of $18,000. During the year, Nuthatch purchases inventory for $230,000 and has the cost of goods sold equal to $233,000. Nuthatch's ending inventory equals:

ⓐ $15,000.
ⓑ $18,000.
ⓒ $21,000.
ⓓ $19,000.

8.2 Inventory records for Deciduous Inc. revealed the following:

Date	Transaction	Number of Units	Unit Cost
April 1	Beginning inventory	500	$2.4
April 15	Purchase	400	2.5

Deciduous sold 700 units of inventory during the month. Ending inventory assuming FIFO would be:

ⓐ $500.
ⓑ $490.
ⓒ $470.
ⓓ $480.

8.3 Consider the following inventory transactions for September:

Date	Transaction	Number of Units	Unit Cost
September 1	Beginning inventory	15	$3.0
September 12	Purchase	20	3.5
September 23	Purchase	10	4.0

For the month of September, the company sold 35 units. What is the cost of goods sold under the weighted-average cost method (round the weighted-average unit cost to four decimals if necessary)?

ⓐ $121
ⓑ $116
ⓒ $124
ⓓ $131

8.4 In a perpetual inventory system, the purchase of inventory is debited to:

ⓐ Purchases.
ⓑ Cost of Goods Sold.
ⓒ Inventory.
ⓓ Accounts Payable.

8.5 Goldfinch Inc. sold inventory for $1,200 that was purchased for $700. Goldfinch records which of the following when it sells inventory using a perpetual inventory system?

ⓐ No entry is required for the cost of goods sold and inventory
ⓑ Debit Cost of Goods Sold $700; credit Inventory $700
ⓒ Debit Cost of Goods Sold $1,200; credit Inventory $1,200
ⓓ Debit Inventory $700; credit Cost of Goods Sold $700

8.6 Merchandise sold FOB shipping point indicates that:

- ⓐ The seller holds the title until the merchandise is received at the buyer's location.
- ⓑ The merchandise has not yet been shipped.
- ⓒ The merchandise will not be shipped until payment has been received.
- ⓓ The seller transfers the title to the buyer once the merchandise is shipped.

8.7 Given the information below, what is the gross profit?

Sales revenue	$320,000
Accounts receivable	50,000
Ending inventory	100,000
Cost of goods sold	250,000
Sales returns and allowances	20,000

- ⓐ $250,000
- ⓑ $70,000
- ⓒ $220,000
- ⓓ $50,000

8.8 Using the information below, determine the ending inventory value by applying the lower of cost or net realizable value method.

Inventory Item	Quantity	Cost	Net Realizable Value
Socks	200	$12	$14
Gloves	400	16	14
Hats	300	15	12

- ⓐ $13,300
- ⓑ $12,000
- ⓒ $11,600
- ⓓ $13,700

8.9 The primary difference between the periodic and perpetual inventory systems is:

a The reported amount of ending inventory is higher under the periodic system.
b The perpetual system maintains a continual record of inventory transactions, whereas the periodic system records these transactions only at the end of the period.
c The reported sales revenue is higher under the periodic inventory system.
d The reported cost of goods sold is higher under the perpetual inventory system.

8.10 In a periodic inventory system, at the time of a sale, the cost of inventory sold is:

a Debited to Accounts Receivable.
b Credited to Cost of Goods Sold.
c Debited to Cost of Goods Sold.
d Not recorded at this time.

CHAPTER 8 Exercises

8.1 Goods in transit

In December 20×1, Lily Wholesale Company sold goods for $3,000 to its customer, Rose Garden Company. The goods were shipped on December 29, 20×1, and arrived at Rose Garden Company's warehouse on January 3, 20×2. The fiscal year-end for both companies is December 31.

Required:

ⓐ Assuming shipping terms of FOB shipping point, which company should report the goods as its inventory?

ⓑ Assuming shipping terms of FOB destination, which company should report the goods as its inventory?

8.2 Periodic vs. perpetual inventory systems

A company has the following transactions during May:

May 3	Purchases inventory on account for $3,500, terms 2/10, n/30.
May 5	Pays freight costs of $200 on inventory purchased on May 3.
May 6	Returns inventory with a cost of $500.
May 12	Pays the full amount due on May 3 purchase.
May 28	Sells all inventory purchased on March 3 for $5,000 on account.

Required:

ⓐ Record all transactions, assuming the company uses a perpetual inventory system.

ⓑ Record all transactions, assuming the company uses a periodic inventory system.

8.3 FIFO method

During 20×1, Bougainvillea Company sells 300 units of inventory for $85 each. The company has the following inventory purchase transactions for 20×1:

Date	Transaction	Number of Units	Unit Cost	Total Cost
January 1	Beginning Inventory	60	$71	$4,260
May 5	Purchase	170	72	12,240
November 3	Purchase	180	74	13,320
	Totals	410		$29,820

Required:

Calculate Ending Inventory and Cost of Goods Sold for 20×1 assuming Bougainvillea uses the periodic FIFO method.

8.4 Different inventory valuation methods (1)

The beginning inventory and subsequent purchases of a product are as follows:

January 1	Balance	10 units @ $11
March 10	Purchase	14 units @ $12
June 12	Purchase	18 units @ $13
September 16	Purchase	16 units @ $14
December 8	Purchase	20 units @ $15

A count of the ending inventory revealed that 32 units were on hand.

Required:

Compute the ending inventory value using the following methods: ⓐ FIFO method, ⓑ LIFO method, and ⓒ weighted-average cost method. The company uses the periodic inventory system.

8.5 Different inventory valuation methods (2)

Baby Boa Company uses the periodic inventory system to account for inventories. Information related to Baby Boa Company's inventory on April 30 is given below:

April 1	Beginning inventory	400	units @ $12.0=	$4,800
8	Purchase	800	units @ $12.4=	9,920
16	Purchase	600	units @ $12.8=	7,680
24	Purchase	200	units @ $13.2=	2,640
	Total units and cost	2,000	units	$25,040

Required:

- ⓐ Show computations to value the ending inventory using the FIFO method if 500 units remain on hand on April 30.
- ⓑ Show computations to value the ending inventory using the weighted-average cost method if 500 units remain on hand on April 30.
- ⓒ Show computations to value the ending inventory using the LIFO method if 500 units remain on hand on April 30.

8.6 Different inventory valuation methods (3)

Marietta Company uses the periodic inventory system and has the following inventory information available:

		Units	Unit Cost	Total Cost
1/ 1	Beginning Inventory	100	$4	$400
1/20	Purchase	500	5	2,500
7/25	Purchase	100	7	700
10/20	Purchase	300	8	2,400
		1,000		$6,000

A physical count of inventory on December 31 reveals 350 units on hand.

Required:

Answer the following independent questions and show computations supporting your answers.

ⓐ Assume that the company uses the FIFO method. The value of the ending inventory on December 31 is $_____________.

ⓑ Assume that the company uses the weighted-average cost method. The value of the ending inventory on December 31 is $_____________.

ⓒ Assume that the company uses the LIFO method. The value of the ending inventory on December 31 is $_____________.

8.7 Different inventory valuation methods (4)

Inventory records for Marlene Company revealed the following:

Date	Transaction	Number of Units	Unit Cost
March 1	Beginning inventory	1,000	$7.20
March 10	Purchase	600	7.25
March 17	Purchase	800	7.30
March 24	Purchase	600	7.35

Marlene sold 2,300 units of inventory during the month.

Required:

ⓐ Determine the Cost of Goods Available for Sale for the month of March.

ⓑ Determine the Cost of Goods Sold assuming the FIFO method is used.

ⓒ Determine the Ending Inventory assuming the Weighted Average method is used.

8.8 Ending inventory

Mulberry Co. started the year with $94,000 of merchandise inventory on hand. During the year, $400,000 in merchandise was purchased on account with credit terms of 1/15, n/45. All discounts were taken. Mulberry paid freight-in charges of $7,500. Merchandise with an invoice amount of $5,000 was returned for credit. The cost of goods sold for the year was $380,000. What is the ending inventory?

8.9 Lower of cost or net realizable value method (1)

Cardinal Ski Shop reports inventory using the lower of cost or net realizable value method. Below is information related to its year-end inventory.

Required:

Calculate the amount to be reported for ending inventory.

Inventory	Quantity	Cost	Net realizable value
Ski Jackets	15	$120	$100
Skis	20	350	400

8.10 Lower of cost or net realizable value method (2)

Parodia Supplies Company reports inventory using the lower of cost or net realizable value method. Below is information related to its year-end inventory.

Inventory	Quantity	Cost	Net realizable value
Furniture Supplies	100	$75	$90
Appliance Supplies	40	300	250

Required:

ⓐ Calculate ending inventory under the lower of cost or net realizable value method.

ⓑ Record any necessary adjustments to inventory.

ⓒ Explain the impact of the adjustment in the financial statements.

8.11 Gross profit method

For the month of March, beginning inventory is $25,000, net purchases are $110,000, and net sales are $250,000. On average, the gross profit rate has been steadily running at 70 percent of net sales. Compute the ending inventory at the end of March using the gross profit method.

8.12 Retail inventory method

Using the retail inventory method, compute the cost of the June 30 inventory.

	Cost	Retail
Inventory-June 1	$24,000	$30,000
Purchases	40,000	60,000
Sales		40,000

ACCOUNTING TERMINOLOGY IN CHAPTER 8

average cost method 평균원가법
beginning inventory 기초재고자산
conservatism 보수주의
consigned goods 위탁품
consignee 수탁인
consignor 위탁인
cost 원가
cost-flow assumption methods 원가흐름가정법
cost of goods available for sale 판매가능원가
cost of goods sold 매출원가
cost-to-retail ratio 원가 대 소매가격 비율
current assets 유동자산
ending inventory 기말재고자산
ending inventory at cost 기말재고원가
finished goods 완제품
first-in-first-out (FIFO) method 선입선출법
FOB destination 도착지인도조건
FOB shipping point 선적지인도조건
goods in transit 적송품
gross profit method 매출총이익법
income summary 집합손익
individual-item basis 개별기준
interim financial statements 중간재무제표
inventory 재고자산
inventory shrinkage 재고자산감모손실
last-in-first-out (LIFO) method 후입선출법
legal title 법적소유권
lower of cost or net realizable value method 저가법
major category basis 조별기준
moving-average cost method 이동평균원가법
net realizable value 순실현가능가치
periodic inventory system 실지재고조사법
perpetual inventory system 계속기록법
public carrier 운송회사
purchase discounts 매입할인
purchase returns and allowances 매입환출및에누리
purchases 매입
raw materials 원재료
retail business 소매업
retail inventory method 소매재고법, 매출가격환원법
retail price 소매가격
sales 판매
specific identification method 개별법
terms of transaction 거래조건
total inventory basis 총계기준
transportation-in 매입운임
transportation-out 판매운임
units available for sale 판매가능수량
weighted-average cost method 총평균원가법
work-in-process 재공품

CHAPTER

9

RECEIVABLES AND PAYABLES

CHAPTER 9

RECEIVABLES AND PAYABLES

9.1 TYPES OF RECEIVABLES

Receivables(수취채권) are claims which are expected to be collected in cash from individuals and companies. Receivables management(수취채권관리) is an essential activity for any company that sells goods or services on account(외상, 신용). Receivables are vital because they represent a firm's most liquid asset after cash.

Receivables are typically classified as accounts receivable, notes receivable, and other receivables. Accounts receivable(외상매출금) are amounts owed by customers on account and result from credit sales of goods or services. Accounts receivable generally are expected to be collected within 30 to 60 days. They are usually the most significant receivables held by a company. Notes receivable(받을어음) represent claims for which formal promissory notes(약속어음) are issued as evidence of debt by the issuers. The credit instrument typically requires the debtor to pay interest and extends up to periods of 60 to 90 days or longer. Accounts receivable and notes receivable that result from sales transactions are often called trade receivables(매출채권). Accounts receivable are informal, short-term, and non-interest-bearing amounts owed by customers. In contrast, note receivables are backed by promissory notes, interest-bearing(이자부), and short- or long-term receivables. Other receivables include non-trade receivables(비매출채권), such as interest receivable, loans receivable, income taxes refundable, and so forth.

9.2 RECOGNITION AND VALUATION OF ACCOUNTS RECEIVABLE

Some customers may fail to pay their payables. Therefore, we need to recognize a provision(비용반영) to reflect the possibility of failing to collect accounts receivable. Recognizing a provision is to comply with two important accounting principles: the matching principle(대응원칙) and measurement at net realizable value(순실현가능가치).

More specifically, we need to recognize Uncollectible Accounts Expense(대손상각비) as a part of operating expenses. As you recall from Chapter 2, we can ensure proper matching between expenses (uncollectible accounts expense) and revenues (credit sales) by recognizing the expense when related sales are recognized. Receivables are reported in the statement of financial position at their net realizable value, representing the amount expected to be collected rather than the gross amount of the receivables.

The direct write-off method(직접차감법) and the allowance method(충당금설정법) are the two accounting methods for uncollectible accounts.

(1) Direct Write-Off Method

Under this method, Uncollectible Accounts Expense is recognized when specific receivables become worthless. In other words, uncollectible accounts expense is not recognized until specific accounts are judged uncollectible. The journal entry when a specific accounts receivable turned out to be uncollectible is:

Uncollectible Accounts Expense	×××	
Accounts Receivable		×××

EXAMPLE 9-1 ***Direct Write-off Method***

Grackle Company sold goods for $1,000 on account to Wren Company on July 6, 20×1. The accounts receivable from Wren was considered uncollectible on February 7, 20×2. Prepare a necessary journal entry to record the write-off of accounts receivable from Wren Company.

The journal entry on February 7 is:

February 7	Uncollectible Accounts Expense	1,000	
	Accounts Receivable - Wren Company		1,000

Note that uncollectible accounts expense may be recorded in the following year after related credit sales are recognized. Therefore, a weakness of the direct write-off method is that it fails to match the uncollectible accounts expense against the revenue in the year of sale. Another weakness of the direct write-off method is that assets are overstated because receivables are reported at the maximum amount. In other words, receivables are shown in the statement of financial position at their gross amount since the possibility of failing to collect some of the receivables is not adequately considered. Therefore, the direct write-off method is not a generally accepted accounting principle(일반적으로 인정된 회계원칙, GAAP).

(2) Allowance Method

The allowance method corrects the drawbacks of the direct write-off method in terms of the matching principle and net realizable value measurement. Under the allowance method, uncollectible accounts expense is reflected in the income statement in the year of credit sale. Therefore, financial statements will be misstated if uncollectible accounts are not properly estimated and reflected. In other words, the purpose of accounting for uncollectible receivables is twofold. First, we need to report the receivables at the net realizable value in the statement of financial position. Second, we need to recognize uncollectible accounts expense when a credit sale is made. As a result, both the statement of financial position and income statement will be appropriately reported.

The following journal entry is made at year's end to record the anticipated credit losses from accounts receivable:

Uncollectible Accounts Expense	×××	
Allowance for Uncollectible Accounts		×××

Allowance for Uncollectible Accounts(대손충당금) is a contra account to accounts receivable. As a result, accounts receivable are reported at the *net realizable value*(순실현가능가치) in the statement of financial position.

Example 9-2 *Allowance Method*

Canine Corporation's accounts receivable balance is $50,000 at the end of an accounting period. It is estimated that $2,000 of the customer balances will be uncollectible. Prepare an appropriate journal entry to record the uncollectible accounts expense at the end of the accounting period and determine the accounts receivable amount in the statement of financial position for Canine Corporation.

The journal entry is:

Uncollectible Accounts Expense	2,000	
Allowance for Uncollectible Accounts		2,000

The statement of financial position shows the estimated net realizable value ($48,000) of the accounts receivable at the end of the year as follows:

Accounts Receivable	$50,000	
Less: Allowance for Uncollectible Accounts	2,000	$48,000

9.3 METHODS OF COMPUTING PROVISION FOR UNCOLLECTIBLE ACCOUNTS

Alternative ways of estimating uncollectible accounts expense are available. We can use an uncollectible percentage of current year net credit sales(순외상매출액), a flat percentage of gross accounts receivable, or an aging schedule approach(연령분석표접근법). The entry to recognize uncollectible accounts expense and reduce accounts receivable to its net amount is considered an adjusting entry and is prepared at the end of the accounting period.

(1) Percent of Credit Sales Method(외상매출액비례법)

This method is an income statement approach(손익계산서접근법) to estimating uncollectible accounts expense. The expense provision is computed by multiplying the current year's net credit sales by a flat uncollectible rate. The rate is based upon past experiences and modified in light of the current environment.

Example 9-3 *Percent of Credit Sales Method*

Credit sales for Grouse Company in 20×1 amount to $220,000. The anticipated uncollectible accounts expense is 1 percent of credit sales. The allowance for uncollectible accounts currently has a credit balance of $1,200 before the adjusting entry at the end of the period. Prepare a proper adjusting journal entry to record uncollectible accounts expense, assuming that Grouse Company uses the percent of credit sales method.

The journal entry is:

	Debit	Credit
Uncollectible Accounts Expense	2,200	
Allowance for Uncollectible Accounts		2,200

The balance in the allowance for uncollectible accounts of $1,200 does not affect the year-end adjustments under this method. This method focuses on measuring an adequate amount of expense in the income statement. The allowance for uncollectible accounts(대손충당금) increases due to recognizing the uncollectible accounts expense. The percent of credit sales method is suitable when a company believes uncollectible receivables are closely related to its volume of credit sales. The method also is suitable to use when preparing interim (e.g., quarterly) financial statements.

(2) Percent of Accounts Receivable Method(채권잔액비례법)

The most commonly used method in estimating uncollectible accounts expense is the statement of financial position approach(재무상태표접근법), which is based on the balance of accounts receivable at year-end. This method emphasizes the measurement of accounts receivable at net realizable value. Under this method, the balance in the allowance for uncollectible accounts affects the year-end journal entry. If the allowance has a credit balance, then the balance must be subtracted from the amounts estimated to be uncollectible. However, seldomly, the allowance may have a debit balance, representing an abnormal (negative) balance. In this unusual circumstance, the balance in the allowance must be added to the amounts estimated to be uncollectible.

EXAMPLE 9-4 *Percent of Accounts Receivable Method*

At the end of December 20×1, Canary Company's Accounts Receivable has a balance of $50,000, and Allowance for Uncollectible Accounts has a credit balance of $500. It is estimated that $2,000 of the customer balances will be uncollectible. Prepare a proper adjusting journal entry to record uncollectible accounts expense, assuming that Canary Company uses the percent of accounts receivable method. Also, show how the accounts receivable will be reported in the statement of financial position prepared on December 31, 20×1.

Additional provision needed in this case is $1,500 ($2,000 − $500).
The journal entry is:

Uncollectible Accounts Expense	1,500	
Allowance for Uncollectible Accounts		1,500

The year-end statement of financial position shows the estimated net realizable value of the accounts receivable:

Accounts Receivable	$50,000	
Less: Allowance for Uncollectible Accounts	2,000	$48,000

(3) Aging Method(연령분석법)

The aging method is a statement of financial position approach in that each customer's account balance is classified into different age groups based on days after sales. The longer the days after the sales, the greater the probability of accounts receivable being uncollectible. Except for the differences in estimating the uncollectible amount, the accounting method is the same as the percent of accounts receivable method.

EXAMPLE 9-5 *Aging Method*

A breakdown of accounts receivable for Canary Company on December 31, 20×1 by age groups is shown below, with the desired balance of allowance for uncollectible accounts for each group and the aggregate.

Age of Accounts Receivable	Year-End Gross Accounts Receivable Balance	Uncollectible Percentage	Amount Needed in Allowance Account at Year's End
1~30 days	$12,000	1%	$120
31~60 days	28,000	3%	840
61~90 days	8,000	5%	400
Over 90 days	2,000	12%	240
	$50,000		$1,600

Prepare an appropriate adjusting entry to record uncollectible accounts expense, assuming that Canary Company uses the aging method.

The year-end journal entry is:

	Debit	Credit
Uncollectible Accounts Expense	400	
Allowance for Uncollectible Accounts		400*

* $1,600 − $1,200 = $400

The aging method fits well when a company feels its uncollectible receivables are closely associated with the age of the receivables. The longer an account receivable is outstanding (unpaid), the more likely the receivable becomes uncollectible.

EXAMPLE 9-6 *Abnormal Balance for Allowance for Uncollectible Accounts*

Assume the same information as in Example 9-5 except that the allowance account has a debit balance of $1,200. Prepare an appropriate adjusting entry to record uncollectible accounts expense, assuming that Canary Company uses the aging method.

The journal entry is:

Uncollectible Accounts Expense	2,800	
Allowance for Uncollectible Accounts		2,800*

* $1,600 + $1,200 = $2,800

After this entry, the allowance account will have the desired balance of $1,600.

9.4 WRITING OFF CUSTOMERS' ACCOUNTS

When it is evident that a customer cannot pay the amount due (for example, the customer has declared bankruptcy), we need to write off(제거) the specific account. The journal entry for the write-off is:

Allowance for Uncollectible Accounts	×××	
Accounts Receivable		×××

Allowance for uncollectible accounts, instead of uncollectible accounts expense, is debited. It is because a part of the allowance provision established at the end of the previous accounting period for future doubtful collectibility has now been used up. If we debit uncollectible accounts expense again for the write-off, the expense is double counted since the year-end adjusting entry in the previous period already reflected the possibility.

Example 9-7 *Write-off of Receivable*

Frigate Company owes Albatross Company $1,000. The account receivable from Frigate Company was deemed worthless on February 6. Prepare an appropriate journal entry to write off the account receivable from Frigate Company.

The journal entry on February 6 is:

Allowance for Uncollectible Accounts	1,000	
Accounts Receivable - Frigate Company		1,000

Note that the net amount of the accounts receivable is not affected by the write-off since the gross receivables and the allowance for uncollectible accounts (contra account) are reduced by the same amount.

9.5 RECOVERY OF WRITTEN-OFF RECEIVABLES

A full or partial recovery of a previously written-off customer account may occur. For example, the customer may unexpectedly receive funds from another source and wish to reinstate its business activities.

Recovery of previously written-off accounts requires two journal entries: one for reinstating the accounts receivable and the other for recording the collection of the accounts receivable. The journal entries are:

Accounts Receivable	×××	
Allowance for Uncollectible Accounts		×××
Cash	×××	
Accounts Receivable		×××

EXAMPLE 9-8 Recovery of Written-off Receivable

Referring to Example 9-7, assume that Frigate Company paid Albatross Company $600. Prepare appropriate journal entries to record the recovery of the previously written-off account from Frigate Company.

The journal entries are:

Accounts Receivable - Frigate Company	600	
Allowance for Uncollectible Accounts		600
Cash	600	
Accounts Receivable - Frigate Company		600

9.6 PROMISSORY NOTES

The issuer of a promissory note(약속어음) agrees to pay a given amount to a payee(수취인) at a future date. Therefore, a promissory note is a note payable (지급어음) to the issuer and a note receivable(받을어음) to the payee.

There are a few advantages to a promissory note. First, the holder may want to cash the note before its maturity by transferring it to a bank. The sale of a note receivable is referred to as *discounting* a note receivable(받을어음의 할인). Second, the note receivable also serves as written evidence of a receivable and, as such, represents a priority lien(선순위담보) compared to an open account(신용계정) receivable, namely accounts receivable.

Interest is usually computed based on a 360-day year (12 months × 30 days per month). The following formula is used to compute interest:

$$\text{Interest} = \text{Principal} \times \text{Interest Rate} \times \text{Time Fraction}$$

The *principal*(원금) is the face value(액면금액) of the note. The *interest rate* (이자율) is the annual interest rate(연리) earned on the note. The *time* is the fraction of the year that the note is held. For example, if a $1,000, 12 percent, 90-day note is issued, the interest is $30, computed as $1,000 × 12% × 90/36. A note receivable(받을어음) is an asset because a claim exists for future collection. Interest earned on the note is credited to the Interest Income(이자수익) account.

EXAMPLE 9-9 Notes Receivable

Cardinal Company has an account receivable of $1,000 from Blue Jay Company. Cardinal Company receives a 90-day, 12 percent note in settlement of the accounts receivable. Prepare journal entries for Cardinal Company to record the receipt of a promissory note in settlement of the account receivable and the cash collection at the maturity date of the promissory note.

Journal entry to record the receipt of a promissory note in settlement of the account receivable is:

	Debit	Credit
Notes Receivable	1,000	
Accounts Receivable		1,000

Interest income is not recorded until it is *due* 90 days later. When the note receivable is collected at maturity, interest income will become a part of the journal entry as follows:

	Debit	Credit
Cash	1,030	
Notes Receivable		1,000
Interest Income		30*

* $1,000 \times 12\% \times 90/360 = \$30$

9.7 DISCOUNTING A NOTE RECEIVABLE

The holder of a promissory note may prompt the receipt of money by transferring the note (either by selling the note or by using it as collateral to borrow money) to a bank or finance company before its maturity date. The sale of a note receivable is referred to as "discounting a note receivable(받을어음의 할인)." The term *discounting* represents the fact that the cash proceeds(현금수령액) received as a result of transferring the note are less than the note's maturity value(만기금액).

The cash proceeds received by the holder from the sale of the note receivable are equal to the maturity value minus the discount (interest charge). The discount(할인액) is based on the period the bank will be holding the note and the note's market interest rate. The market interest rate(시장이자율) charged by the bank need *not* be the same as the stated interest rate(표시이자율) on the note. The difference may be caused by changes in the prevailing interest rate over time due to current money market conditions.

The maturity value of a note is:

Maturity Value = Face Value + Interest to Maturity

The discount is:

Discount = Maturity Value × Discount Rate × Discount Period

The cash proceeds received by the transferor at the time of discounting a note receivable are computed as follows:

Cash Proceeds = Maturity Value − Discount

On the date that a note is discounted, cash is debited for the cash proceeds received, the note receivable is credited for the face value of the note, and interest expense is debited for the *net* interest(순이자) by the transferor. The net interest is computed as the difference between the discount and interest to maturity(만기이자).

If the issuer pays the promissory note at maturity to the bank, no further entry is required by the transferor. In this case, the bank has received the maturity value of the note.

EXAMPLE 9-10 *Discounting a Note Receivable (1)*

Cardinal Company holds a \$100,000, 120-day, 12 percent note dated September 6. It is discounted at 16 percent on October 6.

The interest to maturity on the note:

$$\$100,000 \times 12\% \times 120/360 = \$4,000$$

The maturity value:

$$\$100,000+\$4,000=\$104,000$$

When Cardinal Company discounted the note, it had already held it for 30 days. Hence, the discount period will be 90 days. Cardinal must accrue earned interest income for the 30-day holding period at the discount date.

Accrued interest income:

$$\$100,000\times 12\%\times 30/360=\$1,000$$

The discount:

$$\$104,000\times 16\%\times 90/360=\$4,160$$

The cash proceeds received by Cardinal Company:

$$\$104,000-\$4,160=\$99,840$$

The journal entries to record the accrued interest income and the discounting of the note receivable are:

Account	Debit	Credit
Interest Receivable	1,000	
Interest Income		1,000*
Cash	99,840	
Interest Expense	1,160*	
Notes Receivable		100,000
Interest Receivable		1,000

* Net interest expense is the difference between the interest expense recognized from discounting the note and accrued interest.

Alternatively, we can combine the two journal entries into one as follows:

Account	Debit	Credit
Cash	99,840	
Interest Expense	160	
Notes Receivable		100,000

Also, note that $160 of net interest expense represents the difference between $4,160 discount and $4,000 interest income to maturity on the note receivable if Cardinal Company held it until maturity. You may notice that net interest income can be possible when the discount period is short, and the gap between the discount rate and the stated interest rate is low.

Example 9-11 Discounting a Note Receivable (2)

Assume the same information as in Example 9-10 except that the discount period is 30 days rather than 90 days.

The interest on the note receivable and the maturity value are the same as before. Then, the accrued interest period is 90 days, and the discount period is 30 days.

Accrued interest income:

$$\$100,000 \times 12\% \times 90/360 = \$3,000$$

The discount:

$$\$104,000 \times 16\% \times 30/360 = \$1,387$$

The cash proceeds become:

$$\$104,000 - \$1,387 = \$102,613$$

The entries to record the accrued interest and discounting of the note receivable are now:

Account	Debit	Credit
Interest Receivable	3,000	
Interest Income		3,000*
Cash	102,613	
Interest Expense	387*	
Notes Receivable		100,000
Interest Receivable		3,000

* Net interest income ($3,000 − $387 = $2,613) is the difference between the interest expense recognized from discounting the note and accrued interest or between $4,000 interest income to maturity and $1,387 discount.

Alternatively, we can combine the two journal entries into one as follows:

Account	Debit	Credit
Cash	102,613	
Notes Receivable		100,000
Interest Income		2,613

We can think of discounting a note receivable as consisting of two parts. The first part is the interest-earning period by holding the notes receivable. During the period, the holder earns the interest of "Face Value × Stated Interest Rate × Holding Period." The second part is the interest-paying period since the holder, now in effect, borrows money from the bank using the note receivable as collateral. During the period, the note holder is incurring an interest expense of "Maturity Value × Discount Rate × Discount Period." The concept is illustrated in Figure 9-1.

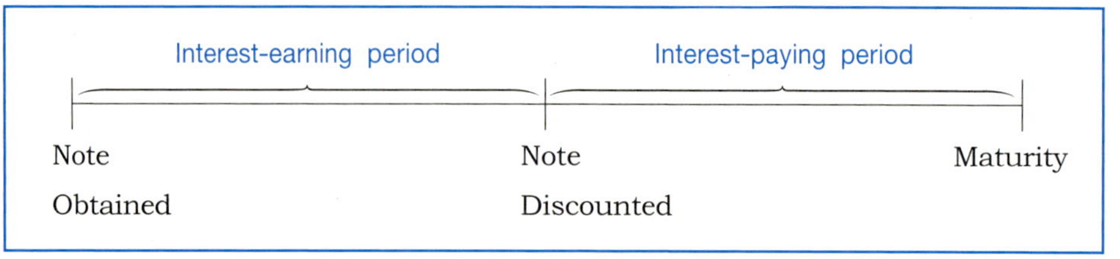

Figure 9-1 Discounting Note Receivable

9.8 NOTES PAYABLE

A note payable(지급어음) may be issued to make a purchase, settle an account payable, or borrow money from a bank. Accounting for notes payable is similar to that of notes receivable, except that notes payable are liabilities.

Example 9-12 *Notes Payable*

Goldfinch Company purchased a machine by issuing a 6%, $5,000 promissory note which matures in six months. The journal entry to record the purchase of the machine and the issuance of the promissory note is as follows:

Machinery	5,000	
Notes Payable		5,000

Example 9-13 *Replacement of Accounts Payable with Notes Payable*

Aspen Company owes an account payable of $6,000 to a supplier. Aspen Company has insufficient cash to pay the account payable when it becomes due. In settlement of the account payable, Aspen Company issued a 90-day promissory note which pays 12 percent annual interest. Prepare journal entries for Aspen Company to record the settlement of accounts payable by issuing a promissory note and the payment of the promissory note at the maturity date.

The journal entry for the exchange of the accounts payable and notes payable is:

Accounts Payable	6,000	
Notes Payable		6,000

The journal entry for the payment of the notes payable is:

Notes Payable	6,000	
Interest Expense	180*	
Cash		6,180

* $6,000 × 12% × 90/360 = $180

A promissory note is typically issued to the bank when a company borrows money from the bank. Often, the bank immediately deducts the interest on the loan from the face value of the note. The borrower receives the net proceeds. The term "borrowing at a discount(할인차입)" or "discounting a note payable" refers to the case if interest is paid in advance at the time of borrowing.

EXAMPLE 9-14 *Borrowing on a Discounted Note*

Phlox Company borrows $10,000 for 60 days at 18 percent from a bank. The loan is arranged on a *discount* basis, where the interest of $200 ($10,000 × 12% × 60/360) is deducted in advance. Prepare journal entries for Phlox Company to record the borrowing of money on a discounted note and the promissory note settlement at the maturity date.

The journal entry at the time of borrowing at a discount is:

Cash	9,800	
Interest Expense	200	
Notes Payable		10,000

The entry for the payment of the debt at the maturity date is:

Notes Payable	10,000	
Cash		10,000

There are two ways to pay interest when you borrow money from a bank. One is to pay interest in advance, and the other is to pay interest at maturity.

To illustrate, assume that you borrow $10,000 from a bank at 12% for three months ($300 interest for three months) by issuing a promissory note of $10,000. Then, the journal entries at the date of borrowing and the maturity date would be as follows under the two alternatives:

Alternative ways of interest payments	Journal Entries					
	Date of Borrowing			Maturity Date		
Interest paid in advance	Cash	9,700		Notes Payable	10,000	
	Interest Expense	300		Cash		10,000
	Notes Payable		10,000			
Interest paid at maturity	Cash	10,000		Notes Payable	10,000	
	Notes Payable		10,000	Interest Expense	300	
				Cash		10,300

CHAPTER 9

Multiple Choice Questions

9.1 Kingbird Inc. estimates uncollectible accounts based on the percentage of accounts receivable. What effect will recording the estimate of uncollectible accounts have on the accounting equation?

ⓐ Increase liabilities and decrease shareholders' equity
ⓑ Decrease assets and decrease liabilities
ⓒ Decrease assets and decrease shareholders' equity
ⓓ Increase assets and decrease shareholders' equity

9.2 On December 31, House Finch Co. reported accounts receivable of $238,000 and an allowance for uncollectible accounts of $600 (credit). An analysis of accounts receivable suggests that the allowance for uncollectible accounts should be 3% of accounts receivable. The amount of the adjustment for uncollectible accounts would be:

ⓐ $6,540.
ⓑ $7,800.
ⓒ $7,140.
ⓓ $7,740.

9.3 On December 31, Meadow Lark Co. reported accounts receivable of $238,000 and an allowance for uncollectible accounts of $600 (debit). An analysis of accounts receivable suggests that the allowance for uncollectible accounts should be 3% of accounts receivable. The amount of the adjustment for uncollectible accounts would be:

ⓐ $6,540.
ⓑ $7,800.
ⓒ $7,140.
ⓓ $7,740.

9.4 Allowance for Uncollectible Accounts is:

- ⓐ An expense account.
- ⓑ A contra asset account.
- ⓒ A contra revenue account.
- ⓓ A liability account.

9.5 Which of the following is recorded by a credit to Accounts Receivable?

- ⓐ Sale of inventory on account
- ⓑ Estimating the annual allowance for uncollectible accounts
- ⓒ Estimating annual sales returns
- ⓓ Write-offs of bad debts

9.6 Collections of accounts receivable that previously have been written off are credited to:

- ⓐ A Gain account.
- ⓑ Accounts Receivable.
- ⓒ Bad Debt Expense.
- ⓓ Retained Earnings.

9.7 When a specific account receivable is uncollectible, which of the following should the company record to write off the account using the allowance method?

- ⓐ A debit to Bad Debt Expense and a credit to Allowance for Uncollectible Accounts
- ⓑ A debit to Allowance for Uncollectible Accounts and a credit to Bad Debt Expense
- ⓒ A debit to Bad Debt Expense and a credit to Accounts Receivable
- ⓓ A debit to Allowance for Uncollectible Accounts and a credit to Accounts Receivable

9.8 When using an aging method for estimating uncollectible accounts:

ⓐ Older accounts are considered less likely to be collected.
ⓑ The number of days the account is past due is not considered.
ⓒ Older accounts are considered more likely to be collected.
ⓓ No estimate of uncollectible accounts is made.

9.9 The primary difference between a note receivable and an account receivable is:

ⓐ A note receivable cannot be classified as a current asset.
ⓑ Borrowers have the option of not paying a note receivable.
ⓒ An account receivable is more likely to be collected.
ⓓ A note receivable is evidenced by a written debt instrument.

9.10 On February 1, 20×1, Miriam Company lends cash and accepts a $1,000 note receivable that offers 12% interest and is due in six months. How much interest revenue will Miriam Company report during 20×1?

ⓐ $120
ⓑ $240
ⓒ $100
ⓓ $60

CHAPTER 9 Exercises

9.1 Percent of sales method

The December 31, 20×1 trial balance of Sunbird Company before adjustments included the following accounts:

	Debit	Credit
Allowance for uncollectible accounts	$2,000	
Sales		$830,000
Sales returns and allowances	10,000	

Sunbird Company estimates its uncollectible accounts expense based upon 2 percent of net sales.

Required:

What amount should Sunbird Company record as uncollectible accounts expense for 20×1?

9.2 Percent of sales method and aging method

The following account balances are for Hummingbird Company:

Accounts Receivable		Sales		Allowance for Uncollectible Accounts	
110,000			320,000		300

Required:

Prepare the adjusting entry to provide for uncollectible accounts expense if the uncollectible expense is estimated ⓐ at 1 percent of net sales and ⓑ by aging the accounts receivable, assuming the needed allowance balance is $3,300.

9.3 Percent of receivable method

On December 31, Tapir's Appliances had account balances in Accounts Receivable of $310,000 and $980 (credit) in Allowance for Uncollectible Accounts. An analysis of Tapir's December 31 accounts receivable suggests that the allowance for uncollectible accounts should be 2% of accounts receivable. Bad debt expense for the year should be:

9.4 Aging method

On December 31, 20×2, Beaver Company has a debit balance of $1,500 for Allowance for Uncollectible Accounts before any year-end adjustment. Beaver Company also has the following information for its accounts receivable and the estimated percentages of bad debts for different past-due amounts:

Age Group (Days past due)	Accounts Receivable	Estimated Percent Uncollectible
0~30	$50,000	5%
31~60	20,000	10%
61~90	10,000	20%

Required:

What amount of bad debt expense will be reported on Beaver Company's financial statements for 20×2?

9.5 Write-off and recovery of uncollectible accounts (1)

On March 13, Weaver Company wrote off a customer's account of $3,800. On June 3, the customer unexpectedly paid the $3,800 balance.

Required:

Using the allowance method, record the write-off on March 13 and the cash collection on June 3.

9.6 Write-off and recovery of uncollectible accounts (2)

Using the allowance method, prepare journal entries for the following transactions:

May 10	Aphid Company's account of $1,100 was deemed uncollectible.
June 20	Thrips Company, who owes us $900, has been declared bankrupt.
July 7	Aphid Company paid us back $800.

9.7 Write-off of specific receivable and bad debt expense

On December 31, 20×1, Pheasant Inc. had balances in Accounts Receivable and Allowance for Uncollectible Accounts of $53,600 and $1,325, respectively. During 20×2, Pheasant wrote off $1,465 in accounts receivable and determined that there should be an allowance for uncollectible accounts of $1,280 on December 31, 20×2. Bad debt expense for 20×2 would be:

9.8 Accounting for uncollectible accounts

Geranium Company uses the allowance method for estimating uncollectible accounts expense.

Required:

Prepare journal entries to record the following transactions:

January 5	Sold merchandise to Magnolia Company for $1,500 on terms of n/15.
April 15	Received $400 from Magnolia Company in settlement of accounts receivable.
August 21	Wrote off as uncollectible the balance of Magnolia Company account when it declared bankruptcy.
October 5	Unexpectedly received a check for $550 from Magnolia Company.

9.9 Notes receivable

On July 1, 20×1, Hummingbird Inc. lends cash and accepts a $10,000 note receivable that offers 10% interest and is due in nine months. How would Hummingbird record the transaction on April 1, 20×2, when the borrower pays Hummingbird the correct amount owed?

9.10 Discounting notes receivable

An $8,000, 90-day, 12 percent note receivable is discounted to a bank after it has been held for 30 days. The bank discount rate is 16 percent.

Required:

Determine the proceeds from the discounting of the note.

9.11 Replacement of accounts payable with notes payable

Dahlia Company owes an account payable of $10,000 to a supplier. Dahlia Company has insufficient cash to pay the account payable when it becomes due. In settlement of the account payable, Dahlia Company issued a 90-day promissory note which pays 12 percent annual interest.

Required:

Prepare journal entries to replace the account payable with the note and the payment of the promissory note at the maturity date.

9.12 Accounting for notes receivable

Journalize the following transactions:

March 1 Received a $3,000, 90-day, 18 percent promissory note in settlement of accounts receivable from Hosta Company.

March 31 Discounted the note to a bank (discount rate=19 percent).

9.13 Notes payable (1)

Cala Company borrowed $8,000 from First Bank and signed a promissory note.

Required:

What entry should Cala Company record?

9.14 Notes payable (2)

Aster Company borrowed $500,000 on November 1, 20×2, and signed a twelve-month note bearing interest at 6%. Principal and interest are payable in full at maturity on October 31, 20×3.

Required:

In connection with this note, at what amount should Aster Company report interest payable on December 31, 20×2?

9.15 Notes payable (3)

On June 1, Marguerite Company borrowed $20,000 from a bank by writing a 60-day, 6%, interest-bearing promissory note.

Required:

Prepare the necessary entries below associated with the note payable on the books of Marguerite Company.

ⓐ Prepare the entry on June 1, when the note was issued.

ⓑ Prepare any adjusting entries necessary on June 30 to prepare the monthly financial statements. Assume no other interest accrual entries have been made.

ⓒ Prepare the entry to record payment of the note at maturity.

9.16 Borrowing at a discount

Linden Company borrows $10,000 for three months at 12 percent from a bank. The loan is borrowed on a discount basis, where the interest of $300 ($10,000 × 12% × 3/12) is deducted in advance.

Required:

Make journal entries at the dates of borrowing and payment at maturity.

ACCOUNTING TERMINOLOGY IN CHAPTER 9

accounts receivable 외상매출금
aging method 연령분석법
aging schedule approach 연령분석표접근법
allowance for uncollectible accounts 대손충당금
allowance method 충당금설정법
annual interest rate 연리
borrowing at a discount 할인차입
cash proceeds 현금수령액
direct write-off method 직접차감법
discount 할인액
discounting notes receivable 받을어음의 할인
face value 액면금액
generally accepted accounting principle (GAAP) 일반적으로 인정된 회계원칙
income statement approach 손익계산서접근법
interest-bearing 이자부
interest income 이자수익
interest rate 이자율
interest to maturity 만기이자
market interest rate 시장이자율
matching principle 대응원칙
maturity value 만기금액
net credit sales 순외상매출액
net interest 순이자
net realizable value 순실현가능가치
non-interest-bearing 무이자부
non-trade receivables 비매출채권
notes payable 지급어음
notes receivable 받을어음
on account 외상, 신용
open account 신용계정
payee 수취인
percent of accounts receivables method 채권잔액비례법
percent of credit sales method 외상매출액비례법
principal 원금
priority lien 선순위담보
proceeds 현금수령액
promissory note 약속어음
provision 비용반영
receivables 수취채권
receivables management 수취채권관리
stated interest rate 표시이자율
statement of financial position approach 재무상태표접근법
trade receivables 매출채권
uncollectible accounts expense 대손상각비
write-off 제거

CHAPTER

10

PROPERTY, PLANT AND EQUIPMENT, AND INTANGIBLE ASSETS

CHAPTER 10

PROPERTY, PLANT AND EQUIPMENT, AND INTANGIBLE ASSETS

10.1 PROPERTY, PLANT, AND EQUIPMENT

Property, plant, and equipment(유형자산, PP&E), also called fixed assets(고정자산), are tangible, long-lived assets used in the operation of a business such as the production and sale of goods or services. They are not held for resale to customers. PP&E and intangible assets are long-lived assets used in the operation of a business. However, they are different because PP&E has physical substances, but intangible assets lack physical substances. Items included in the PP&E category include land(토지), land improvements(구축물), building(건물), machinery(기계), equipment(장비), automobiles(차량운반구), leased property(리스자산), and others.

PP&E is recorded at the cost when acquired. Cost(원가), also called historical cost(역사적원가), can be defined as all the necessary expenditures to make the asset available for its intended use. Therefore, the cost of a piece of PP&E is equal to the purchase price(매입가격) plus all necessary direct costs (직접필요경비) to make the asset available for its intended use and location. The asset's cost does not include unreasonable expenditures, such as the cost of a traffic violation ticket received while having the new machine delivered.

EXAMPLE 10-1 ***Purchase of Machinery***

Rudbeckia Corporation purchased a machine as follows:

Invoice price \$20,000; cash discount \$300; delivery \$535; insurance \$40; installation \$800.

The journal entry to record the purchase of the machine is:

	Dr.	Cr.
Machinery	21,075*	
Cash		21,075

* \$20,000 − \$300 + \$535 + \$40 + \$800 = \$21,075

A cash discount is deducted only when the company utilizes the discount opportunity. Delivery cost, insurance cost, and installation cost are included in the cost of the machine as long as they directly contribute to making it available for its intended use.

10.2 MEASUREMENT AFTER INITIAL RECOGNITION

As indicated earlier, an item of PP&E is recorded at the cost when acquired. An entity shall choose either the cost model(원가모형) or revaluation model(재평가모형) as its accounting policy and apply that policy to an entire class of PP&E. Under the cost model, after initial recognition as an asset, an item of PP&E shall be carried at its cost(원가) minus any accumulated depreciation(감가상각누계액) and any accumulated impairment losses(손상차손누계액). Under the revaluation model, after initial recognition as an asset, an item of PP&E whose fair value can be measured reliably shall be carried at a revalued amount(재평가액). A revalued amount is the fair value at the revaluation date, net of any subsequent accumulated depreciation and impairment losses. Revaluation shall be made with sufficient regularity to ensure that the carrying amount (book value) does not differ materially from what would be determined using fair value at the end of the reporting period.

10.3 DEPRECIATION

10.3.1 Concept of Depreciation

From a financial accounting perspective, PP&E items, except for land, have limited useful life(내용연수) because of physical deterioration(물리적 마모) and obsolescence(진부화). The PP&E items that are subject to depreciation are called depreciable assets(감가상각대상자산). Depreciable assets will eventually be worth only their salvage value(잔존가액, residual value). *Depreciation*(감가상각) is an allocation of the depreciation base(감가상각대상액) of a depreciable asset over its useful life in a rational and systematic manner(합리적이고 체계적인 방식). For accounting purposes, a rational method is the one that can best depict the consumption pattern of the asset's economic benefits. Once a rational method is adopted for depreciation, the method should be used consistently over the asset's useful life. The depreciation base refers to the original cost of the asset minus the estimated salvage value.

Under the accrual-basis accounting(발생주의회계), depreciation expense is recognized in the period the asset is used, not when cash is paid to purchase the asset. Depreciation expense(감가상각비) is an operating expense. The accumulated depreciation(감가상각누계액) of an asset helps report the asset at its *carrying amount*(장부금액, net carrying amount). Accumulated depreciation constitutes the portion of the asset's cost which has been recognized as depreciation expense up to the present time. An asset is reported at its carrying amount on the statement of financial position. As the asset becomes older, its carrying amount declines. Accumulated Depreciation is a contra account, similar to Allowance for Uncollectible Accounts (covered in Chapter 9).

Since land is not subject to depreciation, unlike other PP&E items, land is carried at its original cost when the entity uses the cost model(원가모형) or at a revalued amount when the entity uses the revaluation model(재평가모형).

10.3.2 *Factors Affecting Depreciation*

Three factors affect the computation of depreciation. They are cost, estimated useful life, and estimated salvage value. The cost of an asset is the cash equivalent price(현금등가) which was paid as consideration(대가) for the acquisition of the asset. Useful life is an estimate of the asset's expected productive life, also known as service life. Useful life may be expressed in terms of time, activity units (such as machine hours), or output units. Finally, salvage value, also called residual value or scrap value, is an estimate of the asset's value at the end of its useful life.

EXAMPLE 10-2 *Carrying Amount of Property, Plant, and Equipment*

A machine was acquired for $25,000. The accumulated depreciation at year's end is $7,500. The machine's carrying amount is reported on the statement of financial position as follows:

Machinery	$25,000
Less: Accumulated Depreciation	7,500
Carrying Amount	$17,500

10.3.3 *Depreciation Methods*

The depreciation base(감가상각대상액) of a depreciable asset (original cost minus salvage value) may be charged to expenses over the asset's useful life by choosing a rational method out of alternative methods allowed. The straight-line method(정액법, 직선법) results in equal depreciation charges every period. The accelerated depreciation methods(가속상각법) result in higher depreciation charges in the earlier years and lower depreciation charges in the later years. Two commonly used accelerated depreciation methods are the double-declining-balance method(이중체감잔액법) and the sum-of-the-years'-digits method(연수합계법). Accelerated methods are generally appropriate for measuring the decline in value of depreciable assets (e.g., automobiles) because they are usually most efficient when new. Variable charge methods also exist and depend on asset use. An example is the units-of-production method(생산량비례법), where depreciation expense is directly related to the volume produced.

(1) Straight-Line Method

The straight-line method(정액법) is the easiest and most popular method. It results in equal periodic depreciation charges. The method is most appropriate when the asset's usage is uniform from period to period. Depreciation expense under the straight-line method is equal to:

Depreciation Expense=(Cost−Salvage Value)/Useful Life in Years

Here, cost minus salvage value is a depreciation base or depreciable amount. Hence, under the straight-line method, the depreciation base is divided by the years of useful life to get an annual depreciation.

EXAMPLE 10-3 *Straight-Line Method*

A truck was purchased for $20,000 with an estimated salvage value of $2,000. The truck's estimated useful life is eight years. Depreciation per year equals:

($20,000−$2,000)/8 years=$2,250 per year

An alternative way of computation is to multiply the depreciation base of $18,000 by the annual depreciation rate of 12.5 percent (1/8). The result is the same at $2,250 per year.

The journal entry to record depreciation is:

Depreciation Expense	2,250	
Accumulated Depreciation		2,250

Entries to record depreciation are adjusting entries (covered in Chapter 4) made at the end of the accounting period to appropriately reflect the carrying value of the asset and match period expenses with period revenues.

(2) Sum-of-the-Years'-Digits Method

Under the sum-of-the-years'-digits method(연수합계법, SYD method), annual depreciation expense is calculated by multiplying the depreciation base by an SYD depreciation rate(연수합계법감가상각률). Each year, an SYD deprecation rate is determined by a ratio of the number of remaining useful-life years divided by the sum-of-the-years'-digits (SYD) of the useful life. For example, let us assume that the life expectancy of a machine is eight years. If we write the numbers in reverse order, we have 8, 7, 6, 5, 4, 3, 2, and 1, respectively, as the remaining useful life at the beginning of each accounting period. Therefore, the denominator is the SYD (8+7+6+5+4+3+2+1), which equals 36. Thus, the fraction for the first year is 8/36, while the fraction for the last year is 1/36. As a result, the sum of the eight fractions equals 36/36 or 1. Therefore, the machine is completely written down to its salvage value at the end of eight years.

EXAMPLE 10-4 *Sum-of-the-Years'-Digits Method*

The cost of a truck, having an estimated life of 8 years, is $20,000, and its estimated salvage value is $2,000. So, the depreciation base is $18,000 ($20,000−$2,000). The computation for each year's depreciation expense is shown below.

Year	SYD Depreciation Rate	×	Depreciation Base	=	Depreciation Expense
1	8/36		$18,000		$4,000
2	7/36		18,000		3,500
3	6/36		18,000		3,000
4	5/36		18,000		2,500
5	4/36		18,000		2,000
6	3/36		18,000		1,500
7	2/36		18,000		1,000
8	1/36		18,000		500
Total					$18,000

If the asset has a very long life, the following formula may be used to find the sum-of-the-years'-digits(연수합계, SYD):

$$SYD=N(N+1)/2$$

Here, N represents the number of years of useful life. So, for example, if the useful life is ten years, the SYD is $10\times(10+1)/2=55$.

When an asset is acquired during the year, a pro-rata (i.e., proportionate) amount for depreciation must be computed.

Example 10-5 *Depreciation for Property, Plant, and Equipment Acquired in the Middle of a Year*

A truck was purchased on July 1, 20×1, for \$20,000. Its estimated useful life is eight years, with an estimated salvage value of \$2,000. The company uses the sum-of-the-years'-digits method.

The depreciation expense for 20×1 is:

7/1/20×1~12/31/20×1:	8/36×\$18,000×6/12=	\$2,000

The depreciation expense for 20×2 is:

1/1/20×2~ 6/30/20×2:	8/36×\$18,000×6/12=	\$2,000
7/1/20×2~12/31/20×2:	7/36×\$18,000×6/12=	1,750
		\$3,750

(3) Double-Declining-Balance Method

Under the double-declining-balance method(이중체감잔액법, DDB method), depreciation expense is large in the earlier years and small in the later years. We need to know some important features of the DDB method. First, a depreciation rate is determined by doubling the straight-line depreciation rate. For example, if an asset has an estimated useful life of 10 years, the straight-line depreciation rate is 10 percent, and the double-declining-balance (DDB) depreciation rate is 20 percent. Second, depreciation expense is computed by multiplying the DDB depreciation rate by the beginning carrying amount of the asset. Since the carrying amount declines over time because of depreciation, depreciation expense will become less and less each year as time goes by. Third, the method *ignores* salvage value in the computation of annual depreciation. Lastly, the asset's carrying amount at the end of its useful life cannot be below its salvage value. Therefore, the last year's depreciation expense is simply the difference between the beginning carrying amount of the asset minus its estimated salvage value.

The DDB method is advantageous for tax purposes since higher depreciation charges in the earlier years result in lower taxable income(과세소득) and, thus, smaller taxes to be paid. The tax savings improve cash flows. Over the asset's life, the total depreciation expenses will be the same regardless of the depreciation method used. However, the timing of the tax savings differs.

Example 10-6 *Double-Declining-Balance Method*

A piece of equipment costing $20,000 has an estimated useful life of eight years with an estimated salvage value of $2,000. Assume that the equipment is depreciated using the double-declining-balance method. Since the straight-line depreciation rate is 12.5 percent (1/8), the DDB depreciation rate is 25 percent (2×12.5%). Annual depreciation expenses are computed below.

Year	Beginning balance of carrying amount	×	DDB depreciation rate	=	Depreciation expense	Ending balance of carrying amount
1	$20,000		25%		$5,000	$15,000
2	15,000		25%		3,750	11,250
3	11,250		25%		2,813	8,437
4	8,437		25%		2,109	6,328
5	6,328		25%		1,582	4,746
6	4,746		25%		1,187	3,559
7	3,559		25%		890	2,669
8	2,669		25%		669*	2,000

Since the estimated salvage value is $2,000 and the asset cannot be depreciated below its salvage value, the depreciation expense for the last year should be $669 ($2,669−$2,000).

(4) Activity-based Method

The activity-based method(활동기준법), also called the units-of-production method (생산량비례법), is appropriate when the use of the asset materially varies from period to period. It has the benefit of optimally matching depreciation expense to revenue generated. Under this method, the depreciation expense per unit(단위당감가상각비) or other activity units (e.g., machine hours, kilometers) is first determined by using the following formula:

Depreciation expense per unit = (Cost − Salvage value)/Estimated total units

The depreciation expense for a given year is determined as follows:

Depreciation expense = Depreciation expense per unit × Activity units

Example 10-7 ***Activity-based Method***

The cost of a machine is \$20,000, its salvage value is estimated at \$2,000, and the estimated total usage over the expected life of the machine is 8,000 hours. Assume that the activity-based method is used for depreciation.

The depreciation expense per hour:

(\$20,000 − \$2,000)/8,000 hours = \$2.25

In the first year, the machine is used for 1,600 hours.
Depreciation expense in the first year:

1,600 hours × \$2.25 per hour = \$3,600

10.4 DISPOSAL OF PROPERTY, PLANT, AND EQUIPMENT

Disposal of PP&E can take various forms. Sometimes, they can be discarded, and at other times can be sold for cash or exchanged for other assets.

(1) Discarding Property, Plant, and Equipment

When a PP&E item is no longer useful to the entity, the asset is often sold for its scrap value(폐기가액). If the asset is fully depreciated, then no depreciation is recorded at the time of its disposal. For example, suppose a piece of equipment was purchased for $25,000, and the company decided to discard the asset when it was fully depreciated. Then, the journal entry to derecognize the equipment is:

Accumulated Depreciation	25,000	
Equipment		25,000

If the asset is not fully depreciated at the time of disposal, an entry is needed to update the depreciation so that its carrying amount is updated accordingly. The carrying amount is cost minus accumulated depreciation. If the carrying amount is more than zero and the asset is discarded, then the remaining carrying amount should be recorded as a loss on the disposal of the asset.

EXAMPLE 10-8 *Discarding Property, Plant, and Equipment*

Equipment acquired for $20,000 with accumulated depreciation of $18,000 as of the end of the previous year (December 31) was discarded on March 31. The annual depreciation rate is 10 percent. Then, the three-month depreciation expense (January 1 ~March 31) is $500 ($20,000 × 10% × 3/12).

The journal entry on March 31 to bring the accumulated depreciation up-to-date is:

Depreciation Expense	500	
Accumulated Depreciation		500

The entry to record the disposal of the asset is:

Accumulated Depreciation	18,500	
Loss on Disposal of Equipment	1,500	
Equipment		20,000

The loss account is reported as other expenses in the income statement.

(2) Sale of Property, Plant, and Equipment

Before recording the sale of PP&E, depreciation expense is recognized to the disposal date. The difference between the asset's selling price and the updated carrying amount will result in a gain or loss on disposal(처분손익). If the cash proceeds from the sale are greater than the carrying amount, a gain is recognized. In contrast, a loss is recognized if the cash proceeds from the sale are less than the carrying amount. Of course, in the unlikely case that an asset is sold for an amount identical to its carrying amount, neither a gain nor loss will arise.

EXAMPLE 10-9 *Sale of Property, Plant, and Equipment (1)*

On March 31, 20×2, equipment costing $20,000 with accumulated depreciation of $18,000 as of December 31, 20×1 is sold for $2,600. The annual straight-line depreciation rate is 10 percent. Two journal entries are required. The first is to update the accumulated depreciation account, and the second is to record the sale.

March 31, 20×2		
Depreciation Expense	500*	
Accumulated Depreciation		500
Cash	2,600	
Accumulated Depreciation	18,500	
Equipment		20,000
Gain on Disposal of Equipment		1,100

* $\$20,000 \times 10\% \times 3/12 = \$500$

The gain may be proved by comparing the cash proceeds(현금수취액) from the sale to the carrying amount as follows:

Cash Proceeds		$2,600
Carrying Amount		
Cost	$20,000	
Less: Accumulated Depreciation	(18,500)	1,500
Gain		$1,100

This gain is reported as other income in the income statement.

Now, let's look at a case where a loss on the sale would be recorded because the cash proceeds from the sale are less than the carrying amount.

EXAMPLE 10-10 *Sale of Property, Plant, and Equipment (2)*

If we assume the same information as in Example 10-9 except that the equipment is sold for $1,400, the journal entries are:

March 31, 20×2		
Depreciation Expense	500	
Accumulated Depreciation		500
Cash	1,400	
Accumulated Depreciation	18,500	
Loss on Disposal of Equipment	100	
Equipment		20,000

The loss may be proved by comparing the cash proceeds to the carrying amount.

Cash Proceeds		$1,400
Carrying Amount		
Cost	$20,000	
Less: Accumulated Depreciation	(18,500)	1,500
Loss		$100

(3) Exchange of Property, Plant, and Equipment

One or more items of PP&E may be acquired in exchange for non-monetary assets(비화폐성자산). The cost of PP&E is measured at fair value unless (a) the exchange transaction lacks commercial substance(상업적실질) or (b) the fair value of neither the asset received nor the asset given up is reliably measurable.

When the exchange transaction has commercial substance, the new asset received is recorded at fair value, and the old asset is derecognized, resulting in gain or loss on disposal. On the other hand, when the exchange transaction lacks commercial substance, the new asset is recorded based on the carrying amount of the old asset without recognizing gains or losses on the disposal of the old asset.

Whether an exchange transaction has commercial substance is determined by considering the extent to which its future cash flows are expected to change as a result of the transaction.

An exchange has commercial substance if:

① the risk, timing, and amount of the cash flows of the asset received differ from those of the assets transferred; or
② the company-specific value of the portion of the company's operations affected by the transaction changes as a result of the exchange; and
③ the difference in ① or ② is significant relative to the fair value of the assets exchanged.

Let's compare the two accounting treatments for an exchange transaction, one with commercial substance and the other without commercial substance, in the following two illustrative examples.

EXAMPLE 10-11 *Exchange of Equipment without Commercial Substance*

The following information relates to a trade-in of an old asset for a new asset:

Old Equipment	
Cost	$20,000
Accumulated depreciation at the end of the previous year	17,500
Depreciation expense for the current year up to the time of trade-in	500

New Equipment	
Fair value	$22,000
Trade-in allowance(교환가치인정액)	2,600
Cash paid	$19,400

Assume that the exchange transaction lacks commercial substance.
The entry to bring the depreciation up to date is:

Depreciation Expense	500	
Accumulated Depreciation		500

Before the trade-in is recorded, any gain from the transaction must be determined as follows:

Trade-in allowance	$2,600
Less: Carrying amount of old equipment	(2,000)
Gain	$600

The gain on the exchange of assets is NOT recorded because the exchange transaction lacks commercial substance and hence reduces the cost basis of the new asset as follows:

The fair value of the new equipment	$22,000
Less: Unrecognized gain	(600)
Recorded cost of new equipment	$21,400

The entry to record the exchange when the exchange transaction lacks commercial substance is:

Accumulated Depreciation	18,000	
Equipment (new)	21,400	
Equipment (old)		20,000
Cash		19,400

Let's use the same example except that the exchange transaction has commercial substance.

Example 10-12 Exchange of Equipment with Commercial Substance

Assume the same information as in Example 10-11 except that the exchange transaction has commercial substance. Then, the new asset should be recorded at fair value, and the gain on the disposal of the old asset should be recognized.

The journal entries to update the accumulated depreciation account and to record the exchange transaction are:

Depreciation Expense	500	
Accumulated Depreciation		500
Accumulated Depreciation	18,000	
Equipment (new)	22,000	
Equipment (old)		20,000
Cash		19,400
Gain on Disposal of Equipment		600

10.5 IMPAIRMENT

The carrying amount of PP&E is rarely the same as the recoverable amount(회수가능액). Therefore, when the recoverable amount of a piece of PP&E declines substantially, its value might fall materially below its carrying amount. For example, this may happen because a machine has become obsolete or the market value of the products produced by the machine has declined.

The recoverable amount of an asset is the higher of its fair value(공정가치) or its value in use. Fair value is the market value(시장가치) in principle. Value in use(사용가치) is the present value(현재가치) of the future cash flows expected to be generated by the asset. When an asset's recoverable amount declines below its carrying amount, an impairment must be recognized as a loss. That is, an impairment loss(손상차손) should be recognized immediately in the determination of net income for the period.

10.6 INTANGIBLE ASSETS

Intangible assets(무형자산) lack physical substance and arise from a right granted by the government or contractual agreements with other entities. Intangible assets may be acquired externally or developed internally. Examples of rights granted by the government are patents(특허권), copyrights (저작권), and trademarks(상표권). In contrast, an example of a privilege obtained from a contractual agreement with another entity is a license(라이선스) or franchise(프랜차이즈). Other types of intangibles include leasehold improvements (리스개량자산) and goodwill(영업권). Leasehold improvements are expenditures made by the lessee(임차인) to the leased property, such as the cost of putting up new fixtures on the leased property.

Intangible assets can be divided into two major categories: individually identifiable intangible assets(식별가능무형자산) and goodwill. In other words, all the intangible assets except for goodwill are separable from the company or individually identifiable. Therefore, they can be individually purchased from or sold to other companies. However, goodwill arises from purchasing an entire company, division, or segment.

Some intangible assets are amortized(상각) over their useful lives because they have finite useful lives(한정내용연수), while others are not amortized since they have indefinite useful lives(비한정내용연수). Examples of the former are patents, copyrights, and franchises, whereas examples of the latter are trademarks or trade names and goodwill.

Patent(특허) is an exclusive right that enables the registrant to manufacture, sell, or otherwise control an invention for a certain period (say 20 years) from the date of issue. The initial cost of a patent is the cash or cash equivalent price(현금등가) paid to acquire the patent. Suppose the owner incurs legal costs while successfully defending the patent in an infringement suit. Such costs can be added to the patent account and amortized over the patent's remaining life if the successful lawsuit results in improved economic benefits(경제적효익). However, if the lawsuit only maintained the patent's current economic benefits, the costs should be expensed as incurred. If an intangible asset is suddenly deemed worthless, the asset account should be written off, and an impairment loss should be recognized. An example occurs when a company loses a legal suit involving its patent.

Copyright(저작권) gives the owner an exclusive right to reproduce and sell an artistic or published work. Copyrights extend to the life of the creator plus a certain amount of years (usually 70 years). The cost of copyright consists of the cost of acquiring and defending it. A copyright's useful life is generally significantly shorter than its legal life.

A trademark(상표) or trade name(상호) is a word, phrase, jingle, or symbol that distinguishes or identifies a particular enterprise or product. It helps identify products and generally enhances the sale of the products. A trademark or trade name is usually protected for 20 years and may be renewed indefinitely as long as it is in use. If the trademark or trade name is purchased, the cost is the purchase price plus registration fee if needed. If it is internally developed, the cost includes the attorney's fees, registration fees, design costs, successful legal defense costs, and other expenditures directly related to securing it. Since trademarks or trade names have indefinite useful lives, they are not amortized.

A franchise(프랜차이즈) is a contractual arrangement under which the franchisor(프랜차이즈본사) grants the franchisee(프랜차이즈영업점) the right to sell certain products, to render services, or to use certain trademarks or trade names, usually within a designated geographical area. Another type of franchise granted by a government body permits the company to use public property in performing its services. Examples are public land use for telephone, electricity, cable television lines, and airwaves for broadcasting. Such operating rights are called *licenses*.

Goodwill represents the amount paid to another business in excess of the fair market value of its identifiable net assets(식별가능순자산). For example, if Company A paid $100,000 for Company B's identifiable net assets having a fair market value of $84,000, the amount paid for the goodwill is $16,000. Goodwill can be recorded only when a company *purchases* another business. The amount paid for the goodwill of a business may be based upon the acquired firm's excess earning power over other companies in the industry. Goodwill is not amortized because it is considered to have an indefinite useful life. However, it must be subject to an impairment test(손상검사) at least once a year and must be written down if its recoverable amount(회수가능액) is lower than its carrying amount.

Internally developed goodwill(내부창출영업권), like good customer relations, is *not* recorded as an intangible asset. Some expenditures, like research and development costs, employee training expenses, and advertising expenses, may enhance the company's value. However, these expenditures are expensed as incurred since their contributions to the company's increased value cannot be reliably measured.

EXAMPLE 10-13 *Goodwill*

The books of Cricket Company before the acquisition by Mantis Corporation include the following information:

Cash $50,000; Accounts Receivable $50,000; Inventory $200,000; Property, Plant, and Equipment $500,000; Patent $100,000; Accounts Payable $100,000; Long-term Debt $300,000.

The fair values of the assets and liabilities are the same as the carrying amounts reported above except for inventory and property, plant, and equipment, whose fair market values are determined at $300,000 and $700,000, respectively.

The amount of goodwill is equal to the excess of the purchase cost over the fair value of the identifiable net assets of the acquired company. Assume Mantis Corporation pays $900,000 for the net assets of Cricket Company. The goodwill to be recognized by Mantis Corporation is calculated as follows:

$$\$900{,}000-(\$50{,}000+\$50{,}000+\$300{,}000+\$700{,}000+\$100{,}000-\$100{,}000-\$300{,}000)=\$100{,}000$$

Therefore, Mantis Corporation should prepare the following journal entry to record the acquisition of Cricket Company.

	Debit	Credit
Cash	50,000	
Accounts Receivable	50,000	
Inventory	300,000	
Property, Plant, and Equipment	700,000	
Patent	100,000	
Goodwill	100,000	
Accounts Payable		100,000
Long-term Debt		300,000
Cash		900,000

10.7 ACCOUNTING FOR INTANGIBLE ASSETS

Intangible assets acquired, such as goodwill, should be recorded at cost. Suppose an intangible is acquired for consideration other than cash. In that case, it should be recognized at either the fair value of the consideration(대가) given or the fair value of the right received, whichever is more clearly evident. Intangible assets should not be arbitrarily written off if they still have value.

When identifiable intangible assets are internally developed (e.g., patents), they should be recorded as intangible assets at related direct cost. If they are not identifiable, they should be expensed.

Intangible assets must be *amortized* over the periods benefited when they have finite useful lives(한정내용연수). However, when they have indefinite useful lives(비한정내용연수), they are subject to impairment accounting(손상차손회계)

rather than amortization accounting(상각회계). Examples of intangible assets with indefinite useful lives include trademarks, trade names, and goodwill. Impairment accounting for goodwill deserves special attention since it is not easy to verify the cost of goodwill in many cases objectively. Therefore, goodwill is required to be subject to an impairment test at least once a year.

Amortization(상각) is a term used to describe the systematic allocation of the acquisition cost of intangible assets to expense over their economic useful lives. The straight-line method(정액법) of amortization is generally used. The amortization entry is:

Amortization Expense	×××	
Intangible Asset		×××

A credit entry is made directly to the particular intangible asset account. This method is called the direct method(직접법) since a specific asset account is directly written off as a result of amortization. The direct method is appropriate for amortizing intangible assets because intangible assets are usually not material in terms of amounts. However, it would not be incorrect to use the indirect method(간접법), which credits an accumulated amortization (상각누계액) account.

Example 10-14 *Amortization of Intangible Assets*

On January 1, 20×1, Chameleon Company paid $1,700 to obtain a patent that has a life of 17 years. The appropriate adjusting entry to record the amortization for 20×1 is:

Amortization Expense	100	
Patents		100

An amortization expense of $100 is shown in the income statement for 20×1. In addition, the patent account of $1,600 ($1,700 − $100) is shown under Intangible Assets on the statement of financial position as of December 31, 20×1.

CHAPTER 10

Multiple Choice Questions

10.1 Heather Inc. purchased land for $75,000 cash. They also incurred commissions of $4,500, property taxes of $5,000, and title insurance of $800. The $5,000 in property taxes includes $4,000 in back taxes paid by Heather on behalf of the seller and $1,000 due for the current year after the purchase date. For what amount should Heather record the land?

a. $83,500
b. $84,300
c. $85,300
d. $75,000

10.2 Halifax Company purchased a piece of equipment by paying $5,000 cash. It also incurred a shipping cost of $400 to get the equipment to its factory. The fair value of this equipment is $7,000. For what amount should Halifax record the equipment?

a. $5,000
b. $5,400
c. $7,000
d. $7,400

10.3 Productive assets that are physically used up or depleted are:

a. Equipment.
b. Land.
c. Land improvements.
d. Natural resources.

10.4 The statement of financial position of Cattleman Inc. shows assets of $86,400 and liabilities of $15,000. The fair value of the assets is $90,000, and the fair value of its liabilities is $15,000. Longhorn paid Cattleman $95,000 to acquire it. Longhorn should record goodwill on this purchase of:

ⓐ $3,600.
ⓑ $5,000.
ⓒ $20,000.
ⓓ $23,600.

10.5 Which of the following subsequent expenditures would be capitalized?

ⓐ Ordinary repair
ⓑ Costs that increase the service life of an asset
ⓒ Routine maintenance
ⓓ Both ⓐ and ⓑ

10.6 Which of the following is considered a "contra" account?

ⓐ Unearned Revenue
ⓑ Goodwill
ⓒ Accumulated Depreciation
ⓓ Costs of Goods Sold

10.7 The depreciable cost used in calculating depreciation expense is:

ⓐ Its service life.
ⓑ The amount allowable under tax depreciation methods.
ⓒ The difference between its replacement value and cost.
ⓓ The asset's cost minus its estimated residual value.

10.8 A machine was acquired at $15,000, with an estimated residual value of $3,000 and an estimated useful life of four years. The machine is being depreciated on a straight-line basis. At the end of the second year, what amount will be reported for accumulated depreciation?

ⓐ $9,000
ⓑ $6,000
ⓒ $7,500
ⓓ $3,000

10.9 During 20×1 and 20×2, Flicker Inc. drove the truck 15,000 and 22,000 kilometers, respectively, to deliver merchandise to its customers. The company purchased the truck at the beginning of 20×1 for $175,000. If the truck has an estimated life of 10 years and 300,000 kilometers, with an estimated residual value of $25,000, how much deprecation expense should Flicker Inc. record in 20×2 using the activity method?

ⓐ $11,000
ⓑ $18,500
ⓒ $7,500
ⓓ $16,000

10.10 On January 1, 20×1, Junco Inc. purchased a commercial truck for $48,000 and uses the straight-line depreciation method. The truck has a useful life of eight years and an estimated residual value of $8,000. On December 31, 20×3, Junco Inc. sold the truck for $30,000. How much gain or loss should Junco Inc. record on December 31, 20×3?

ⓐ Gain, $22,000
ⓑ Loss, $18,000
ⓒ Gain, $5,000
ⓓ Loss, $3,000

CHAPTER 10

Exercises

10.1 Acquisition of equipment (1)

Oak Brook Company purchased a piece of equipment for $5,000. It also incurred a shipping cost of $400 to get the equipment to its factory. The list price of this equipment was $7,000 at the time of purchase.

Required:

At what amount should Oak Brook Company record the equipment?

10.2 Acquisition of equipment (2)

Boxwood Company purchased a piece of equipment having a list price of $75,000. Because the equipment was immediately paid for, the company was entitled to a 2 percent discount. Costs incurred to make the equipment ready for use included: freight, $3,000; installation, $485; electrical wiring, $700; repair expense due to improper handling, $100; and rental of a special crane, $435. What is the acquisition cost of the equipment?

10.3 Straight-line depreciation method

On January 1, 20×1, a piece of equipment was purchased for $30,000. The estimated life is six years, and the salvage value is $1,500.

Required:

Determine the annual depreciation using the straight-line method.

10.4 Activity-based depreciation method

During 20×2 and 20×3, Chrysanthemum Catering Company drove its truck 15,000 and 22,000 kilometers, respectively, to deliver merchandise to its customers. The company purchased the truck at the beginning of 20×2 for $175,000.

Required:

If the truck has an estimated life of 10 years and 300,000 kilometers, with an estimated residual value of $25,000, how much depreciation expense should Chrysanthemum Catering Company record in 20×3 using the activity method?

10.5 Accelerated depreciation methods

A fixed asset costs $48,000 and has an estimated salvage value of $6,000. The anticipated life is 10 years.

Required:

Fill in the following tables.

Sum-of-the-Years'-Digits Method

Year	Depreciation Expense	Accumulated Depreciation	Year-End Carrying Amount
1			
2			
3			

Double-Declining-Balance Method

Year	Depreciation Expense	Accumulated Depreciation	Year-End Carrying Amount
1			
2			
3			

10.6 Different depreciation methods

Slug Inc. purchased equipment for $40,000. Residual value at the end of an estimated four-year service life is expected to be $8,000. The machine operated for 2,200 hours in the first year, and the company expects it to operate for 10,000 hours over its four-year life. Calculate depreciation expense for the first year using each of the following depreciation methods: ⓐ straight-line, ⓑ double-declining-balance, and ⓒ activity-based methods.

10.7 Carrying amount of equipment

The following information is available for Ginkgo Company, which has an accounting year-end of December 31, 20×3.

ⓐ A van was purchased on June 1, 20×2, for $40,000. It was estimated to have a $4,000 salvage value after being driven 100,000 kilometers. During 20×3, the van was driven 30,000 kilometers. The units-of-activity method of depreciation is used.

ⓑ A building was purchased 22 years ago for $6,600,000. It is estimated to have a $60,000 salvage value at the end of its 40-year useful life. The straight-line method of depreciation is being used.

ⓒ Office equipment was purchased on January 1, 20×2, for $60,000. The office equipment would have a $6,000 salvage value at the end of its 5-year useful life. The double-declining-balance method of depreciation is being used.

Required:

Complete the table shown below by filling in the appropriate amounts.

Assets	Accumulated Depreciation 1/1/20×3	Depreciation Expense for 20×3	Carrying Amount 12/31/20×3
Van	$12,600	$	$
Building	$3,433,500	$	$
Office equipment	$24,000	$	$

10.8 Change in estimated useful life

Oriole Corp. purchased equipment at the beginning of 20×1 for $650,000. In 20×1 and 20×2, Oriole depreciated the asset using the straight-line method with an estimated useful life of 8 years and a $10,000 residual value. In 20×3, due to technological changes, Oriole revised the useful life to a total of six years (four more years) with zero residual value. What depreciation expense would Oriole record for the year 20×3 on this equipment?

10.9 Disposal of equipment (1)

Equipment costing $19,500 with accumulated depreciation of $12,000 is discarded. There is no salvage value.

Required:

Prepare the appropriate journal entry for its disposal.

10.10 Disposal of equipment (2)

On January 1, 20×1, Bentgrass Company purchased a commercial truck for $48,000 and uses the straight-line depreciation method. The truck has a useful life of eight years and an estimated residual value of $8,000. On December 31, 20×3, Bentgrass Company sold the truck for $30,000.

Required:

How much gain or loss should Bentgrass Company record on December 31, 20×3?

10.11 Derecognition of equipment

Sawgrass Company purchased equipment in 20×1 for $80,000 and estimated an $8,000 salvage value at the end of the equipment's 10-year useful life. On December 31, 20×7, there was $50,400 in the Accumulated Depreciation account for this equipment using the straight-line depreciation method. On April 30, 20×8, the equipment was sold for $22,000.

Required:

Prepare appropriate journal entries to derecognize the equipment from the books of Sawgrass Company on April 30, 20×8.

10.12 Exchange of assets

Hedgehog Inc. exchanges long-term assets with Lizard Inc. Hedgehog receives a delivery truck and gives up a piece of machinery. The machinery's fair value and carrying amount were $27,000 and $25,000 (original cost of $35,000 less accumulated depreciation of $10,000), respectively. Since the delivery truck was worth $32,000, Hedgehog paid Lizard an additional $5,000 in cash. Record the exchange for Hedgehog.

10.13 Intangible assets

Identify the intangible asset being described by writing its letter on the line next to the description.

a. Copyright
b. Franchise
c. Goodwill
d. Patent
e. Trademark

1. ______ This intangible asset is recorded only when one company purchases another company and pays more for that company than the fair value of the net assets acquired.
2. ______ This intangible asset gives a company the right to sell products or services using the operating techniques and/or trademarks of another company within a geographical area.
3. ______ This intangible asset protects the graphic images and words used to represent a company or its product or service.
4. ______ This intangible asset represents the rights over artistic works, music, or written words and allows the holder to sell or reproduce these creations.
5. ______ This intangible asset gives rights to the developer and owner of a physical process or invention used to manufacture and sell products.

10.14 Goodwill (1)

Siskin Corporation purchased Grosbeak Company for $350,000. At the time of acquisition, Grosbeak's assets and liabilities reflect the following fair values:

Cash	$20,000	Accounts payable	$21,000
Trading securities	45,000	Taxes payable	5,000
Accounts receivable	18,000	Short-term note payable	9,000
PP&E	389,000	Mortgage payable	207,000
Copyright	30,000		

Required:

What amount of goodwill will be recorded by Siskin Corporation when it acquires Grosbeak Company?

10.15 Goodwill (2)

On July 1, 20×1, Grizzly Inc. acquired all the outstanding ordinary shares of Salmon Inc. for $68,000 in cash. The carrying amounts and market values of Salmon's assets and liabilities were as follows:

	Carrying amounts	Fair Value
Current assets	$24,000	$30,000
Property, plant, and equipment	44,000	56,000
Other assets	4,000	6,000
Current liabilities	16,000	16,000
Long-term liabilities	24,000	22,000

Required:

Calculate the amount paid for goodwill.

10.16 Amortization of intangibles

Spoonbill Company recently obtained a patent for a manufacturing process related to mobile phone technology. The patent has a legal life of 20 years, but the company's finance director, engineers, and marketing executive agree the patent's useful life will be close to 7 years. They also estimate that the patent will have no residual value. Spoonbill paid $84,000 for the patent.

Required:

Prepare the adjusting entry to record the first full year's patent amortization expense.

ACCOUNTING TERMINOLOGY IN CHAPTER 10

accelerated depreciation method 가속상각법
accrual-basis accounting 발생주의회계
accumulated amortization 상각누계액
accumulated depreciation 감가상각누계액
accumulated impairment losses 손상차손누계액
activity-based method 활동기준법
amortization 상각
amortization accounting 상각회계
automobiles 차량운반구
buildings 건물
carrying amount 장부금액
cash equivalent price 현금등가
cash proceeds 현금수취액
commercial substance 상업적실질
consideration 대가
copyright 저작권
cost 원가
cost model 원가모형
depreciable assets 감가상각대상자산
depreciation 감가상각
depreciation base 감가상각대상액
depreciation expense 감가상각비
depreciation expense per unit 단위당감가상각비
depreciation rate 감가상각률
direct method 직접법
direct necessary costs 직접필요경비
double-declining-balance (DDB) method 이중체감잔액법
economic benefits 경제적효익
fair value 공정가치
finite useful life 한정내용연수
fixed assets 고정자산
franchise 프랜차이즈
franchisee 프랜차이즈영업점
franchisor 프랜차이즈본사
gain or loss on disposal 처분손익
goodwill 영업권
historical cost 역사적원가
identifiable intangible assets 식별가능무형자산
identifiable net assets 식별가능순자산
impairment 손상
impairment accounting 손상차손회계
impairment loss 손상차손
impairment test 손상검사
indefinite useful lives 비한정내용연수
indirect method 간접법
intangible assets 무형자산
internally developed goodwill 내부창출영업권
land 토지
land improvements 구축물
leased property 리스자산
leasehold improvements 리스개량자산
lessee 임차인
license 라이선스
machinery 기계
market value 시장가치

net carrying amount 장부금액
non-monetary assets 비화폐성자산
obsolescence 진부화
patent 특허권
physical deterioration 물리적 마모
present value 현재가치
property, plant, and equipment (PP&E) 유형자산
purchase price 매입가격
rational and systematic manner 합리적이고 체계적인 방식
recoverable amount 회수가능액
residual value 잔존가액
revaluation model 재평가모형
revalued amount 재평가액
salvage value 잔존가액
scrap value 폐기가액
straight-line method 정액법
sum-of-the-years'-digits (SYD) 연수합계
sum-of-the-years'-digits (SYD) method 연수합계법
taxable income 과세소득
trade name 상호
trade-in allowance 교환가치인정액
trademark 상표권
units-of-production method 생산량비례법
useful life 내용연수
value in use 사용가치

CHAPTER

11

LIABILITIES

CHAPTER 11

LIABILITIES

11.1 INTRODUCTION

Liabilities(부채) are obligations of an entity that require future cash payment, delivery of goods, or rendering of services. An essential characteristic of a liability is that the entity has a present obligation. An obligation is a duty or responsibility to act or perform in a certain way. Obligations may be legally enforceable due to a binding contract or statutory requirement. Obligations also arise from normal business practices, customs, and a desire to maintain good business relations or act equitably. Liabilities result from past transactions or other past events. Thus, for example, acquiring goods and using services on account give rise to trade payables.

Examples of liabilities are accounts payable, taxes payable, accrued expenses, unearned revenues, bonds payable, mortgages payable, and leases payable. Liabilities can be classified into current liabilities or noncurrent liabilities.

11.2 CURRENT LIABILITIES

Current liabilities(유동부채) are claims due within one year or an operating cycle(영업주기) of the business, whichever is longer. Current liabilities are typically paid out of current assets. Current liabilities are of the following types:

ⓐ ***Accounts payable***(외상매입금). Obligations for goods or services that have been acquired on account.

ⓑ ***Notes payable***(지급어음). Written promises to pay money at a future date.

ⓒ ***Accrued expenses***(발생비용, accrued liabilities 미지급부채). Liabilities relating to expenses incurred but not paid, such as accrued salaries and interest.

ⓓ ***Withholdings payable***(원천징수예수금). Amounts withheld from employees' salaries that are to be remitted to central and local tax agencies or are for employee benefit plans or union dues. Examples are income taxes, health insurance, and retirement plans. Sometimes, the company can also withhold employee membership dues(회비).

ⓔ ***Unearned revenues***(선수수익, deferred revenues 이연수익). Revenues received in advance but not earned yet, such as receipt of advance payments for rental income and subscription revenue(구독료수익). These obligations are in the form of future delivery of goods or services rather than cash obligations. If long-term advances are made (extending beyond one year), they are classified as noncurrent liabilities.

ⓕ ***Short-term debts***(단기차입금). Borrowings to be paid within a year.

ⓖ ***Other current liabilities***(기타유동부채). Any other current liabilities that do not belong to the above categories may be reported as other current liabilities.

EXAMPLE 11-1 *Payroll Accounting(급여회계)*

Juniper Company's weekly payroll is $5,000. Employee withholdings are as follows: Income taxes $1,300, and health insurance $170.

The appropriate journal entry is:

Salaries Expense	5,000	
Income Taxes Payable		1,300
Health Insurance Payable		170
Cash		3,530

When the company pays the withholdings to the appropriate party, the payable is debited, and cash is credited.

Remember that such withholdings are not expenses for the company. Instead, the company deducts these amounts from employees' paychecks and remits the amounts to the government, insurance company, or retirement benefit plan.

11.3 NONCURRENT LIABILITIES

Noncurrent liabilities(비유동부채) are sometimes used to finance noncurrent assets. The expectation is that the returns generated from the long-term asset will be sufficient to meet the interest(이자) and principal(원금) payment of the debts. Long-term liabilities include:

ⓐ ***Bonds payable***(회사채). Written promises by the company to repay amounts borrowed at its face amount (also called face value or principal) at the maturity date and to make periodic interest payments during the bond's duration. Periodic interest payments are typically made semi-annually or annually. Debt financing(차입금조달) has several advantages compared to equity financing(주식발행조달). Interest expense is tax deductible, whereas dividend payments are not. During inflationary periods, debts are paid back in cheaper dollars because the borrowers pay fixed interest and principal amounts. However, there are drawbacks to debt financing, including the risk of not being able to meet the fixed interest and principal at maturity and restrictions placed on the company under the bond agreement, such as minimum working capital(운전자본) requirements.

ⓑ ***Long-term Debts***(장기차입금). Borrowings not expected to be paid within a year. Sometimes, a promissory note is issued for long-term borrowings. When a long-term note payable(장기성지급어음) is issued, funds are obtained from a specific lender rather than through the issuance of bonds payable to the general public (i.e., to many lenders).

ⓒ ***Mortgages payable***(담보부채무). Mortgage-backed borrowings. A mortgage represents a lien on the property in case of default.

ⓓ ***Lease Liabilities***(리스부채). Liabilities arising from a lease agreement between the company and a lease provider, called a lessor. The lessee(리스이용자) uses the property in return for periodic rental payments to the lessor(리스회사).

11.4 BONDS PAYABLE

Corporations often finance their operations by issuing bonds. A bond(회사채) is an interest-bearing debt certificate(채무증권). A bond requires periodic interest payments, and the face value must be repaid at maturity. Bondholders are creditors of the issuing corporation. Therefore, bondholders have priority in claiming their claims on the corporation's assets before shareholders.

Bond issuance is typically divided into many individual bonds. Usually, the face value(액면금액) of each bond, also called the principal, is $1,000 or a multiple of $1,000. The interest on bonds may be payable annually, semi-annually, or quarterly.

When all bonds of an issue mature at the same time, they are called term bonds(정기상환사채). If the maturities are spread over several years, they are called serial bonds(연속상환사채). Bonds that may be exchanged for other securities, such as ordinary shares, are called convertible bonds(전환사채). Bonds that a corporation reserves the right to redeem before their maturities are called callable bonds(수의상환사채). The issuing company usually provides collateral as a security for the protection of bondholders if the company may not keep the promise to pay interest and principal at maturity. The bonds with collateral are called secured bonds(담보부사채). Bonds issued based on the general credit of the corporation are called debentures(무담보사채).

When a corporation issues bonds, the price that buyers are willing to pay for the bonds depends on four factors: face value(액면금액), maturity date(만기일), stated interest rate(표시이자율), and market interest rate(시장이자율) at the issuance date. Bonds are issued at par when the stated interest rate equals the market interest rate. Bonds are issued at a premium when the stated interest rate is higher than the market interest rate. Finally, bonds are issued at a discount when the stated interest rate is less than the market interest rate.

When bonds are issued at their face value, the entry is to debit cash and credit bonds payable. The entry to record the interest payment is to debit interest expense and credit cash. Interest expense is computed as follows:

Interest expense = Face value of bond × Annual interest rate × Time fraction

Example 11-2 Bonds Payable

On January 1, 20×1, Fern Corporation issued $50,000, 10-year, 10 percent bonds. The bonds were sold at face value. Interest is payable semi-annually on July 1 and January 1. The entries for 20×1 are:

Date	Account	Debit	Credit
20×1 January 1	Cash	50,000	
	Bonds Payable		50,000
July 1	Interest Expense	2,500*	
	Cash		2,500
December 31	Interest Expense	2,500	
	Interest Payable		2,500

* $50,000 × 10% × 6/12 = $2,500

Note that on January 1, 20×2, the interest payment date, the entry would be:

Date	Account	Debit	Credit
20×2 January 1	Interest Payable	2,500	
	Cash		2,500

The market price of a bond will most likely be different from its face value. For example, if a bond's stated interest rate is much lower than the market interest rate, the market price of the bond will be considerably lower than its face value. If the stated interest rate is higher (lower) than the market interest rate, the bond will be issued at a premium (discount).

The difference between the selling price of a bond and its face value is recorded as Premium on Bonds Payable(사채할증발행차금) when the issuance price exceeds the face value. Conversely, the difference is recorded as a Discount on Bonds Payable(사채할인발행차금) when the issue price is less than the face value.

The face value of a bond can be stated as 100 percent. Therefore, a bond issued at a premium would be sold at more than 100 percent. Conversely, a bond issued at a discount would be sold at less than 100 percent. For example, the proceeds of a $1,000 bond issued at 108 (an 8 percent premium) would be $1,080 ($1,000 × 108%). However, if the bond were sold at 93 (a 7 percent discount), the proceeds would be $930 ($1,000 × 93%).

PREMIUM ON BONDS PAYABLE(사채할증발행차금)

A bond will be sold at a premium if its stated interest rate(표시이자율) exceeds the market interest rate(시장이자율) for a comparable quality bond. The premium should not be considered income. Instead, it is interest received in advance(선수이자) that will make the effective interest expense(유효이자비용) lower than the cash interest payment. The premium account is amortized over the bond's life as a reduction of interest expense. The entry for amortization is to debit Premium on Bonds Payable and credit Interest Expense. The effective interest expense (net cost of borrowing) for a given year is the face interest (cash interest) less the amortization of the premium. In the statement of financial position, the unamortized premium is added to the face value of the bonds payable to compute the carrying amount of the bond. At the maturity date, the carrying amount of the bond will equal its face value since the premium must have been fully amortized by the date. Therefore, the principal of the bond must be paid at that time.

EXAMPLE 11-3 *Bonds Issued at a Premium*

On January 1, Ponderosa Corporation sold $50,000, 10-year, 10 percent bonds at 105. Interest is payable semi-annually on June 30 and December 31. The entry to record the issuance is:

		Debit	Credit
January 1	Cash	52,500	
	Bonds Payable		50,000
	Premium on Bonds Payable		2,500

The entries for the semiannual interest payment are:

June 30	Interest Expense	2,500	
	Cash		2,500
December 31	Interest Expense	2,500	
	Cash		2,500

The annual premium amortization under the straight-line method is $250 ($2,500/10). The entry is:

December 31	Premium on Bonds Payable	250	
	Interest Expense		250

The Interest Expense account at year's end appears below.

Interest Expense

June 30	2,500	December 31	250
December 31	2,500		

The Interest Expense account has a balance of $4,750, representing the year's net borrowing cost.

The balance in the premium account at year's end is $2,250, as shown below.

Premium on Bonds Payable

December 31	250	January 1	2,500

The statement of financial position on December 31 shows the carrying amount of the bonds at $52,250:

Long-Term Liabilities

Bonds Payable	$50,000
Add: Premium on Bonds Payable	2,250*
Carrying Amount	$52,250

* Unamortized amount

At the end of the tenth year, the carrying amount of the bonds will equal their maturity value of $50,000. The journal entry to pay the maturity value is as follows:

Bonds Payable	50,000	
Cash		50,000

DISCOUNT ON BONDS PAYABLE(사채할인발행차금)

A bond would be sold at a discount when its stated interest rate is below the market interest rate. The discount is considered an incremental interest expense, which is amortized over the bond's life. The entry for amortization is to debit Interest Expense and credit Discount on Bonds Payable. The effective interest expense (net borrowing cost) for a given year is, therefore, the cash interest plus the discount amortization(사채할인발행차금 상각액). In the statement of financial position, the unamortized discount is subtracted from bonds payable to compute the carrying amount of the bond. Therefore, the unamortized discount is a contra account. At maturity, the unamortized discount account(미상각사채할인발행차금) will be reduced to zero, and hence the carrying amount of the bond will equal its face value.

EXAMPLE 11-4 *Bonds Issued at a Discount*

Assume the same facts as in Example 11-3 except that the bonds are sold at 94. The entry to record the issuance of the bonds is:

January 1	Cash	47,000	
	Discount on Bonds Payable	3,000	
	Bonds Payable		50,000

At the date the bonds are issued, the carrying amount of the bonds payable is equal to the proceeds received for them. For example, if a statement of financial position was prepared immediately after the issuance of the bonds, the liability would be $47,000:

Noncurrent Liabilities	
Bonds Payable	$50,000
Less: Discount on Bonds Payable	3,000
Carrying Amount	$47,000

Over the life of the bonds, the carrying amount increases gradually until it equals the maturity value.

The entries to record the interest payments are:

June 30	Interest Expense	2,500	
	Cash		2,500
December 31	Interest Expense	2,500	
	Cash		2,500

The annual discount amortization under the straight-line method is $300 ($3,000/10). The entry is:

December 31	Interest Expense	300	
	Discount on Bonds Payable		300

Note that interest expense has increased, but cash interest is the same as in Example 11-3.

The following T-account shows the entries in the Interest Expense account for the year:

Interest Expense

June 30	2,500		
December 31	2,500		
December 31	300		

Interest Expense for the year is $5,300.

The balance in the Discount on Bonds Payable account at year's end is $2,700, as indicated below:

Discount on Bonds Payable

January 1	3,000	December 31	300

The statement of financial position on December 31 shows the carrying amount of the bonds at $47,300:

Noncurrent Liabilities

Bonds Payable	$50,000
Less: Discount on Bonds Payable	2,700
Carrying Amount	$47,300

At the end of the tenth year, the carrying amount of the bonds will be the same as their face value, $50,000.

11.5 BONDS ISSUED BETWEEN INTEREST DATES

The purchasers must pay the interest accrued after the last interest payment date when bonds are sold between interest dates. It is because the purchaser will receive the interest for the entire period at the next interest date. The net effect is that the purchasers will earn the interest they are entitled to for the period they hold the bond. For example, bonds can be sold on August 31 when interest is payable on June 30 and December 31. The purchaser must pay accrued interest for two months, from July 1 to August 31. On December 31, the purchaser will receive interest for six months, from July 1 to December 31. The net effect is that the purchaser has earned interest for four months, from September 1 to December 31.

When bonds are sold at face value between interest dates, the entry on the seller's books is:

Cash	×××	
Bonds Payable		×××
Interest Expense (or Interest Payable)		×××

EXAMPLE 11-5 *Bonds Sold between Interest Dates*

On March 1, 20×1, Papyrus Company issued \$50,000, 10-year, 12 percent bonds at face value. The bonds were dated January 1, 20×1. Interest is payable on January 1 and July 1.

The entry to record the issuance is:

March 1, 20×1	Cash	51,000	
	Bonds Payable		50,000
	Interest Expense		1,000*

* Accrued interest is for two months from January 1 to March 1: \$50,000 × 12% × 2/12 = \$1,000

The accrued interest collected from purchasers for the bonds issued between interest dates is returned to them on the next interest payment date. On July 1, semiannual interest for the full six months is paid. The entry for interest payment is:

July 1, 20×1	Interest Expense	3,000*	
	Cash		3,000

* \$50,000 × 12% × 6/12 = \$3,000

If interest payable is credited on March 1 for the issuance of the bonds, the following journal entry is needed on the following interest payment date.

July 1, 20×1	Interest Payable	1,000	
	Interest Expense	2,000*	
	Cash		3,000

* \$50,000 × 12% × 4/12 = \$2,000

The Interest Expense account now appears as follows:

Interest Expense

July 1	3,000	March 1	1,000

The $2,000 balance in the Interest Expense account represents the net interest cost to the issuer for four months, from March 1 to July 1.

An adjusting entry is required at year's end for the accrued interest:

December 31, 20×1	Interest Expense	3,000	
	Interest Payable		3,000

When the interest is paid at the next interest date, the entry is:

January 1, 20×2	Interest Payable	3,000	
	Cash		3,000

11.6 REDEMPTION OF BONDS(사채상환)

When bonds are redeemed at their maturities, either premium or discount must have been fully amortized. Therefore, the following journal entry will be entered when bonds are redeemed at maturity.

Bonds Payable	×××	
Cash		×××

If a callable option(수의상환선택권) exists, a company may redeem its bonds prior to maturity. The company, the call option holder, may choose to exercise the call option when the interest rate on the debt is considerably higher than current market interest rates. In this case, the company will profit by issuing new bonds at a lower interest rate and use the funds to reacquire the original, higher interest bonds. The call price(상환가격) is usually slightly higher than the face value. Even if a call provision(수의상환조항) does not exist, the company may still retire its bonds early by purchasing them in the open market(공개시장).

Example 11-6 *Early Redemption of Bonds*

Crabapple Corporation has outstanding bonds payable of $100,000 with an unamortized premium of $5,000. The call price on the bonds is 102. If all the bonds are redeemed, the journal entry is:

Bonds Payable	100,000	
Premium on Bonds Payable	5,000	
Cash		102,000
Gain on Redemption of Bonds		3,000

11.7 PROVISION AND CONTINGENT LIABILITIES

A business may face potential liabilities arising from previous events. However, uncertainty exists with regard to the amount, if any, of the company's liability. For example, if the maker of a promissory note discounted to a bank by the company defaults on maturity, the company will be required to pay.

A provision(충당부채) is a recognized contingent liability of uncertain timing and amount. A provision is recognized when:

① an entity has a present obligation as a result of a past event;
② it is probable that an outflow of resources will be required to settle the obligation; and
③ a reliable estimate can be made of the amount of the obligation.

Examples of provisions include product warranties(제품보증), refund liability(반품부채), pending lawsuits(계류중인 소송), and so on.

A contingent liability(우발부채), not recognized as a provision, is a possible obligation that arises from past events and whose existence will be confirmed only by the occurrence or non-occurrence of uncertain future events not wholly within the control of the entity. A contingent liability is a present obligation that arises from a past event but is unrecognized because it is not probable that an outflow of resources will be required or because the amount of the obligation cannot be measured with sufficient reliability. An unrecognized contingent liability shall be disclosed in the notes to the financial statements unless the possibility of an outflow of resources is remote.

A contingent asset(우발자산) is a possible asset that arises from past events and whose existence will be confirmed only by the occurrence or non-occurrence of future events not wholly within the control of the entity. Contingent assets usually arise from unplanned or unexpected events that give rise to the possibility of an inflow of resources to the entity. Contingent assets are not recognized in financial statements since this may result in recognizing income that may never be realized. However, when the realization of income is virtually certain, then its recognition is appropriate.

EXAMPLE 11-7 *Provision*

Heather Company provides warranties at the point of sale to purchasers of its products. Under the terms of the warranty, Heather undertakes to repair or replace items that fail to perform satisfactorily for one year from the date of sale. In 20×1, Heather sold $5,000,000 of products to purchasers. Based on past experience, Heather estimates that about 2% of product sales need to be reflected as provisions for the product warranty. Assume that Heather already incurred $45,000 of warranty expense with this year's sales. Then, Heather should record the estimated liability as follows:

Product Warranty Expense	55,000	
Product Warranty Liability		55,000*

* $5,000,000 × 2% − $45,000 = $55,000

CHAPTER 11

Multiple Choice Questions

11.1 Which of the following is not a current liability?

- ⓐ Accounts payable
- ⓑ A note payable due in 2 years
- ⓒ Current portion of long-term debt
- ⓓ Salaries payable

11.2 In December 20×1, Narwhal Company received magazine subscriptions for 20×2 from a customer who paid $500 in cash. What would be the appropriate journal entry for this event?

- ⓐ Debit Cash $500, Credit Subscription Revenue $500
- ⓑ Debit Cash $500, Credit Unearned Revenue $500
- ⓒ Debit Subscription Revenue $200, Credit Cash $200
- ⓓ No journal entry is necessary.

11.3 The sale of gift cards by a company is a direct example of:

- ⓐ Unearned revenues.
- ⓑ Sales tax payable.
- ⓒ Current portion of long-term debt.
- ⓓ Deferred taxes.

11.4 The current portion of long-term debt should be:

- ⓐ Reported as a current liability on the statement of financial position.
- ⓑ Reported as a long-term liability on the statement of financial position.
- ⓒ Combined with the rest of the long-term debt on the statement of financial position.
- ⓓ Paid immediately.

11.5 Beluga Company has a $50 million liability on December 31, 20×1, of which $10 million is payable in 20×2. In its December 31, 20×1 statement of financial position, the company reports the $50 million debt as:

- ⓐ A $50 million current liability.
- ⓑ A $50 million long-term liability.
- ⓒ A $10 million current liability and a $40 million long-term liability.
- ⓓ A $40 million current liability and a $10 million long-term liability.

11.6 If management can estimate the amount of loss that will occur due to litigation against the company, and the likelihood of the loss is probable, a contingent liability should be:

- ⓐ Disclosed but not reported as a liability.
- ⓑ Disclosed and reported as a liability.
- ⓒ Neither disclosed nor reported as a liability.
- ⓓ Reported as a liability but not disclosed.

11.7 Caterpillar Inc. estimates warranty expense at 2% of sales. Sales were $4 million during the year, and warranty expenditures were $44,000. What was the balance in the Warranty Liability account at the end of the year?

- ⓐ $44,000
- ⓑ $80,000
- ⓒ $36,000
- ⓓ $480,000

11.8 Term bonds are:

ⓐ bonds issued above the face amount.
ⓑ bonds that mature in installments.
ⓒ bonds that mature all at once.
ⓓ bonds issued below the face amount.

11.9 The price of a bond is equal to:

ⓐ the future value of the face amount only.
ⓑ the present value of the interest only.
ⓒ the present value of the face amount plus the present value of the stated interest payments.
ⓓ the future value of the face amount plus the future value of the stated interest payments.

11.10 Which of the following is true for bonds issued at a discount?

ⓐ The stated interest rate is greater than the market interest rate.
ⓑ The market interest rate is greater than the stated interest rate.
ⓒ The stated interest rate and the market interest rate are equal.
ⓓ The stated interest rate and the market interest rate are unrelated.

CHAPTER 11 Exercises

11.1 Payroll

Gross salaries for the week total $23,000. The following amounts were withheld from employee salaries: income taxes $3,100; social security $1,200; and union dues $320.

Required:

Prepare the necessary journal entry to record the payroll payment and related withholdings payable.

11.2 Unearned revenue

On January 1, 20×1, *The Perennial Newsweek* received cash from customers for three-year subscriptions totaling $60,000. Prepare all appropriate journal entries for 20×1.

11.3 Accounting terms for bonds

Listed below are four bond terms followed by a list of definitions. Match (by number) the bond terms with their definitions. Each letter is used only once.

- (a) Matures in installments
- (b) Secured only by the "full faith and credit" of the issuing corporation
- (c) Matures on a single date
- (d) Supported by specific assets pledged as collateral by the issuer

1. ______ Serial bond
2. ______ Term bond
3. ______ Secured bond
4. ______ Unsecured bond

11.4 Price of bonds

On January 1, 20×1, Wombat Inc. issued $20 million of 8% bonds, due in ten years, with interest payable semi-annually on June 30 and December 31 each year.

Required:

ⓐ If the market rate is 7%, will the bonds issue at face amount, a discount, or a premium?

ⓑ If the market rate is 8%, will the bonds issue at face amount, a discount, or a premium?

ⓒ If the market rate is 9%, will the bonds issue at face amount, a discount, or a premium?

11.5 Bonds payable – Par

On June 1, 20×1, Arborvitae Company issued $100,000 of 10-year, 10% bonds at face value. The bonds are dated March 1, 20×1. Interest is payable on March 1 and September 1.

Required:

Make necessary journal entries on the following dates:

ⓐ June 1, 20×1 for the issuance of the bonds.

ⓑ September 1, 20×1 for the payment of semiannual interest.

ⓒ December 31, 20×1 for the year-end adjusting entry.

11.6 Bonds payable – Premium (1)

On May 1, 20×1, Yew Company issued $50,000 of 10-year, 12 percent bonds at 110. The bonds are dated January 1, 20×1. Interest is payable on January 1 and July 1. The bonds will be outstanding for 9 years and 8 months, or 116 months.

Required:

Make appropriate journal entries on the following dates:

ⓐ May 1, 20×1

ⓑ July 1, 20×1

ⓒ December 31, 20×1

ⓓ January 1, 20×2

11.7 Bonds payable - Premium (2)

On January 1, 20×1, Magnolia Corporation issued $200,000, 8 percent, 5-year bonds at 103. Interest is payable on July 1 and January 1.

Required:

Prepare appropriate journal entries for 20×1 for the issuance of the bonds, the recording of interest, and the amortization of premium.

11.8 Bonds payable - Discount

Tulip Company issues $200,000 of 8%, 5-year bonds on January 1, 20×1 at 97. Interest is payable semi-annually on July 1 and January 1.

Required:

ⓐ Journalize the entries for the bonds on (1) January 1, 20×1, (2) July 1, 20×1, and (3) December 31, 20×1.

ⓑ Show the statement of financial position presentation of the bonds on December 31, 20×1.

ⓒ Assume on July 1, 20×2 after paying interest, Tulip calls bonds having a face value of $100,000. The call price is 101. Record the redemption of the bonds.

11.9 Bonds payable

Raven Inc. issues a bond with a stated interest rate of 10%, face value of $50,000, and due in 5 years. Interest payments are made semi-annually. The company uses the straight-line amortization method.

Required:

ⓐ Assume that the bond was issued at 95. Prepare journal entries to record the bond issuance and the first interest payment.

ⓑ Assume that the bond was issued at 105. Prepare journal entries to record the bond issuance and the first interest payment.

11.10 Bonds sold between interest dates

On March 1, 20×1, Walnut Company issued $10,000 of 10-year, 6 percent bonds at face value. The bonds are dated January 1, 20×1. Interest is payable on January 1 and July 1.

Required:

Prepare journal entries to record the issuance of the bonds on March 1 and the interest payment on July 1.

11.11 Bond Interest Expense

On January 1, 20×1, Green Fields Corporation sold $50,000, 4-year, 12 percent bonds at 96. Interest is payable annually on December 31.

Required:

Compute the bond interest expense that the firm will recognize in 20×1. Show your work.

11.12 Redemption of bonds payable (1)

Impatiens Corporation has outstanding bonds payable of $100,000 with an unamortized premium of $5,000. The call price on the bonds is 103. Assume that only 20 percent of the outstanding bonds are redeemed.

Required:

Make a necessary journal entry to record the redemption of the bonds.

11.13 Redemption of bonds payable (2)

Cattail Company retires a $20,000 bond at its market value when the carrying value of the bond is $19,500, but its market value is $21,000.

Required:

Prepare a necessary journal entry to record the retirement of the bonds.

11.14 Provision for pending lawsuit

There is a pending lawsuit against Fir Corporation that may result in future damages of $30,000.

Required:

What recognition should be given to it in the financial statements?

11.15 Provision for warranty

At the beginning of 20×2, Dianthus Corporation began offering a 1-year warranty on its products. The warranty program was expected to cost Dianthus 4% of net sales. Net sales made under warranty in 20×2 were $180,000. The warranty incurred by the end of 20×2 was $5,300.

Required:

What is the provision for the warranty that Dianthus needs to report at the end of 20×2?

ACCOUNTING TERMINOLOGY IN CHAPTER 11

accounts payable 외상매입금
accrued expenses 발생비용
accrued liabilities 미지급부채
bond 회사채
bonds payable 회사채
call price 상환가격
call provision 수의상환조항
callable bonds 수의상환사채
callable option 수의상환선택권
contingent asset 우발자산
contingent liability 우발부채
convertible bonds 전환사채
current liabilities 유동부채
debentures 무담보사채
debt certificate 채무증권
debt financing 차입금조달
deferred revenue 이연수익
discount amortization 사채할인발행차금상각액
discount on bonds payable 사채할인발행차금
effective interest expense 유효이자비용
equity financing 주식발행조달
face value (face amount) 액면금액
interest 이자
interest received in advance 선수이자
lease liabilities 리스부채
lessee 리스이용자
lessor 리스회사
liabilities 부채
long-term debts 장기차입금
long-term notes payable 장기성지급어음
market interest rate 시장이자율
maturity date 만기일
membership dues 회비
mortgages payable 담보부채무
noncurrent liabilities 비유동부채
notes payable 지급어음
open market 공개시장
operating cycle 영업주기
payroll accounting 급여회계
pending lawsuits 계류중인 소송
premium on bonds payable 사채할증발행차금
principal 원금
product warranty 제품보증
provision 충당부채
redemption of bonds 사채상환
refund liability 반품부채
secured bonds 담보부사채
serial bonds 연속상환사채
short-term debts 단기차입금
stated interest rate 표시이자율
subscription revenue 구독료수익
term bonds 정기상환사채
unamortized discount account 미상각사채할인발행차금
unearned revenues 선수수익
withholdings payable 원천징수예수금
working capital 운전자본

CHAPTER

12

SHAREHOLDERS' EQUITY

CHAPTER 12

SHAREHOLDERS' EQUITY

12.1 INTRODUCTION

A corporation(주식회사) is a legal entity(법인) created by law with an *indefinite life*. It is owned by shareholders who hold shares(주식) of the corporation.

The advantages of the corporate form of business include the following:

① Shareholders are only accountable for the amount they have invested in the event the corporation fails (limited liability, 유한책임).
② Ownership may easily be transferred by selling the shares (transferability of ownership, 소유권이전).
③ The corporation continues to exist even with the death of a shareholder (going concern, 계속기업).
④ Contracts can be entered into in the corporate name (legal entity, 법인).
⑤ A significant amount of funds can be raised through the sale of shares to the public (fund-raising ability, 자금조달능력).

The disadvantages of the corporate form of business include the following:

① Shareholders are taxed twice in that corporate income, the source of dividends, is subject to corporate income taxes, and the dividends received by shareholders are themselves subject to personal income taxes (double taxation, 이중과세).
② Regulation over corporate affairs is strict.
③ The cost of compliance is high. Corporations are required to file financial reports with regulatory bodies such as the Financial Supervisory Service (FSS, 금융감독원) and the Securities and Exchange Commission (SEC, 증권거래위원회) in the United States, and to disclose information to investors and creditors as required by securities exchanges(증권거래소).

12.2 TERMINOLOGY

A *stockholder or shareholder*(주주) is an owner of the corporation. Shareholders have such rights as voting rights(의결권), dividends rights(배당참여권), liquidation rights(청산참여권) if the corporation fails, and participation rights to purchase additional shares on a proportionate basis if the corporation increases the number of shares outstanding (preemptive rights, 주식선매권). As a part of the voting rights, shareholders can also elect a *board of directors*(이사회) who make corporate policy decisions and appoint corporate officers(임원).

Shares are issued as evidence of ownership in the corporation. The *share certificate*(주권) typically has a *par value*(액면금액) printed on it. The par value represents an arbitrary amount assigned to it per the corporation's charter or bylaws(정관). The market price of the share is what the share is currently selling for in the stock exchange(주식시장).

Authorized shares(수권자본) are the maximum number of shares that a corporation can issue according to the articles of incorporation(정관). However, the corporation may, at a later date, increase the number of authorized shares. *Issued shares*(발행주식) are the number of shares that have been sold to the public. The difference between authorized shares and issued shares represents *unissued shares*(미발행주식). *Treasury shares*(자기주식) represent the issued shares that the corporation has repurchased. *Outstanding shares*(유통주식) are those shares being *held by shareholders*. Outstanding shares equal issued shares minus treasury shares. Dividends(배당) are based on outstanding shares. *Subscribed shares*(청약주식) are those shares under contract at a specified price for which a down payment has usually been made to the corporation by the subscribed shareholders. The shares will not be issued until full payment is received from the subscribers.

EXAMPLE 12-1 *Outstanding Shares*

Elm Corporation is authorized to issue 100,000 shares. During 20×1, 80,000 shares were issued. During the year, Elm Corporation repurchased 5,000 of its own shares. The outstanding shares at year's end are determined as follows:

Issued Shares	80,000
Less: Treasury Shares	(5,000)
Outstanding Shares	75,000

Dividends will be paid on the outstanding shares of 75,000.

12.3 TYPES OF SHARES

Corporations can issue two types of shares. They are *ordinary shares*(보통주, common stocks) and *preference shares*(우선주, preferred stocks). If a corporation only has one type of share, it is *ordinary share*. Ordinary shareholders have voting rights(의결권). In contrast, Preference shareholders do not have voting rights but have preference over ordinary shareholders in the event of liquidation(청산) and the distribution of dividends. However, the amount of dividends paid to preference shareholders is typically limited to a given percentage of par value(액면금액). Most of the preference shares are *cumulative preference shares*(누적적우선주), which means that if no dividends are paid in a given year, those dividends must be paid in the following years before any dividends are distributed to ordinary shareholders. The skipped dividends for preference shares are called dividends in arrears(연체배당금). *Noncumulative* preference share(비누적적우선주) means that skipped dividends are not paid in the following years.

Preference shares are typically *nonparticipating*(비참가적), which means that preference shareholders receive pre-determined fixed dividends only. On the other hand, *participating* preference shares(참가적우선주), which are not common, means that in addition to the specified regular dividends, preference shareholders will participate in additional dividends if ordinary shareholders receive more dividends.

EXAMPLE 12-2 *Cumulative Preference Shares*

Hornet Corporation has 10,000 cumulative, nonparticipating preference shares paying dividends of $2 per share. Hornet Corporation also has 35,000 ordinary shares. In 20×1 and 20×2, no dividends were paid. In 20×3, Hornet paid $82,000 in dividends. The dividend distribution in 20×3 is:

Allocation of Dividends	
Preference shares (10,000 shares×$2×3 years)	$60,000
Ordinary shares ($82,000−$60,000)	22,000
Total Dividends	$82,000

12.4 SHAREHOLDERS' EQUITY

The shareholders' equity(소유주지분) section of the statement of financial position consists of share capital, share premium (or additional paid-in capital), retained earnings, and total shareholders' equity.

ⓐ ***Share Capital***(자본금). This section shows the par value(액면가) of the shares issued. The share capital from preference shares is listed before the share capital from ordinary shares because preference shareholders have priority in their claims for liquidation and dividends distribution.

ⓑ ***Share Premium***(주식발행초과금). This section shows the amount received in excess of the par value of the shares issued. Share premium is also called *additional paid-in capital* or *paid-in capital in excess of par value*. On the other hand, when shares are issued below the par value, it is called a *share discount*(주식할인발행차금).

ⓒ ***Paid-in Capital***(납입자본). This section includes share capital and share premium. Paid-in capital is also called *contributed capital*, indicating that paid-in capital is a part of shareholders' equity formed by the contribution of shareholders.

ⓓ ***Retained Earnings***(이익잉여금, 유보이익). Retained earnings represent the accumulated earnings of the corporation since its inception, minus the total dividends distributed so far.

ⓔ ***Total Shareholders' Equity***(총소유주지분, 자본총계). This section shows the sum of the share capital, share premium, retained earnings, and other components of shareholders' equity.

12.5 ISSUANCE OF SHARES(주식의 발행)

A journal entry is prepared when the company issues shares to shareholders. However, when shareholders sell their shares to other shareholders, the company does not record the transfer of shares between shareholders since the company is not involved in the transaction. However, the company records payments of dividends to its shareholders.

When shares are issued at par value, cash is debited, and the particular security (ordinary shares or preference shares) is credited.

EXAMPLE 12-3 *Issuance of shares at Par Value*

Wasp Corporation issued at par 1,000 shares of $10 par value ordinary shares. The journal entry to record the share issuance is:

Cash	10,000	
Ordinary Shares		10,000

Typically, the market price of a company's shares will be different from its par value. Plausible reasons for the discrepancy include inflation, financial position, financial performance, business conditions, and other factors. However, par value is based on a legal concept of creditor protection with minimal economic implications for capital markets.

When shares are sold at a price different from par value, cash is debited for the amount received, and the particular share (ordinary shares or preference shares) is credited at par value. The difference will either represent share premium or share discount. When shares are sold above par value, the excess is called a share premium(주식발행초과금). Share premium is separately reported in the shareholders' equity. Share premium is *not* an income statement account since the company earns profits by selling goods and services to outsiders, *not* by issuing shares. Therefore, a company cannot generate profits or losses from the transactions with its owners. Profit or loss originates from non-owner transactions. In other words, transactions with a company's owners, which are called capital transactions(자본거래), do not affect profit or loss. If shares are issued at a price lower than the par value, a share discount(주식할인발행차금) account results. The issuance of shares at a discount is very rare. In most cases, it is prohibited.

EXAMPLE 12-4 *Share Premium and Discount*

(1) Grasshopper Corporation issued 50,000 shares of $10 par value ordinary shares for $15 a share. The journal entry to record the share issuance at a premium is:

Cash	750,000	
Ordinary Shares		500,000
Share Premium - Ordinary Shares		250,000

(2) Grasshopper Corporation issued 10,000 shares of $20 par value preference shares for $19 a share. The journal entry to record the share issuance at a discount is:

Cash	190,000	
Share Discount - Preference Shares	10,000	
Preference Shares		200,000

The shareholders' equity section has many components. They are share capital(자본금), share Premium(주식발행초과금), retained earnings(이익잉여금), accumulated other comprehensive income(기타포괄손익누계액, AOCI), and capital adjustments(자본조정). Companies usually have the first three items at least. Some companies may have the last two items also. Therefore, the shareholders' equity section should clearly show them separately.

Example 12-5 *Shareholders' Equity*

Using the information in Example 12-4, assuming Grasshopper Corporation's retained earnings balance is $40,000, we can show the shareholders' equity section as follows:

Statement of Financial Position (Partial)		
Shareholders' Equity		
Share Capital		
Preference Shares,		
$20 par value, issued and outstanding 10,000 shares	$200,000	
Ordinary Shares,		
$10 par value, issued and outstanding 50,000 shares	500,000	$700,000
Share Premium		
Share Discount on preference shares	($10,000)	
Share Premium on ordinary shares	250,000	240,000
Retained Earnings		40,000
Total Shareholders' Equity		$980,000

If shares are issued for considerations other than cash, the asset received is recorded at its fair market value.

EXAMPLE 12-6 ***Exchange of Shares with Assets***

Baboon Corporation issued 1,000 shares of $5 par value ordinary shares in exchange for land whose fair value is $5,500. The journal entry to record the exchange of shares with the land is:

Land	5,500	
Ordinary Shares		5,000
Share Premium - Ordinary Shares		500

12.6 TREASURY SHARES

Treasury shares(자기주식) represent issued shares that the company has repurchased. The reasons for the repurchase include having shares available for a share option plan or the acquisition of another company and attempting to support the market price of shares. Treasury shares are not entitled to dividends or voting rights. Treasury shares are shown in the statement of financial position as a reduction to shareholders' equity since treasury shares are treated like unissued shares in essence.

The most common method of accounting for treasury shares is the cost method(원가법). The par value and original issue price are not considered. The journal entry to record the purchase of treasury shares under the cost method is:

Treasury Shares	×××	
Cash		×××

When treasury shares are resold, the difference between the selling price and the cost is reflected in an account called Share Premium from Treasury Shares(자기주식자본잉여금, 자기주식처분손익). If the selling price exceeds the purchase cost, the journal entry is:

Cash	×××	
Treasury Shares		×××
Share Premium from Treasury Shares		×××

EXAMPLE 12-7 *Treasury Shares*

Dugong Company's shareholders' equity section of its statement of financial position as of December 31, 20×1 appears below.

Statement of Financial Position (Partial) December 31, 20×1	
Shareholders' Equity	
Share Capital	
Ordinary shares, $10 par value, authorized 40,000 shares; issued and outstanding 20,000 shares	$200,000
Share Premium	
Premium on Ordinary Shares	15,000
Retained Earnings	20,000
Total Shareholders' Equity	$235,000

The company had the following transactions during 20×2:

April 1	Purchased 1,000 shares of outstanding ordinary shares at $18 per share
August 1	Sold 400 shares of treasury shares at $20 per share
December 6	Sold 250 shares of treasury shares at $16 per share

The appropriate journal entries for the above transactions are:

April 1	Treasury Shares	18,000	
	Cash		18,000
August 1	Cash	8,000	
	Treasury Shares		7,200*
	Share Premium from Treasury Shares		800
December 6	Cash	4,000	
	Share Premium from Treasury Shares	500	
	Treasury Shares		4,500**

* 400 shares × $18 = $7,200

** 250 shares × $18 = $4,500

Assume that net income for the year was $3,000. The shareholders' equity section of the statement of financial position on December 31, 20×2 follows:

Statement of Financial Position (Partial) December 31, 20×2		
Shareholders' Equity		
Share Capital		
Ordinary shares, $10 par value, authorized 40,000 shares; issued 20,000 shares		$200,000
Share Premium		
Premium on Ordinary Shares	$15,000	
Premium from Treasury Shares	300*	15,300
Retained Earnings		23,000
Subtotal		$238,300
Less: Treasury Shares (350 shares at cost)		(6,300)**
Total Shareholders' Equity		$232,000

* $800－$500＝$300
** $18,000－$7,200－$4,500＝$6,300

12.7 DIVIDENDS

Dividends(배당) are paid out of retained earnings. Therefore, dividends reduce retained earnings. Dividends are usually paid in cash. However, shares are sometimes distributed as dividends. When a cash dividend is declared, it becomes a company's liability. Three important dates associated with dividends are:

ⓐ ***Declaration date***(배당선언일). The date on which a dividend is declared by the board of directors(이사회) or shareholders' meeting(주주총회).

ⓑ ***Date of record***(배당기준일). The date on which a shareholder must hold the share to be entitled to receive the dividends.

ⓒ ***Payment date***(배당지급일). The date the company pays the dividends to its shareholders.

Journal entries are prepared on the declaration and payment dates. No entry is made on the date of record.

(1) Cash Dividends(현금배당)

The standard type of dividends is cash dividends. A cash dividend is typically expressed on a dollar-per-share basis. However, dividends are sometimes expressed as a percentage of par value.

EXAMPLE 12-8 *Cash Dividends - Ordinary Shares*

On November 15, 20×1, a cash dividend of $1.5 per share was declared on 10,000 shares of $10 par value ordinary shares. The record date is December 20, 20×1. Payment is to be made on January 15, 20×2. The journal entries are:

November 15, 20×1	Retained Earnings	15,000*	
	Dividends Payable		15,000
December 20, 20×1	No Entry		
January 15, 20×2	Dividends Payable	15,000	
	Cash		15,000

* 10,000 shares × $1.5 = $15,000

Note that dividends payable are a current liability account.

(2) Share Dividends(주식배당)

A share dividend involves the issuance of additional shares to shareholders. A share dividend may be declared when the cash position of a firm is inadequate. It is also used when a firm wishes to increase the liquidity of its shares by lowering the market price of its shares by increasing the number of shares outstanding.

A share dividend can be accounted for using the market value method(시가법) or the carrying amount method(장부금액법). Traditionally, the market value method is believed to be appropriate for share dividends of *less* than 20-25 percent of the outstanding shares. On the other hand, the carrying amount method is appropriate for share dividends of more than 20-25 percent of the outstanding shares.

Under the market value method, the following entry is needed when a share dividend is declared:

Retained Earnings	×××	
(based on the market value of the shares)		
Share Dividends Distributable		×××
(based on the par value of the shares)		
Share Premium on Ordinary Shares		×××

Under the carrying amount method, the following entry is needed when a share dividend is declared:

Retained Earnings	×××	
(based on the par value of the shares)		
Share Dividends Distributable		×××
(based on the par value of the shares)		

The entry for the actual share issuance is the same whether there is a small or large share dividend:

Share Dividends Distributable	×××	
(based on the par value of the shares)		
Ordinary Shares		×××
(based on the par value of the shares)		

The share dividends distributable(미배당주식) account is shown under the share capital section of shareholders' equity. The share capital section shows not only the par value of the shares issued but also the par value of shares that will be issued at a later date. Examples of shares to be issued are share dividends and shares subscribed. Therefore, share dividends distributable is *not a liability* account but a shareholders' equity account.

EXAMPLE 12-9 *Share Dividends*

Termite Corporation has 40,000 shares of $10 par value ordinary shares outstanding. On December 1, 20×1, it declared a 5 percent share dividend to the shareholders of record on December 31, 20×1. On December 1, the market price of the share was $25 per share. The issuance date is February 6, 20×2. Appropriate journal entries follow:

Date	Account	Debit	Credit
December 1, 20×1	Retained Earnings	50,000*	
	Share Dividends Distributable		20,000**
	Premium on Ordinary Shares		30,000
December 31, 20×1	No Entry		
February 6, 20×2	Share Dividends Distributable	20,000	
	Ordinary Shares		20,000

* 40,000 shares × 5% × $25 = $50,000
** 2,000 shares × $10 = $20,000

As can be seen from the journal entries, there is no effect on shareholders' equity for a share dividend since all the accounts involved are shareholders' equity accounts. Retained earnings has decreased, but Ordinary shares and Premium on ordinary shares have increased by the same total amount. A share dividend, therefore, provides *no* income for shareholders. It increases the shares held, but the proportionate interest of each shareholder in the company remains the same. In other words, if a shareholder had a 2 percent interest in the company before a share dividend, the shareholder will still have the same 2 percent interest after the share dividend. For illustration, suppose Jane Lim owns 200 shares of Tarantula Company. Outstanding shares are 10,000. She thus has a 2 percent interest. Suppose that a share dividend of 10 percent is issued. Jane Lim will now have 220 shares out of 11,000 issued shares. Her proportionate interest has remained at 2 percent (220/11,000).

(3) Dividends for Preference Shares and Ordinary Shares

When there are preference shares as well as ordinary shares, preference shareholders have priority in receiving dividends. Preference shareholders have the preferential right to a specified amount of dividends (a stated amount per share or a percentage of par value per share). If the board of directors declares dividends, preference shareholders will receive the designated dividends before ordinary shareholders receive any. Furthermore, preference shares are usually cumulative shares, implying that if dividends are skipped in one year, they must be paid before the current year's dividends are paid.

EXAMPLE 12-10 *Dividends for Preference Shares and Ordinary Shares*

Condor Corporation has two classes of shares: 5%, cumulative, $100 par value preference shares, and $10 par value ordinary shares. 500 preference shares and 1,000 ordinary shares have been outstanding since the beginning of 20×1. There were no additional share transactions during 20×1 and 20×2. Condor did not pay dividends to shareholders in 20×1. However, on December 31, 20×2, Condor declared dividends of $8,000.

Prepare the appropriate journal entry on the declaration date, assuming that Condor has sufficient retained earnings to pay dividends.

December 31, 20×2	Retained Earnings	8,000	
	Dividends Payable - Preference Shares		5,000*
	Dividends Payable - Ordinary Shares		3,000**

* 500 shares × 5% × $100 × 2 years = $5,000
** $8,000 − $5,000 = $3,000

12.8 SHARE SPLIT

A share split(주식분할) involves issuing a substantial number of additional shares and reducing the par value of the share on a proportionate basis. *No entry* is needed because none of the company's accounts will change due to a share split. However, there should be a *memorandum* describing the share split. A share split is often prompted by a desire to increase the liquidity of its shares by reducing the market price per share to stimulate investor buying.

EXAMPLE 12-11 Share Split

Falcon Corporation has 1,000 shares of $20 par value ordinary shares. The total par value is thus $20,000. The company announced a two-for-one share split. As a result, there will now be 2,000 shares with a $10 par value. The total par value remains at $20,000. Theoretically, the market price per share should also drop to one-half of what it was before the split.

12.9 RETAINED EARNINGS

Retained earnings(이익잉여금, 유보이익) is the accumulated earnings of the business that have not been distributed to shareholders. A profitable business will have a credit balance. However, the account will have a debit balance (deficit) if accumulated losses and dividends exceed accumulated earnings. Retained earnings is increased by net income but reduced by a net loss or dividends.

Retained earnings may be either *unappropriated* (available for dividend distribution) or *appropriated* (reserved and unavailable for dividend distribution). When an appropriation(적립, 처분) is made, unappropriated retained earnings (미처분이익잉여금) is reduced, and the specific appropriated retained earnings(처분이익잉여금) account is created. Therefore, the company's total retained earnings consist of the balance in the unappropriated retained earnings account and the balances in the appropriated retained earnings accounts. In addition, different appropriations may exist, such as appropriations for contingencies, business expansion, and treasury shares. When an appropriation is established, the following entry is made:

Retained Earnings	×××	
Appropriated Retained Earnings		×××

When the appropriation is no longer needed, the above entry is reversed:

Appropriated Retained Earnings	×××	
Retained Earnings		×××

EXAMPLE 12-12 Appropriation of Retained Earnings

Capybara Corporation has a balance in retained earnings of $80,000. The company decides to establish a reserve for plant expansion of $15,000. The entry is:

Retained Earnings	15,000	
Appropriation for Plant Expansion		15,000

The company also establishes a reserve for the acquisition of $5,000 of treasury shares. The entry for the appropriation is:

Retained Earnings	5,000	
Appropriation for Treasury Shares		5,000

Under the shareholders' equity section, retained earnings would be broken down as follows:

Statement of Financial Position (Partial)		
Unappropriated Retained Earnings		$60,000*
Appropriated Retained Earnings:		
For Plant Expansion	$15,000	
For Treasury Shares	5,000	20,000
Total Retained Earnings		$80,000

* $80,000−$15,000−$5,000=$60,000

CHAPTER 12

Multiple Choice Questions

12.1 Outstanding ordinary share refers to the total number of shares:

a Issued.
b Issued plus treasury share.
c Issued less treasury share.
d Authorized.

12.2 Authorized ordinary shares refer to the total number of shares:

a Outstanding.
b Issued.
c Issued and outstanding.
d That can be issued.

12.3 Preference shares have two preferences over ordinary shares. These preferences relate to the following:

a Dividends and voting rights.
b Par value and dividends.
c The preemptive right and voting rights.
d Dividends and distribution of assets if the corporation is dissolved.

12.4 Treasury shares are normally reported as:

- ⓐ A reduction of total shareholders' equity.
- ⓑ An asset account.
- ⓒ A liability account.
- ⓓ An expense account.

12.5 When treasury shares are resold at a price above cost:

- ⓐ A gain account is credited.
- ⓑ A loss is reported.
- ⓒ A revenue account is credited.
- ⓓ Share premium is increased.

12.6 Retained Earnings represent a company's:

- ⓐ Net income minus dividends since the company first started.
- ⓑ Undistributed net assets.
- ⓒ Extra paid-in capital.
- ⓓ Undistributed cash.

12.7 Journal entries to record cash dividends are made on the:

- ⓐ declaration date, record date, and payment date.
- ⓑ record date and payment date.
- ⓒ declaration date and payment date.
- ⓓ declaration date and record date.

12.8 Both cash dividends and stock dividends:

- ⓐ reduce total assets.
- ⓑ reduce total liabilities.
- ⓒ reduce total shareholders' equity.
- ⓓ reduce retained earnings.

12.9 The statement of shareholders' equity shows:

- a Only the ending balance in each shareholders' equity account.
- b How each equity account changed over time.
- c Only the beginning balance in each shareholders' equity account.
- d Less information than the shareholders' equity section in the statement of financial position.

12.10 Financial information for Robin Company includes the following selected data:

Net income (in millions)	\$145
Preference share dividends (in millions)	\$25
Shares outstanding (in millions)	240
Share price	\$10

What is the company's earnings per share?

- a \$0.60
- b \$0.71
- c \$0.50
- d \$0.05

CHAPTER 12 Exercises

12.1 Share issuance

On January 1, Barracuda Corporation started its business. It was authorized to issue 50,000 ordinary shares and 40,000 preference shares. On January 1, it issued 6,000 shares of $10 par value ordinary shares for cash. On June 20, the company issued an additional 5,000 ordinary shares and 1,500 shares of 5 percent, a $100 par value preference shares. All shares were issued at par value.

Required:

Prepare the appropriate journal entries.

12.2 Paid-in capital

Birch Corp. was organized on January 3, 20×1. The firm was authorized to issue 100,000 shares of $5 par value ordinary shares. During 20×1, Birch had the following transactions relating to shareholders' equity:

Issued 30,000 ordinary shares at $7 per share.
Issued 20,000 ordinary shares at $8 per share.
Reported a net income of $100,000.
Paid dividends of $50,000.

Required:

What is the total paid-in capital at the end of 20×1?

12.3 Shareholders' equity section (1)

On January 1, Barracuda Corporation started its business. It was authorized to issue 50,000 ordinary shares and 40,000 preference shares. On January 1, it issued 6,000 shares of $10 par value ordinary shares for cash. On June 20, the company issued an additional 5,000 ordinary shares and 1,500 shares of 5 percent, $100 par value preference shares. All shares were issued at par value.

Required:

Prepare the shareholders' equity section of the statement of financial position as of June 30.

12.4 Shareholders' equity section (2)

Lily Inc. has the following balances in its shareholders' equity accounts on December 31, 20×1: Treasury share, $375,000; Share Capital - Ordinary, $400,000; Preference share, $1,200,000; Retained Earnings, $1,680,000; and Share Premium, $3,200,000.

Required:

Prepare the shareholders' equity section of the statement of financial position for Lily Inc. as of December 31, 20×1.

12.5 Share issuance and shareholders' equity

Gladiolus Corporation is authorized to issue 20,000 preference shares and 30,000 ordinary shares. In addition, the company issued 3,000 shares of 5 percent, $70 par value preference shares at $68, and 4,000 shares of $35 par value ordinary shares at $40.

Required:

ⓐ Prepare appropriate journal entries.

ⓑ Prepare the shareholders' equity section of the statement of financial position.

12.6 Share transactions (1)

Hibiscus Company's shareholders' equity section of the statement of financial position as of January 1 follows:

Statement of Financial Position (Partial)		
Shareholders' equity		
Share Capital		
Preference share, 5%, $100 par value, authorized 30,000 shares, issued and outstanding 18,000 shares	$1,800,000	
Ordinary share, $50 par value, authorized 120,000 shares; issued and outstanding 80,000 shares	4,000,000	$5,800,000
Share Premium		
Premium on preference shares	$40,000	
Premium on ordinary shares	100,000	140,000
Retained Earnings		600,000
Total Shareholders' Equity		$6,540,000

Selected transactions occurred as follows:

April 8	Issued 6,000 preference shares at $104.
July 10	Purchased 10,000 ordinary shares as treasury shares for $400,000.
October 20	Sold 5,000 shares of treasury shares for $250,000.
December 15	Sold 3,000 shares of treasury shares for $102,000.
December 31	Net income for the year was $30,000.

Required:

Prepare journal entries (including a closing entry for income summary to retained earnings) for the above transactions.

12.7 Share transactions (2)

Dalia Inc. has the following transactions during the year related to shareholders' equity:

January 1	Issued 3,000 shares of no-par value ordinary shares for $20 per share.
March 1	Issued 800 shares of $20 par value preference shares for $22 per share.
December 1	Declared a cash dividend of $1 per share to all shareholders of record (both ordinary and preference shares) on October 15.
December 15	Date of record.
December 31	Paid the cash dividends declared on October 1.

Required:

Record each of these transactions.

12.8 Shareholders' equity

Redbud Inc. was organized on January 1, 20×1. The firm was authorized to issue 100,000 shares of $5 par value ordinary shares. During 20×1, Redbud had the following transactions relating to shareholders' equity:

Issued 10,000 ordinary shares at $7 per share.
Issued 20,000 ordinary shares at $8 per share.
Reported a net income of $100,000.
Paid dividends of $50,000.
Purchased 3,000 treasury shares at $10 (part of the 20,000 shares issued at $8).

Required:

What is total shareholders' equity at the end of 20×1?

12.9 Cash dividends (1)

Marlin Corporation has 10,000 shares of ordinary shares outstanding. On March 5, the company declared a cash dividend of $5 per share, payable to the shareholders of record on April 5. The payment of the dividend was made on June 1.

Required:

Prepare appropriate journal entries.

12.10 Cash dividends (2)

Quail Corporation has outstanding 20,000 shares of $10 par value, 10 percent preference shares. On October 15, 20×1, a cash dividend was declared to the shareholders of record as of December 15, 20×1. The payment date is January 15, 20×2.

Required:

Prepare necessary journal entries on October 15, 20×1 (declaration date), December 15, 20×1 (record date), and January 15, 20×2 (payment date).

12.11 Dividends allocation (1)

Wood Duck Corporation has two classes of shares: 5%, cumulative, $50 par value preference shares, and $10 par value ordinary shares. 1,000 preference shares and 2,000 ordinary shares have been issued and outstanding since the beginning of 20×1. There were no additional share transactions during 20×1 and 20×2. Wood Duck Corporation did not pay dividends to shareholders in 20×1. On December 31, 20×2, Wood Duck Corporation declared dividends of $12,000.

Required:

Prepare the appropriate journal entry on the declaration date, assuming Wood Duck Corporation has sufficient retained earnings to pay dividends.

12.12 Dividends allocation (2)

Hydrangea Inc. issues 1,000 shares of 6%, $100 par value preference share at the beginning of 20×1. All remaining shares are ordinary shares. The company was not able to pay dividends in 20×1 but plans to pay dividends of $18,000 in 20×2. Assuming the preference share is cumulative, how much of the $18,000 dividend will be paid to preference shareholders and how much will be paid to ordinary shareholders in 20×2?

12.13 Share dividends

Flax Corporation has 10,000 shares of $10 par value ordinary shares outstanding. On December 1, 20×1, it declared a 5 percent share dividend to the shareholders of record on December 31, 20×1. On December 1, the market price of the share was $20 per share. The issuance date is February 1, 20×2.

Required:

Prepare appropriate journal entries for the share dividends.

12.14 Share transactions and dividends (1)

On January 1, 20×1, Mulberry Company had 60,000 shares of $1 par value ordinary shares issued and outstanding. During the year, the following transactions occurred:

March 1	Issued 40,000 ordinary shares for $600,000.
June 1	Declared a cash dividend of $3.00 per share to the shareholders of record on June 15.
June 30	Paid the $3.00 cash dividend.
December 1	Purchased 4,000 ordinary shares as treasury shares for $22 per share.
December 15	Declared a cash dividend of $3.25 per share to the outstanding shareholders of record on December 31.

Required:

Prepare journal entries to record the above transactions.

12.15 Share transactions and dividends (2)

Blueberry Company has the following transactions during the year related to shareholders' equity:

February 1	Issues 5,000 no-par value ordinary shares for $15 per share.
June 1	Issues 500 $10 par value preference shares for $12 per share.
October 1	Declares a cash dividend of $0.75 per share to all shareholders of record (both ordinary and preference shares) on October 15.
October 15	Date of record.
October 31	Pays the cash dividend declared on October 1.

Required:

Record each of these transactions.

12.16 Appropriation of retained earnings

Fir Corporation has a balance in retained earnings of $180,000. The company decides to establish a reserve for overseas expansion of $30,000. The company also establishes a reserve for the repurchase of $10,000 of treasury shares.

Required:

ⓐ What is the journal entry to record the appropriation for overseas expansion and treasury share repurchase?

ⓑ Prepare a partial statement of financial position showing the retained earnings section of the shareholders' equity.

12.17 Share issuance and repurchase

Anchovy Company has two classes of shares authorized: 8%, $10 par preference shares, and $1 par value ordinary shares. The following transactions affect shareholders' equity during 20×2, its first year of operations:

January 2	Issued 100,000 ordinary shares for $25 per share.
March 1	Issued 2,000 8% preference shares for $12 per share.
June 5	Repurchased 10,000 treasury shares for $30 per share.
December 5	Reissued 5,000 treasury shares at $35 per share.

Required:

Record each of these transactions.

12.18 Treasury shares

Sycamore Inc. had 100,000 outstanding ordinary shares. On June 1, 20×1, Sycamore repurchased 20,000 shares at $30 per share. On July 23, 20×1, Sycamore resold 10,000 treasury shares at $28 per share.

Required:

Prepare journal entries for the share transactions on June 1 and July 23, 20×1.

12.19 Statement of shareholders' equity

Mackerel Corporation designs and produces a line of golf equipment and golf apparel. Mackerel has 100,000 ordinary shares outstanding as of the beginning of 20×2. In addition, Mackerel has the following transactions affecting shareholders' equity in 20×2:

March 1	Issued 55,000 additional shares of $1 par value ordinary share for $52 per share.
May 10	Repurchased 5,000 treasury shares for $55 per share.
June 1	Declared a cash dividend of $1.5 per share to all shareholders of record on June 15. (Hint: Dividends are not paid on treasury shares.)
July 1	Paid the cash dividends declared on June 1.
October 21	Reissued 2,500 treasury shares purchased on May 10 for $60 per share.

Mackerel Corporation has the following beginning balances in its shareholders' equity accounts on January 1, 20×2:

Ordinary shares $100,000; Share Premium $4,500,000; Retained Earnings $2,000,000

Net income for the year ended December 31, 20×2 was $600,000.

Required:

Prepare the statement of shareholders' equity for Mackerel Corporation for the year ended December 31, 20×2 using the format provided.

Mackerel Corporation
Statement of Shareholders' Equity
For the Year Ended December 31, 20×2

	Ordinary Shares	Share Premium	Retained Earnings	Treasury Shares	Total
Balance, January 1	$100,000	$4,500,000	$2,000,000	0	$6,600,000
Issued ordinary shares					
Purchased treasury shares					
Cash dividends					
Sale of treasury shares					
Net income					
Balance, December 31					

ACCOUNTING TERMINOLOGY IN CHAPTER 12

accumulated other comprehensive income (AOCI) 기타포괄손익누계액
additional paid-in capital 주식발행초과금
appropriated retained earnings 처분이익잉여금
appropriation 적립(처분)
articles of incorporation 정관
authorized shares 수권자본
board of directors 이사회
capital adjustments 자본조정
capital transactions 자본거래
carrying amount method 장부금액법
cash dividends 현금배당
charter (bylaws) 정관
common stocks 보통주
contributed capital 납입자본
corporate officers 임원
corporation 주식회사
cost method 원가법
cumulative preference share 누적적우선주
date of record 배당기준일
declaration date 배당선언일
dividends 배당
dividends in arrears 연체배당금
dividends rights 배당참여권
double taxation 이중과세
Financial Supervisory Service 금융감독원
fund-raising ability 자금조달능력
going concern 계속기업
issuance of shares 주식의 발행
issued shares 발행주식
legal entity 법인
limited liability 유한책임
liquidation 청산
liquidation rights 청산참여권
market value method 시가법
noncumulative preference share 비누적적우선주
nonparticipating 비참가적
ordinary share 보통주
outstanding shares 유통주식
paid-in capital 납입자본
paid-in capital in excess of par value 주식발행초과금
par value 액면금액
participating preference share 참가적우선주
payment date 배당지급일
preemptive right 주식선매권
preference shares 우선주
preferred stocks 우선주
premium from treasury shares 자기주식자본잉여금
retained earnings 이익잉여금
Securities and Exchange Commission 증권거래위원회
security exchanges 증권거래소

shares 주식
share capital 자본금
share certificate 주권
share discount 주식할인발행차금
share dividends 주식배당
share dividends distributable 미배당주식
share premium 주식발행초과금
share split 주식분할
shareholders 주주
shareholders' equity 소유주지분
shareholders' meeting 주주총회
stock exchange 주식시장
stockholders 주주
subscribed shares 청약주식
total shareholders' equity 총소유주지분, 자본총계
treasury shares 자기주식
unappropriated retained earnings 미처분이익잉여금
unissued shares 미발행주식
voting rights 의결권

CHAPTER

13

STATEMENT OF CASH FLOWS

13.1 PURPOSE OF THE STATEMENT OF CASH FLOWS

13.2 CASH FLOWS BY ACTIVITIES

13.3 TYPES OF CASH INFLOWS AND OUTFLOWS

13.4 METHODS FOR PREPARING THE STATEMENT OF CASH FLOWS

13.5 THE DIRECT METHOD

13.6 THE INDIRECT METHOD

13.7 INTERPRETING INFORMATION IN THE STATEMENT OF CASH FLOWS

CHAPTER 13

STATEMENT OF CASH FLOWS

13.1 PURPOSE OF THE STATEMENT OF CASH FLOWS

The primary purpose of the *statement of cash flows*(현금흐름표) is to provide information about cash receipts(현금수입), cash payments(현금지출), and the net change in cash(현금순변화) resulting from the operating, investing, and financing activities of a company during the period. In the statement of cash flows, activities involving cash are reported in a format that reconciles the beginning and ending cash balances. Reporting the causes of changes in cash is useful because investors, creditors, and other interested parties want to know what is happening to a company's cash.

The statement of cash flows is also called the statement of changes in financial position(재무상태변동표). The reason for the alternative name comes from the fact that the statement of cash flows has the ability to explain changes in the statement of financial position(재무상태표).

The statement of cash flows provides answers to the following important questions concerning an enterprise:

① Where did the cash come from during the period?
② What was the cash used for during the period?
③ What was the change in the cash balance during the period?

The statement of cash flows also provides clues about whether dynamic companies will be able to thrive and invest in new opportunities or whether a struggling company will survive or perish.

13.2 CASH FLOWS BY ACTIVITIES

The statement of cash flows classifies cash receipts and payments into operating, investing, and financing activities. Transactions within each activity are as follows:

ⓐ ***Operating activities***(영업활동) include the cash effects of transactions that create revenues and expenses and thus enter into the determination of net income.
ⓑ ***Investing activities***(투자활동) include (a) purchasing and disposing of noncurrent assets such as investments, PP&E (property, plant, and equipment), intangible assets, and other noncurrent assets using cash and (b) lending money and collecting the loans.
ⓒ ***Financing activities***(재무활동) include (a) obtaining cash from issuing debts and repaying the amounts borrowed and (b) obtaining cash from shareholders and paying dividends to shareholders.

The information in the statement of cash flows should help the users of financial statements evaluate the following aspects of the company's financial position.

First, the company's ability to generate future cash flows can be evaluated. By examining relationships between items in the statement of cash flows, the users of financial statements can better predict the amounts, timing, and uncertainty of future cash flows.

Second, the company's ability to pay dividends and meet obligations can be assessed. Employees, creditors, shareholders, and customers should be particularly interested in this statement because it shows the flows of cash in a business.

Third, the reasons for the difference between net income and net cash provided (used) by operating activities can be understood. Many financial statement users investigate the reasons for the difference between net income and cash flows from operating activities. As a result, they can assess the quality of the income statement numbers.

Finally, the investing and financing transactions during the period can be examined. As a result, financial statement users can better understand how assets and liabilities increased or decreased during the period by examining a company's investing and financing activities.

Cash flow from operations (or cash provided by operating activities) is the most important information about cash flows because it shows the cash provided or used by operating activities. From the difference between net income and cash flow from operating activities, we can compute "accruals"(발생액) which can be used to measure the degree of earnings management(이익관리). Cash flow from operating activities is generally considered to be the best measure of whether a company can generate sufficient cash to continue as a going concern(계속기업) and to expand.

13.3 TYPES OF CASH INFLOWS AND OUTFLOWS

As explained above, business activities can be classified into operating, investing, and financing activities. Accordingly, the statement of cash flows reports changes in cash flows during the period caused by the three business activities: cash flow from operating activities(영업활동현금흐름), cash flow from investing activities(투자활동현금흐름), and cash flow from financing activities(재무활동현금흐름). Each activity involves cash inflows and cash outflows. However, they are reported at net cash flows by subtracting outflows from inflows.

As indicated above, the statement of cash flows can explain the changes in the statement of financial position. In other words, changes in individual accounts reported in the comparative statements of financial position(비교재무상태표) can be explained by one of the three business activities. Therefore, we can express the relationship between the statement of financial position and three types of business activities in the statement of financial position, as depicted in Figure 13-1.

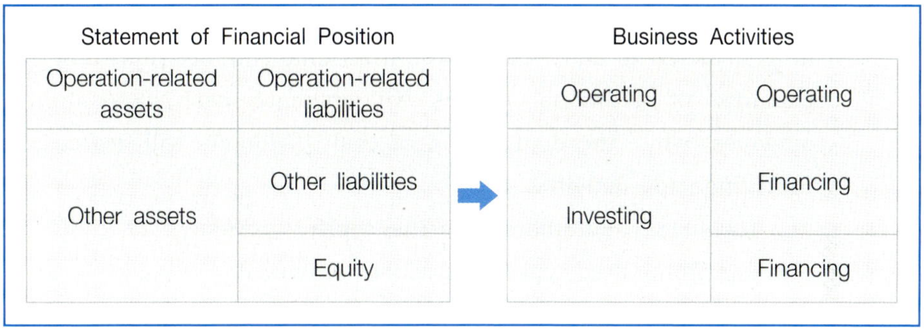

Figure 13-1 Decomposition of Statement of Financial Position from the Perspectives of Business Activities

Some assets and liabilities result from operating activities. Examples of the assets and liabilities that result from operating activities include accounts receivable(매출채권), inventories(재고자산), prepaid expenses(선급비용), accounts payable(매입채무), and accrued liabilities(미지급부채). Therefore, any increase or decrease in those operation-related assets and liabilities(영업활동관련자산부채) affects cash flows from operations.

Other assets are considered to have no direct relationship with the firm's operating activities for the period or from a short-term viewpoint. These types of assets are considered to have resulted from investing activities. Even though some may argue that all the assets are somehow related to operating activities from a long-term perspective, those assets have not resulted from the operating activities on a short-term basis. Those assets which do not have direct relationships with the operating activities of the current period include investments(투자자산), PP&E(유형자산), intangible assets(무형자산), and other noncurrent assets. Therefore, changes in those assets that do not have direct relationships with the operating activities in the current period affect cash flows from investing activities. For example, a purchase of equipment requires cash outflows for investing activities.

Liabilities that do not have direct relationships with the operating activities in the current period are considered to have resulted from financing activities. For example, debts(차입금) and bonds payable(사채) result from financing activities. Therefore, changes in these types of liabilities affect cash flows from financing activities.

Changes in equity, except for a change caused by net income or loss, are all considered to affect cash flows from financing activities. For example, the issuance of additional shares will increase cash flows from financing activities, while the distribution of cash dividends will decrease cash flows from financing activities.

Table 13-1 summarizes some typical examples of cash inflows and outflows from three types of business activities.

Companies can classify some cash flows resulting from the original investing/financing activities as operating cash flows or investing/financing cash flows. Companies can classify them as operating cash flows since related items are reported in the income statement. In this case, an alignment between the statement of cash flows and the income statement is emphasized. However, they can be classified as investing or financing cash flows to align

Table 13-1 Cash Inflows and Outflows from Three Types of Business Activities

Business Activities	Cash Flows	
	Inflows	Outflows
Operating Activities	• sale of goods or services • returns on investments such as interest income or dividends income	• purchases of goods or services • tax payment • interest payment • other expenses
Investing Activities	• sale of PP&E • sale of investments • collection of loans	• purchase of PP&E • purchase of investments • making loans to others
Financing Activities	• issuance of equity securities • issuance of debt securities or borrowings	• distributions of cash dividends to shareholders • redemption of debt securities or borrowings • purchase of treasury shares

the resulting cash flows with the underlying original investing or financing activities. For example, receipts of investment revenue (interest and dividend income) and payments of interest to lenders are classified as operating activities because these items are reported in the income statement or as investing activities or financing activities because the assets or liabilities on which they are based are related to investing/financing activities.

As a general rule, operating activities involve income statement items. Investing activities involve cash flows resulting from changes in investments and noncurrent assets such as PP&E, intangible assets, and other noncurrent assets. Financing activities involve cash flows resulting from changes in debts and shareholders' equity items.

Some noncurrent assets can be acquired by incurring debts or issuing shares without affecting cash. In other words, there are some significant non-cash investing and financing activities(중요한 비현금 투자 및 재무활동). Since one of the purposes of the statement of cash flows is to summarize business activities that occurred during the period, it is desirable to report these non-cash investing and financing activities in the statement of cash flows. Examples of significant non-cash investing and financing activities include the following:

① Issuance of ordinary shares to purchase assets
② Conversion of bonds into ordinary shares
③ Issuance of debts to purchase assets
④ Exchanges of property, plant, and equipment

Significant non-cash investing and financing activities are not reported in the body of the statement of cash flows. Instead, they are reported in notes to the financial statements. The reporting of significant activities not affecting cash in notes to financial statements is to comply with the full disclosure principle(완전공시의 원칙).

The three activities—operating, investing, and financing—plus the significant non-cash investing and financing activities make up the general format of the statement of cash flows. The section on cash flows from operating activities always appears first, followed by cash flows from investing activities and cash flows from financing activities. Finally, the individual inflows and outflows from investing and financing activities are reported separately.

The reported operating, investing, and financing activities result in either net cash provided or used by each activity. The net cash provided or used by each activity is totaled to show the net increase (decrease) in cash for the period. The net increase (decrease) in cash for the period is then added to or subtracted from the beginning cash balance to obtain the ending cash balance. Any significant non-cash investing and financing activities are reported in the notes(주석) to the statement of cash flows.

13.4 METHODS FOR PREPARING THE STATEMENT OF CASH FLOWS

The information to prepare the statement of cash flows comes from three sources.

① Information in the *comparative statements of financial position*(비교재무상태표) indicates the amount of changes in assets, liabilities, and shareholders' equity from the beginning to the end of the period.
② Information in the *income statement* helps the users determine the amount of cash provided or used by operations during the period.
③ *Additional information*(추가정보) includes transaction data that are needed to determine how cash was provided or used during the period.

In order to determine cash flow from operating activities, net income must be converted from an accrual basis(발생주의) to a cash basis(현금주의). There are two methods to convert net income or loss to cash flows from operating activities. They are the direct method(직접법) and the indirect method(간접법). Both methods arrive at the same total amount for "cash flow from operating activities." However, they differ in disclosing the items that make up the total amount. Note that the two different methods affect only the operating activities section. The investing and financing activities sections are not affected by choice of methods.

Even though both methods are allowed, the indirect method is used extensively in practice. Companies favor the indirect method for three reasons. First, it is easier to prepare. Second, it focuses on the relationship between net income and net cash flows from operating activities. Third, it tends to reveal less company information to competitors.

The direct method is more consistent with the objective of the statement of cash flows because it shows operating cash receipts and payments.

Presented below is information from the comparative statements of financial position for the years 20×1 and 20×2, the income statement for the year ended on December 31, 20×2, and additional information for Jade Company.

Jade Company
Comparative Statements of Financial Position

Assets	**20×2**	**20×1**	**Increase/Decrease**
Cash	$382,000	$318,000	$64,000 increase
Accounts receivable	36,000	30,000	6,000 increase
Inventory	248,000	320,000	72,000 decrease
Prepaid expenses	12,000	16,000	4,000 decrease
Land	360,000	160,000	200,000 increase
Equipment	520,000	200,000	320,000 increase
Accumulated depreciation	(92,000)	(60,000)	32,000 increase
Total	$1,466,000	$984,000	
Liabilities and Shareholders' Equity			
Accounts payable	$104,000	$120,000	$16,000 decrease
Accrued liabilities	30,000	40,000	10,000 decrease
Income taxes payable	64,000	40,000	24,000 increase
Bonds payable	280,000	100,000	180,000 increase
Ordinary shares	800,000	600,000	200,000 increase
Retained earnings	188,000	84,000	104,000 increase
Total	$1,466,000	$984,000	

Jade Company Income Statement For the Year Ended December 31, 20×2		
Revenues from sales		$1,950,000
Cost of goods sold	$1,320,000	
Operating expenses (excluding depreciation)	334,000	
Depreciation expense	36,000	
Loss on sale of equipment	2,000	1,692,000
Income before interest and taxes		258,000
Interest expense		18,000
Income tax expense		72,000
Net income		$168,000

Additional Information

(a) Jade declared and paid cash dividends of $64,000.
(b) Jade issued bonds at a face value of $180,000.
(c) Jade purchased equipment for $360,000 in cash.
(d) Jade sold equipment costing $40,000 for $34,000 cash when its carrying amount was $36,000.
(e) Jade issued ordinary shares of $200,000 to acquire land.
(f) Interest expense incurred during the period was paid.

Using the information above, let's now learn how to prepare the statement of cash flows under the direct and indirect methods.

13.5 THE DIRECT METHOD

It is easier to prepare a statement of cash flows by going through specific steps. In addition, it is easier to use a summary entry(요약분개) or worksheet journal entry(정산표분개) system to prepare the statement of cash flows. The summary entries are not formal ones recorded in the accounting books. The summary entries are used only to help prepare the statement of cash flows. We will learn how to prepare the statement of cash flows by going through those steps one by one.

STEP 1 *Determining the net increase or decrease in cash*

The comparative statements of financial position of Jade Company show a beginning cash balance of $318,000 and an ending cash balance of $382,000. Thus, there is a net increase in cash of $64,000 in 20×2. The ending balance of cash will be proven when the statement of cash flows is completed since it requires showing how the three sources of cash flows are reconciled to arrive at the ending balance of cash.

STEP 2 *Determining net cash flows from operating activities*

ⓐ ***Cash receipts from customers***(고객으로부터의 현금수령). Since accounts receivable increased by $6,000, cash receipts from customers are smaller than revenue. Cash receipts from customers are $1,944,000, computed as follows:

Revenues from sales	$1,950,000
Deduct: Increase in accounts receivable.	(6,000)
Cash receipts from customers	$1,944,000

Alternatively, we can compute cash receipts from customers by using the following summary entry, Crediting Sales revenue, debiting Accounts receivable for an increase, and debiting Cash received from customers to balance the journal entry:

Cash received from customers	1,944,000	
Accounts receivable	6,000	
Sales revenue		1,950,000

ⓑ ***Cash payments to suppliers***(공급업자에게 현금지불). For 20×2, we can compute purchases using the cost of goods sold of $1,320,000 from the income statement and a decrease in inventory by $72,000 from the comparative statements of financial position. Purchases are then adjusted for the decrease in accounts payable by $16,000. Cash payments to suppliers are $1,264,000, computed as follows:

Cost of goods sold	$1,320,000
Deduct: Decrease in inventory	(72,000)
Purchases	1,248,000
Add: Decrease in accounts payable	16,000
Cash payments to suppliers	$1,264,000

Alternatively, we can compute cash payments to suppliers by using the following summary entry, recording the Cost of goods sold, crediting Inventory for a decrease, debiting Accounts payable for a decrease, and crediting Cash paid to suppliers to balance the journal entry:

Cost of goods sold	1,320,000	
Accounts payable	16,000	
Inventory		72,000
Cash paid to suppliers		1,264,000

ⓒ ***Cash payments for operating expenses***(영업비용 현금지불). Prepaid expenses decreased by $4,000 during the year. The decrease in prepaid expenses is deducted from operating expenses to determine cash payments for operating expenses. Accrued liabilities decreased by $10,000 during the period. The decrease in accrued liabilities is added to operating expenses. Cash payments for operating expenses are $340,000, computed as follows:

Operating expenses	$334,000
Deduct: Decrease in prepaid expenses	(4,000)
Add: Decrease in accrued liabilities	10,000
Cash payments for operating expenses	$340,000

Alternatively, we can compute cash payments for operating expenses by using the following summary entry, recording operating expenses, crediting Prepaid expenses for a decrease, debiting Accrued liabilities for a decrease, and crediting Cash payments for operating expenses to balance the journal entry:

Operating expenses	334,000	
Accrued liabilities	10,000	
Prepaid expense		4,000
Cash payments for operating expenses		340,000

ⓓ ***Cash payments for income taxes***(법인세 현금지불). Income taxes payable increased by $24,000. Therefore, cash payments for income taxes are $48,000 ($72,000 − $24,000).

Alternatively, we can compute the payments for income taxes using the following summary entry, debiting Income tax expense, crediting Income taxes payable for its increase, and crediting Cash payments for income taxes to balance the journal entry:

Income tax expense	72,000	
Income taxes payable		24,000
Cash payments for income taxes		48,000

ⓔ ***Depreciation expense and loss on sale of equipment***. Depreciation expense in 20×2 is $36,000. Depreciation expense is not shown in the statement of cash flows under the direct method because it is a non-cash charge. The loss on sale of equipment of $2,000 is also a non-cash charge.

STEP 3 ***Determine the reporting format for cash flows from operating activities***

Some items must be separately reported in reporting cash flows from operating activities. First, cash receipts from customers and cash payments to suppliers are required to be separately reported. Second, interest and income taxes are also required to be separately reported. Third, companies typically divide cash payments to suppliers into those suppliers and other operating expenses. Fourth, some firms report an intermediate item, "Cash generated from operations(영업에서 창출된 현금)," before reporting interest paid and income taxes paid. Lastly, "Net cash flows from operating activities(영업활동순현금흐름)" is reported.

STEP 4 *Determining net cash flows from investing and financing activities*

ⓐ ***Increase in land.*** Additional information indicates that ordinary shares were issued to purchase land. The issuance of ordinary shares for land does not affect cash. But it is a significant non-cash investing and financing transaction that requires disclosure.

ⓑ ***Increase in equipment.*** The increase of $320,000 resulted from two investing transactions: (1) Equipment costing $360,000 was purchased for cash; (2) Equipment costing $40,000 was sold for $34,000 when its carrying amount was $36,000. The $360,000 purchase of equipment was an outflow of cash, and the $34,000 sale of equipment was an inflow of cash. The two amounts should not be netted but should be shown separately.

ⓒ ***Increase in bonds payable.*** The additional information indicates that bonds with a face value of $180,000 were issued for $180,000. The issuance of bonds is a financing activity. Therefore, there is an inflow of cash for $180,000 from the issuance of bonds payable.

ⓓ ***Increase in ordinary shares.*** The issuance of ordinary shares is a financing activity. However, additional information indicates that land was acquired from the issuance of ordinary shares. Therefore, the transaction is a significant non-cash investing and financing transaction that needs to be disclosed.

ⓔ ***Increase in retained earnings.*** Net income increases retained earnings by $104,000. The additional information indicates that the company declared and paid a cash dividend of $64,000. Net income is not reported in the statement of cash flows under the direct method. However, cash dividends paid are reported in the financing activities section as an outflow of cash.

The statement of cash flows prepared for the year ended December 31, 20×2 for Jade Company using the direct method is presented below:

Jade Company Statement of Cash Flows - Direct Method For the Year Ended December 31, 20×2		
Cash flows from operating activities		
Cash receipts from customers	$1,944,000	
Cash payments to suppliers	(1,264,000)	
Cash payments for operating expenses	(340,000)	
Cash generated from operations	340,000	
Interest paid	(18,000)	
Income taxes paid	(48,000)	
Net cash flows from operating activities		$274,000
Cash flows from investing activities		
Sale of equipment	34,000	
Purchase of equipment	(360,000)	
Net cash used in investing activities		(326,000)
Cash flows from financing activities		
Issuance of bonds payable	180,000	
Distribution of cash dividends	(64,000)	
Net cash provided by financing activities		116,000
Net increase in cash		64,000
Add: Beginning balance - January 1, 20×2		318,000
Ending balance - December 31, 20×2		$382,000

Notes

Ordinary shares of $200,000 were issued to purchase land.

13.6 THE INDIRECT METHOD

The statement of cash flows prepared by the indirect method starts with income before interest and taxes. It then adds or deducts items not affecting cash to arrive at "net cash generated from operations." It is further adjusted for cash paid for interest and cash paid for income taxes because these two items are required to be shown separately in the statement of cash flows. Finally, cash flows from operating activities are shown after adjusting interest paid and income taxes paid from the cash generated from operations.

Just like the direct method, it is easier to go through steps in preparing the statement of cash flows using the indirect method.

STEP 1 ***Determine the net increase/decrease in cash***

Cash increased by $64,000 ($382,000 − $318,000).

STEP 2 ***Determine net cash from operating activities***

Net income under the accrual basis must be adjusted to arrive at net cash flows from operating activities by going through two procedures. First, "cash generated from operations" must be determined by adjusting non-cash income statement items and changes in operation-related assets and liabilities to income before interest and taxes. Then, interest paid and income taxes paid must be subtracted from cash generated from operations to arrive at net cash flows from operating activities. We discuss the explanations for the adjustments to accrual basis net income for Jade Company for 20×2 below.

(1) Determination of Cash Generated from Operations

ⓐ ***Income before interest and taxes***(이자및법인세차감전이익). For 20×2, Jade Company reported income before interest and taxes of $258,000. Cash flows from operating activities start with income before interest and taxes, which needs to be adjusted for non-cash expenses (losses) and revenues (gains), and changes in operation-related assets and liabilities.

A worksheet (summary) journal entry for this is:

Cash from Operating Activities	258,000	
Retained Earnings		258,000

ⓑ ***Depreciation expense***(감가상각비). For 20×2, Jade Company reported a depreciation expense of $36,000. Depreciation expense is a non-cash charge. Thus, it is added back to income before interest and taxes to arrive at net cash flows from operating activities. Other non-cash expenses, such as amortization of intangible assets, are treated similarly to depreciation.

A worksheet journal entry for depreciation expense is:

Cash from Operating Activities	36,000	
Accumulated Depreciation		36,000

ⓒ ***Loss on sale of equipment***. Jade Company reported a $2,000 loss on equipment sale (cost $40,000; accumulated depreciation $4,000; cash proceeds $34,000). The loss reduces income before interest and taxes but does not reduce cash. Therefore, the $2,000 loss is added to income before interest and taxes to convert the accrual income to net cash flows from operating activities.

The worksheet journal entry is:

Cash from Investing Activities	34,000	
Accumulated Depreciation	4,000	
Cash from Operating Activities	2,000	
Equipment		40,000

ⓓ ***Increase in accounts receivable***. Accounts receivable increased because cash receipts were lower than revenues reported on the accrual basis. To convert the accrual income to net cash flows from operating activities, the increase in accounts receivable of $6,000 must be subtracted from income before interest and taxes.

A worksheet journal entry for this is:

Accounts Receivable	6,000	
Cash from Operating Activities		6,000

ⓔ ***Decrease in inventory***. There is a decrease in inventory of $72,000. The decrease in inventory means that more inventory was sold than purchased during the period, resulting in increased cash from sales. To convert the accrual income to net cash flows from operating activities, the decrease in inventory must be added to income before interest and taxes.

A worksheet journal entry for this is:

Cash from Operating Activities	72,000	
Inventory		72,000

ⓕ ***Decrease in prepaid expenses.*** Prepaid expenses decreased during the period because cash paid for expenses was smaller than expenses reported under the accrual basis. Therefore, to convert the accrual income to net cash flows from operating activities, the decrease in prepaid expense of $4,000 must be added to income before interest and taxes.

A worksheet journal entry for this is:

Cash from Operating Activities	4,000	
Prepaid Expense		4,000

ⓖ ***Decrease in accounts payable.*** The decrease in accounts payable of $16,000 must be subtracted from income before interest and taxes to compute net cash flows from operating activities.

A worksheet journal entry for this is:

Accounts Payable	16,000	
Cash from Operating Activities		16,000

ⓗ ***Decrease in accrued liabilities.*** A decrease in accrued liabilities means that cash has been used during the period to decrease accrued liabilities. Therefore, the decrease in accrued liabilities must be subtracted from income before interest and taxes.

A worksheet journal entry for this is:

Accrued Liabilities	10,000	
Cash from Operating Activities		10,000

ⓘ ***Increase in income taxes payable.*** An increase in income taxes payable means that the company's tax payment was less than its income tax expense incurred during the period, resulting in less cash paid for operating purposes. Therefore, the increase must be added to income before interest and taxes.

A worksheet journal entry for this is:

Cash from Operating Activities	24,000	
Income Taxes Payable		24,000

After all the necessary adjustments are made to income before interest and taxes, Jade Company's cash generated from operations is determined as follows:

Income before interest and taxes	$258,000
Adjustments for:	
Depreciation expense	36,000
Loss on sale of equipment	2,000
Increase in accounts receivable	(6,000)
Decrease in inventory	72,000
Decrease in prepaid expenses	4,000
Decrease in accounts payable	(16,000)
Decrease in accrued liabilities	(10,000)
Cash generated from operations	$340,000

Notes

Increase in income taxes payable is not included in Cash generated from operations because it is to be reported as separate items, together with income taxes paid.

(2) Determination of Cash Flows from Operating Activities

Interest paid and taxes paid must be separately shown in the cash flows from operating activities section. Therefore, interest paid and taxes paid must be subtracted from cash generated from operations to arrive at cash flows from operating activities as follows:

Cash generated from operations	$340,000
Interest paid (from the income statement)	(18,000)*
Income taxes paid	(48,000)**
Net cash flows from operating activities	$274,000

* From the income statement. There is no interest payable, indicating interest expense equals interest paid.

** $72,000 (from the income statement) − $24,000 increase in taxes payable = $48,000

STEP 3 *Determine net cash flows from investing and financing activities*

After determining cash flows from operating activities, the remaining changes in the statement of financial position accounts must be analyzed to determine cash flows from investing and financing activities.

ⓐ ***Purchase and sale of equipment.*** Equipment costing $360,000 was acquired during the period. This transaction is a cash outflow reported in the investing activities section.

A worksheet journal entry for this is:

Equipment	360,000	
Cash from Investing Activities		360,000

Additional information indicates that Jade sold equipment costing $40,000 for $34,000 when its carrying amount was $36,000. Therefore, the accumulated depreciation on the equipment sold is $4,000.

A worksheet journal entry for the sale of equipment is:

Cash from Investing Activities	34,000	
Accumulated Depreciation	4,000	
Loss on sale of equipment	2,000	
Equipment		40,000

The purchase and sale of equipment during the period show that a net increase in equipment amounts to $320,000. In addition, the loss on sale of equipment is a non-cash item. Therefore, it is not reported in cash flows from operating activities under the direct method.

ⓑ ***Increase in bonds payable.*** Bonds were issued for $180,000 during the period. The bond issuance is an inflow of cash from financing activities.

A worksheet journal entry for this is:

Cash from Financing Activities	180,000	
Bonds Payable		180,000

ⓒ ***Increase in retained earnings.*** Retained earnings increased by $104,000 during the period. Net income of $168,000 increases retained earnings, while cash dividends of $64,000 decrease it. We have not taken into account Jade Company's payment of dividends yet. Therefore, we need to account for the impact of the dividend payment on cash flows. A dividend payment is a cash outflow from financing activities.

A worksheet journal entry for cash dividends is:

Retained Earnings	64,000	
Cash from Financing Activities		64,000

STEP 4 *Identify Significant Non-cash Investing and Financing Activities*

Additional information indicates that Jade acquired land by the issuance of ordinary shares. Land acquisition is an investing activity, while the issuance of ordinary shares is a financing activity. Therefore, the transaction is a significant non-cash investing and financing transaction that needs to be disclosed.

We can now verify cash flows from the three different activities by preparing worksheet T-accounts as follows:

Cash from Operating Activities

Income before interest and taxes	258,000	Increase in accounts receivable	6,000
Depreciation expense	36,000	Decrease in accounts payable	16,000
Loss on sale of equipment	2,000	Decrease in accrued liabilities	10,000
Decrease in inventory	72,000	Interest paid	18,000
Decrease in prepaid expenses	4,000	Income taxes paid	72,000
Increase in taxes payable	24,000		
Total	396,000	Total	122,000
Increase	274,000		

Cash from Investing Activities

Sale of equipment	34,000	Purchase of equipment	360,000
Total	34,000	Total	360,000
		Decrease	(326,000)

Cash from Financing Activities

Issuance of bonds	180,000	Cash dividends paid	64,000
Total	180,000	Total	64,000
Increase	116,000		

The statement of cash flows prepared by the indirect method for Jade Company for the year ended December 31, 20×2 is shown below:

Jade Company
Statement of Cash Flows - Indirect Method
For the Year Ended December 31, 20×2

Cash flows from operating activities		
Income before interest and taxes	$258,000	
Adjustments for:		
Depreciation expense	36,000	
Loss on sale of equipment	2,000	
Increase in accounts receivable	(6,000)	
Decrease in inventory	72,000	
Decrease in prepaid expenses	4,000	
Decrease in accounts payable	(16,000)	
Decrease in accrued liabilities	(10,000)	
Cash generated from operations	340,000	
Interest paid	(18,000) *	
Income taxes paid	(48,000) **	
Net cash flows from operating activities		$274,000
Cash flows from investing activities		
Sale of equipment	34,000	
Purchase of equipment	(360,000)	
Net cash used in investing activities		(326,000)
Cash flows from financing activities		
Issuance of bonds	180,000	
Distribution of cash dividends	(64,000)	
Net cash from financing activities		116,000
Net increase in cash		64,000
Add: Beginning balance - January 1, 20×2		318,000
Ending balance - December 31, 20×2		$382,000

* From the income statement. There is no interest payable, indicating interest expense equals interest paid.

** $72,000 (from the income statement) − $24,000 increase in taxes payable = $48,000

Notes

Ordinary shares of $200,000 were issued to purchase land.

13.7 INTERPRETING INFORMATION IN THE STATEMENT OF CASH FLOWS

What can the statement of cash flows tell users about a company's financial situation and the patterns of cash use over the company's life? For example, it might reveal something about the company's life cycle or stage of development, and it could uncover patterns of activity that raise concerns for shareholders and creditors. This section of the chapter highlights a few patterns that might be observed in the statement of cash flows and explains what these patterns can signal about a company.

Pattern #1: Start-up companies and/or first years of a company's life

Garnet Company began business operations in the current year. However, it hasn't yet earned positive net income (i.e., incurred net losses each quarter) and has been unable to generate cash inflows from operating activities. What might be a typical pattern of cash flows observed on such a company's year-end statement of cash flows?

There likely would be a net inflow of cash from financing activities, represented by an increase in cash from issuing shares to shareholders and increases in cash obtained through borrowing from banks. This inflow of cash from financing activities would be used to acquire property, plant, and equipment, an investing activity. Thus, you would observe a net cash outflow in the investing activities classification. Additionally, the cash from issuing shares and borrowing could be used to support the business's daily operations. Until the time when Garnet Company generates cash from its operating activities, it needs to use cash provided from financing activities to pay for operating expenses.

Pattern #2: Mature companies with steady growth

Onyx Company has been in business for many years. It has steady growth in net income and consistently reports cash inflows from operations. So, what pattern of operating, investing, and financing cash flows might we expect to see in Onyx's statement of cash flows?

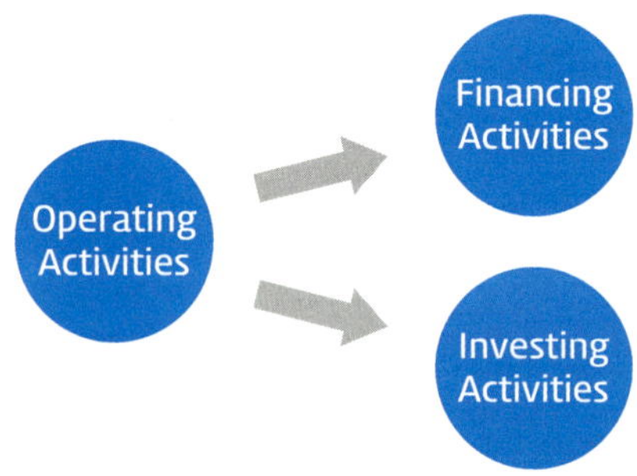

Users probably would find that the statement of cash flows shows the net inflow of cash from operating activities is used for two purposes. Onyx Company could use the cash generated from operations to acquire fixed and intangible assets, make loans to other companies, or buy shares (i.e., make investments) in other companies. The cash obtained from operations can also be applied toward various transactions classified as financing activities. For example, Onyx might use this cash to reduce its liabilities by paying down long-term debt balances. In addition, it might choose to pay dividends to shareholders or repurchase treasury shares. Therefore, it would not be unusual to observe net cash inflows from operating activities and net cash outflows in both investing and financing activities.

Pattern #3: Companies experiencing operational troubles

Over the past several years, Amber Company has had net cash outflows from operations and reported net losses on its income statement. In addition, the company is burdened with large accounts receivable and payables balances; these significantly affect Amber's cash flows from operations. So, what will users of Amber's statement of cash flows notice when they read it?

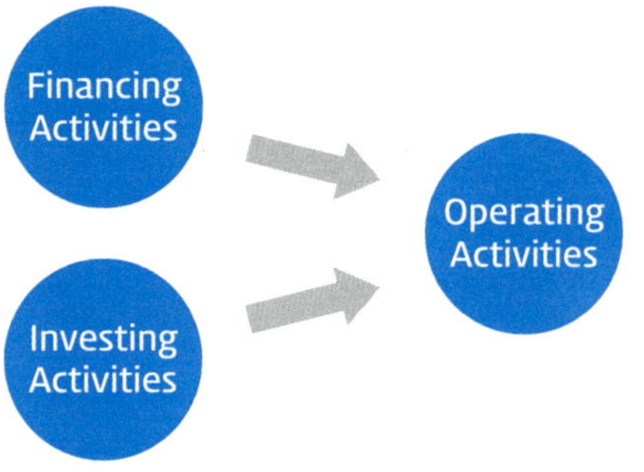

Like a start-up company or a firm in the early years of its life, Amber may fail to generate net cash inflows from operating activities. So, where does Amber get the cash to pay its suppliers and employees and cover its other operating costs? The answer is not good; cash comes from investing and financing activities. In other words, there are net cash inflows from the investing and financing activities. But this cash is then used to pay for Amber's many operating expenses. In the investing category, cash inflows result when the company disposes of its fixed or intangible assets or sells investments it made in other companies. What is the source of Amber's net cash inflows from financing activities? They come from borrowing from banks and selling treasury shares. A company might be able to take this path for a short time while it tries to overcome its operational problems. But in the long run, this is not a sustainable cash flow pattern.

CHAPTER 13 Multiple Choice Questions

13.1 The statement of cash flows reports cash flows from the activities of:

a Operating, purchasing, and investing.
b Borrowing, paying, and investing.
c Financing, investing, and operating.
d Using, investing, and financing.

13.2 Operating cash flows would exclude:

a Payment of employee salaries.
b Receipt of cash from customers.
c Payment of dividends.
d Payment for advertising.

13.3 Cash flows from investing do not include cash flows from:

a Lending.
b The sale of equipment.
c Borrowing.
d The purchase of a building.

13.4 Cash flows from financing activities include:

a Lending.
b Salaries paid.
c The sale of land.
d Dividends paid.

13.5 Investing cash flows would include which of the following?

ⓐ Payment of cash dividends to shareholders
ⓑ Purchase of office supplies with cash
ⓒ Purchase of a building with cash
ⓓ Cash sales to customers

13.6 Issuing ordinary shares for cash is considered a(n):

ⓐ Operating cash flow.
ⓑ Investing cash flow.
ⓒ Financing cash flow.
ⓓ Not a cash flow.

13.7 Transactions of a company involving external sources of funding are referred to as:

ⓐ Investing activities.
ⓑ Financing activities.
ⓒ External activities.
ⓓ Operating activities.

13.8 Transactions related to the purchase and sale of long-term productive assets are referred to as:

ⓐ Investing activities.
ⓑ Financing activities.
ⓒ Expenditure activities.
ⓓ Operating activities.

13.9 Transactions related to the primary business activities of the company, such as selling goods and services to customers, are referred to as:

ⓐ Investing activities.
ⓑ Management activities.
ⓒ Operating activities.
ⓓ Financing activities.

13.10 Which cash flows can be presented using either direct or indirect methods?

ⓐ Operating activities
ⓑ Investing activities
ⓒ Financing activities
ⓓ Lending activities

CHAPTER 13

Exercises

13.1 Cash flows from operating activities

Ray Company reported income before interest and taxes of $150,000 for the current year. Depreciation recorded on buildings and equipment amounted to $80,000 for the year. Interest and income tax expenses incurred and paid during the year amount to $15,000 and $40,500, respectively. Balances of the current asset and current liability accounts at the beginning and end of the year are as follows:

	End of Year	Beginning of Year
Cash	$20,000	$15,000
Accounts receivable	19,000	30,000
Inventories	55,000	65,000
Prepaid expenses	7,500	5,000
Accounts payable	12,000	16,000

Required:

Prepare the cash flows from the operating activities section of the statement of cash flows using the indirect method.

13.2 Identification of cash flows

Consider the following transactions:

ⓐ Pay employees' salaries.
ⓑ Repay borrowing to the bank.
ⓒ Purchase equipment with note payable.
ⓓ Provide services to customers on account.
ⓔ Pay dividends to shareholders.
ⓕ Collect cash from customers for services provided.
ⓖ Purchase supplies on account.
ⓗ Pay for supplies purchased in the transaction ⓖ above.

Required:

For each transaction, indicate the type of cash flow involved based on the classifications in the statement of cash flows. If a transaction does not involve cash, write 'No Cash.'

13.3 Cash flows different business activities (1)

Determine cash flows from different business activities for the following independent situations:

ⓐ A company provides services on account during the current year totaling $400,000. By the end of the year, $350,000 of this amount had been received. In addition, $75,000 was received on account from customers for services provided in the prior year. Determine the amount of operating cash flows the company will report as received from customers in the current year.

ⓑ During the current year, a company purchases equipment for $250,000, paying $50,000 immediately and promising to pay the remainder within 30 days after the end of the year. Determine the amount of investing cash flows the company will report in the current year.

ⓒ At the beginning of the current year, a company issued ordinary shares for $100,000 and borrowed $50,000 from the bank. By the end of the year, the company had provided services of $80,000 for cash, paid employee salaries of $30,000, and paid utilities of $10,000. Determine the amount of financing cash flows the company will report in the current year.

ⓓ During the year, a company issues ordinary shares for $50,000 and repays previously borrowed amounts of $75,000. In addition, the company pays dividends of $5,000 to shareholders. Determine the amount of financing cash flows the company will report in the current year.

13.4 Cash flows different business activities (2)

A company had the following transactions during the year:

- ⓐ Paid rent for the next two years, $8,000.
- ⓑ Purchased office supplies on account, $2,400.
- ⓒ Purchased equipment, paying $12,000 cash and issuing a note payable for $4,000.
- ⓓ Borrowed from the bank, $6,000.
- ⓔ Paid employee salaries, $7,200.
- ⓕ Paid $2,000 on account related to the transaction ⓑ above.
- ⓖ Paid dividends to shareholders, $2,800.
- ⓗ Sold land for $10,000 purchased in a prior year for $7,500.
- ⓘ Collected cash from customers for services provided, $25,700.

Required:

Calculate cash flows from operating activities, investing activities, and financing activities.

13.5 Statement of cash flows - Indirect method (1)

Recent comparative statements of financial position of Armadillo Company are presented below, along with an income statement for the most recent year.

Armadillo Company
Comparative Statements of Financial Position
December 31

Assets	20×3	20×2
Cash	$25,000	$13,300
Accounts receivable	84,000	68,000
Inventories	14,300	10,800
Prepaid expenses	2,000	1,200
Land	80,000	30,000
Plant and equipment	300,000	300,000
Accumulated depreciation - plant and equipment	(45,000)	(37,500)
Total assets	$460,300	$385,800

Liabilities and Shareholders' Equity		
Accounts payable	$24,200	$42,000
Accrued liabilities	1,500	3,800
Mortgages payable	80,000	50,000
Ordinary shares ($5 par)	200,000	150,000
Retained earnings	154,600	140,000
Total liabilities and shareholders' equity	$460,300	$385,800

Armadillo Company
Income Statement
For the Year Ended December 31, 20×3

Revenues		$135,000
Cost of goods sold	$57,250	
Operating expenses	28,750	86,000
Income before interest and taxes		$49,000
Interest expense		6,800
Income tax expense		12,600
Net income		$29,600

Additional Information

1. Operating expenses include a depreciation expense of $7,500.
2. Cash dividends of $15,000 were declared and paid in 20×3.
3. Interest expense amounting to $6,800 was paid in cash.
4. Land costing $50,000 was purchased. Armadillo paid $20,000 in cash and borrowed the remaining $30,000, providing the purchased land as collateral.
5. Ordinary shares ($5 par) of $50,000 were issued for cash.
6. All accounts payable pertain to merchandise purchases on account.

Required:
Prepare a statement of cash flows for Armadillo Company using the indirect method.

13.6 Statement of cash flows - Indirect method (2)

A comparative statement of financial position of Sturgeon Corporation is presented below:

Sturgeon Corporation
Comparative Statements of Financial Position
December 31

Assets	**20×2**	**20×1**
Cash	$51,000	$31,000
Accounts receivable (net)	75,000	60,000
Prepaid insurance	22,000	17,000
Land	22,000	40,000
Equipment	70,000	60,000
Accumulated depreciation	(20,000)	(13,000)
Total assets	$220,000	$195,000
Liabilities and Shareholders' Equity		
Accounts payable	$13,000	$6,000
Bonds payable	30,000	19,000
Ordinary shares	140,000	115,000
Retained earnings	37,000	55,000
Total liabilities and shareholders' equity	$220,000	$195,000

Additional Information

1. Loss before interest and taxes for 20×2 is $8,000. Interest expense incurred and paid was $6,000. Net sales for 20×2 are $250,000.
2. Cash dividends of $4,000 were declared and paid in 20×2.
3. Land was sold for cash at a loss of $5,000. This was the only land transaction during the year.
4. Equipment with a cost of $15,000 and accumulated depreciation of $10,000 was sold for $5,000 cash.
5. $14,000 of bonds were retired during the year at the carrying amount.
6. Equipment was acquired for ordinary shares. The fair market value of the shares at the time of the exchange was $25,000.

Required:

Prepare a statement of cash flows for the year ended 20×2 using the indirect method.

13.7 Cash payments for operating expenses - Direct method

Flounder Company had total operating expenses of $150,000 in 20×2, which included a depreciation expense of $20,000. Also, during 20×2, prepaid expenses increased by $5,000, and accrued expenses decreased by $8,700.

Required:

Calculate the amount of cash payments for operating expenses in 20×2 using the direct method.

13.8 Cash receipts and payments from operating activities - Direct method

The general ledger of Trout Company provides the following information:

	End of Year	Beginning of Year
Accounts Receivable	$60,000	$94,000
Inventory	350,000	230,000
Accounts Payable	40,000	65,000

The company's net sales for the year were $1,000,000, and the cost of goods sold amounted to $700,000.

Required:

Compute the following:

ⓐ Cash receipts from customers.

ⓑ Cash payments to suppliers.

13.9 Cash flows from operating activities – Direct method (1)

The income statement of Salmon Corporation for the year ended December 31, 20×2 reported the following condensed information:

Service revenues	$550,000
Operating expenses	330,000
Income from operations	220,000
Income tax expense	90,000
Net income	$130,000

Salmon Corporation's statements of financial position contained the following comparative data on December 31:

	20×2	20×1
Accounts receivable	$60,000	$40,000
Accounts payable	35,000	41,000
Income taxes payable	6,000	3,000

Salmon Corporation has no depreciable assets. Accounts payable pertains to operating expenses.

Required:

Prepare the operating activities section of the statement of cash flows using the direct method.

13.10 Cash flows from operating activities - Direct method (2)

The income statement of Lobster Company is shown below:

Lobster Company
Income Statement
For the Year Ended December 31, 20×2

Sales		$6,000,000
Cost of goods sold		4,200,000
Gross profit		1,800,000
Operating expenses		
Selling expenses	$400,000	
Administrative expense	700,000	
Depreciation expense	90,000	
Amortization expense	30,000	1,220,000
Income before taxes		580,000
Income tax expense		174,000
Net income		$406,000

Additional Information

1. Accounts receivable increased by $400,000 during the year.
2. Inventory increased by $200,000 during the year.
3. Prepaid expenses increased by $200,000 during the year.
4. Accounts payable to merchandise suppliers increased by $100,000 during the year.
5. Accrued expenses payable increased by $180,000 during the year.

Required:

Prepare the operating activities section of the statement of cash flows for the year ended December 31, 20×2 for Lobster Company, using the direct method.

ACCOUNTING TERMINOLOGY IN CHAPTER 13

accounts payable 매입채무
accounts receivable 매출채권
accrual basis 발생주의
accruals 발생액
accrued liabilities 미지급부채
bonds payable 사채
cash basis 현금주의
cash flows from financing activities 재무활동현금흐름
cash flows from investing activities 투자활동현금흐름
cash flows from operating activities 영업활동현금흐름
cash generated from operations 영업에서 창출된 현금
cash payments 현금지출
cash payments for income taxes 법인세 현금지불
cash payments for operating expenses 영업비용 현금지불
cash payments to suppliers 납품업자에게 현금지불
cash receipts 현금수입
cash receipts from customers 고객으로부터의 현금수령
comparative statements of financial position 비교재무상태표
debts 차입금
depreciation expense 감가상각비
direct method 직접법
earnings management 이익관리
financing activities 재무활동
full disclosure principle 완전공시의 원칙
going concern 계속기업
income before interest and taxes 이자및법인세차감전이익
indirect method 간접법
intangible assets 무형자산
inventories 재고자산
investing activities 투자활동
investments 투자자산
net cash flows from operating activities 영업활동순현금흐름
net change in cash 현금순변화
notes 주석
operating activities 영업활동
operation-related assets and liabilities 영업활동관련자산부채
prepaid expense 선급비용
property, plant, and equipment (PP&E) 유형자산
significant non-cash investing and financing activities 중요한 비현금 투자 및 재무 활동
statement of cash flows 현금흐름표
statement of changes in financial position 재무상태변동표
statement of financial position 재무상태표
summary entries 요약분개
worksheet journal entries 정산표분개

CHAPTER

14

REVENUE RECOGNITION

CHAPTER 14

REVENUE RECOGNITION

14.1 INTRODUCTION

Companies generate revenue by providing goods or services to customers. Revenues(수익) are defined as inflows or other enhancements of assets or settlements of liabilities (or a combination of both) from delivering goods(재화의 인도), rendering services(용역의 제공), or other activities to customers. There are two essential accounting issues related to revenue. The two issues are when we recognize revenue and how we determine the amount of revenue.

The core revenue recognition principle states that firms recognize revenue when goods or services are transferred to customers for the amount the company expects to be entitled to receive in exchange for those goods and services.

14.2 FIVE STEPS TO REVENUE RECOGNITION

There are five steps to follow in revenue recognition. The five steps are summarized in Table 14-1.

Table 14-1 Five steps to recognize revenue

Step	Description
Step 1	Identify the contract with a customer
Step 2	Identify the performance obligation(s) in the contract
Step 3	Determine the transaction price
Step 4	Allocate the transaction price to each performance obligation
Step 5	Recognize revenue when (or as) each performance obligation is satisfied

The first step is to identify the contract with a customer. The contract with a customer sets the legal rights and obligations of the seller and customer. A contract with a customer(고객과의 계약) can take various forms, such as written contract or verbal contract. However, the contract should have a commercial substance(상업적실질) to be considered a contract. For example, if a contract can be canceled without a penalty by any party to the contract, it is not considered a contract. So, irrespective of the form of the contract, a commercial substance is the critical feature of a contract.

The second step is to identify the performance obligations(수행의무) in the contract. A performance obligation is a promise to transfer a distinct good or service, which is the case if the good or service is both capable of being distinct and separately identifiable. A contract can have a single performance obligation or multiple performance obligations.

The third step is to determine the transaction price(거래가격). The transaction price is the amount the seller is entitled to receive from the customer. The transaction price may consist of a fixed price(확정가격) only or fixed price and variable considerations(변동대가).

The fourth step is to allocate the transaction price to performance obligations. The seller allocates the transaction price to performance obligations based on relative standalone selling prices(상대판매가격) of goods or services in each performance obligation.

The last step is to recognize revenue when each performance obligation is satisfied. A performance obligation is satisfied when a good or service specified in the contract is transferred from the seller to the customer. A performance obligation can be satisfied at a point in time(단일시점) or over a period of time(일정기간). Therefore, revenue recognition takes only two forms of recognition for each performance obligation: a revenue recognition at a point in time(단일시점수익인식) and a revenue recognition over time(기간수익인식). Step 5 is applied to each performance obligation even though a contract can have multiple performance obligations. Therefore, a contract can have performance obligation(s) to which a point in time revenue recognition is applied and other performance obligation(s) to which over-time revenue recognition is applied.

Table 14-2 summarizes some key considerations when applying the five steps to revenue recognition, depending on whether a contract has only a single performance obligation or multiple performance obligations.

Table 14-2 Key considerations when applying the five steps to revenue recognition

<table>
<tr><td>1. Identify the contract</td><td colspan="3">Legal rights of seller and customer established</td></tr>
<tr><td>2. Identify the performance obligation(s)</td><td colspan="2">Single</td><td>Multiple</td></tr>
<tr><td>3. Determine the transaction price</td><td colspan="3">The amount the seller is entitled to receive from the customer</td></tr>
<tr><td>4. Allocate the transaction price</td><td colspan="2">No allocation is required</td><td>Allocate a portion to each performance obligation using the relative standalone selling price method</td></tr>
<tr><td>5. Recognize revenue when (or as) each performance obligation is satisfied</td><td>At a point in time</td><td>Over time</td><td>At whatever time is appropriate for each performance obligation</td></tr>
</table>

14.3 PERFORMANCE OBLIGATIONS

Sellers account for a promise to provide a good or service as a performance obligation if that good or service is distinct from other items in the contract. A good or service is distinct if it is both:

① Capable of being distinct
② Separately identifiable from other goods or services in the contract

Some examples of not satisfying performance obligations include prepayments(선수금, 선급금), quality-assurance warranty(품질보증형보증), and right of return(반품권). Prepayments represent part of the transaction price received in advance from the customer. Therefore, prepayments are not considered a separate performance obligation. Quality-assurance warranty is not considered a separate performance obligation because it represents a part of the performance obligation to deliver goods and services free of defects. Some goods or services will not sell without quality assurance. Likewise, the right of return represents a part of the performance obligation to deliver acceptable goods and services. Some goods or services will not sell without the right of return given to the customer.

However, extended warranties(연장형보증) or service-type warranties(용역형보증) are considered a separate performance obligation. A warranty is an extended warranty if the customer has the option to purchase the warranty separately or if the warranty provides a service to the customer beyond quality assurance. For example, suppose a $1,000 laptop computer comes with a default one-year warranty with no additional charge by the customer. Then, the one-year warranty is considered a quality-assurance warranty to make the laptop sellable. However, suppose a customer wants to get covered for five years and has to pay more for the warranty. In that case, the extended warranty is a separate performance obligation because the customer has the option to purchase the extended warranty at a higher price. Like the extended warranty, if the seller provides the customer with an option on a material right that the customer would not get otherwise, then the customer option(고객선택권) is considered a separate performance obligation. A material right is something the customer wouldn't get otherwise, so the seller is obligated to provide it.

14.4 TIMING OF REVENUE RECOGNITION: A POINT IN TIME OR OVER TIME RECOGNITION

After identifying performance obligations, we need to determine whether we apply a point in time or over-time recognition to the performance obligation. The nature of the performance obligations determines what type of revenue recognition we need to apply.

Performance obligations can be a point in time revenue recognition type or an over-time revenue recognition type. The former includes goods or services delivered at a point in time. In contrast, the latter typically includes services to be provided over a period of time, such as cleaning and security services. Sometimes, a contract includes goods to be delivered and following services related to the goods delivered over a period. There can be various combinations of goods or services.

Example 14-1 *Performance Obligation to Which a Point in Time Revenue Recognition is Applied*

ComTech sells laptops with a default one-year free-of-charge warranty for $570. ComTech received an order to deliver ten laptops on January 1, 20×1. ComTech delivered ten laptops on January 10, 20×1, and collected accounts receivable on January 20, 20×1.

Prepare appropriate journal entries on the dates related to the sale of laptops during January 20×1.

January 1, 20×1:
No entry is recorded since the performance obligation is not satisfied yet.

January 10, 20×1:
The performance obligation is satisfied by delivering the laptops. The journal entry is as follows:

Accounts receivable (10×$570)	5,700	
Sales revenue		5,700

January 20, 20×1:
The collection of accounts receivable is recorded as follows:

Cash	5,700	
Accounts receivable		5,700

A performance obligation is satisfied over time if at least one of the following three criteria is met:

① The customer consumes the benefit of the seller's work as it is performed,
② The customer controls the asset as it is created, or
③ The seller is creating an asset with no alternative use to the seller, and the seller can receive payment for its progress even if the customer cancels the contract.

If a performance obligation is an over-time recognition type, revenue is recognized over a period in proportion to the amount of performance obligation that has been satisfied.

EXAMPLE 14-2 *Recognizing Revenue Over Time*

Shiny Cleaning Industries provides cleaning services to some office buildings over a one-year period for $10 per square meter. On January 1, 20×1, Shiny Cleaning Industries signed a contract with a 12,000-square-meter building customer to provide daily cleaning service for one year. Prepare journal entries that Shiny Cleaning will record on January 1, 20×1, and January 31, 20×1, assuming that cash for the cleaning services is collected on the fifth day of the following month after providing services daily.

January 1, 20×1:
No entry is recorded at the date of signing the contract since the performance obligation is yet to be performed.

January 31, 20×1:
One month of service has been performed. Therefore, the following journal entry is prepared:

Accounts receivable	10,000*	
Service revenue		10,000

* $10 × 12,000 square meters × 1/12 = $10,000

14.5 ALLOCATION OF TRANSACTION PRICE TO PERFORMANCE OBLIGATIONS

Suppose a contract consists of multiple performance obligations. In that case, the transaction price should be allocated to each performance obligation based on the relative standalone selling prices of the performance obligations included in the contract. Relative standalone selling prices(상대적판매가격) are expressed as a percent allocated to each performance obligation. For example, suppose there are two performance obligations with standalone selling prices of $300 and $100, respectively when sold separately. If performance obligations A and B are sold together as a package, the bundle is sold for $360 per package. Then, the transaction price of $360 is allocated based on the relative standalone selling prices as follows:

Relative standalone selling price of A = $300/($300 + $100) = 3/4 or 75%
Relative standalone selling price of B = $100/($300 + $100) = 1/4 or 25%
The transaction price allocated to A = $360 × 3/4 = $270
The transaction price allocated to B = $360 × 1/4 = $90

Example 14-3 Contract Containing Multiple Performance Obligations

MPG Game Inc. sells the MPG system, a multiplayer gaming system allowing players to compete with each other over the Internet. The MPG system includes a game console and a one-year subscription to the MPG system platform of internet-based games. MPG Game sells the game console for $720 and a one-year subscription allowing access to the MPG system platform for $180. The game console and the one-year subscription are considered separate performance obligations because they are capable of being distinct. MPG Game sells the MPG system (console plus subscription) as a package for $750.

On January 1, 20×1, MPG Game delivers 100 MPG systems to GalaxyShop for $750 per system and receives $75,000 from GalaxyShop.

Allocate the transaction price between the two performance obligations using the relative standalone selling price method.

Relative standalone selling price of the game console = $720 ÷ ($720 + $180) = 80%
Relative standalone selling price of the subscription = $180 ÷ ($720 + $180) = 20%
Allocation of the transaction price of $75,000 to the console = $75,000 × 80%
= $60,000
Allocation of the transaction price of $75,000 to the subscription = $75,000 × 20%
= $15,000

Firms sometimes provide customers with coupons to encourage them to purchase other goods at a discount price when they purchase goods. Then, the coupons are considered a separate performance obligation. We need to estimate the standalone selling price of the customer coupons by considering both the discount amount and the probability of exercising the coupons.

EXAMPLE 14-4 *Customer Option, Allocation of the Transaction Price, and Revenue Recognition*

ComTech offers a promotional coupon with every laptop it sells for the normal price of $570. The coupon allows the laptop customer to buy an earbud set for $50 that usually sells for $100 (a 50% discount). The coupon must be redeemed within one year of the laptop purchase. ComTech estimates that 60% of customers will take advantage of the coupon. How would ComTech account for the cash sale of 100 laptops sold under this promotion on January 1, 20×1?

The estimated standalone selling price of the coupon (a customer option):

Discount = $100 × 50% = $50
Estimated standalone selling price of the coupon = $50 × 60% = $30
Total standalone selling prices for the laptop and coupon = $570 + $30 = $600

Allocation of the transaction price to each performance obligation:

Laptop: $570/$600 = 95%; $570 × 95% × 100 = $54,150
Earbud set coupon: $30/$600 = 5%; $570 × 5% × 100 = $2,850

Journal Entries on January 1, 20×1:

Cash	57,000	
Sales revenue - Laptop		54,150
Deferred revenue - Coupon		2,850

Suppose the customers exercised 40% of the coupon in the first month. Then, the following journal entry is needed:

Deferred revenue - Coupon	1,140	
Cash (40×$50)	2,000	
Sales revenue - Earbuds		3,140

14.6 RECOGNIZE REVENUE AS EACH PERFORMANCE OBLIGATION IS SATISFIED

The seller recognizes revenue as the seller satisfies the performance obligation in the contract. If there are multiple performance obligations in a contract, the seller recognizes revenue as each performance obligation is satisfied.

Example 14-5 *Revenue Recognition When Multiple Performance Obligations Exist in a Contract*

MPG Game Inc. sells the MPG system, a multiplayer gaming system allowing players to compete with each other over the Internet. The MPG system includes a game console and a one-year subscription to the MPG system platform of internet-based games. MPG Game sells the game console for $720 and a one-year subscription allowing access to the MPG system platform for $180. The game console and the one-year subscription are considered separate performance obligations because they are capable of being distinct. MPG Game sells the MPG system (console plus subscription) as a package deal for $750.

On January 1, 20×1, MPG Game delivers 100 MPG systems to GalaxyShop for $750 per system and receives $75,000 from GalaxyShop.

Prepare journal entries on January 1, 20×1, and January 31, 20×1, as MPG Game recognizes monthly revenue. Use the allocated amount of the transaction price to the console and the subscription as given in Example 14-3 for journal entries.

Journal entry on January 1, 20×1:

On January 1, MPG Game satisfied the performance obligation of delivering the consoles. Therefore, sales revenue from the delivery of the consoles is recognized on the date. However, the subscription service is yet to be performed for one year. Therefore, the subscription service is recorded as a deferred revenue, a liability to provide service over the one-year period. Therefore, the January 1, 20×1 journal entry is as follows:

	Debit	Credit
Cash	75,000	
Sales revenue		60,000
Deferred revenue - Subscription		15,000

Journal entry on January 31, 20×1:
MPG Game records the following monthly entry to recognize MPG system subscription revenue.

	Debit	Credit
Deferred revenue ($15,000÷12)	1,250	
Service revenue		1,250

Commonly, some goods are sold with extended warranties to meet the customers with extended protection at a higher price than those with only quality-assurance warranties. If so, the extended warranty is treated as a separate performance obligation. So, the transaction price needs to be allocated to two performance obligations. In addition, revenue is recognized when each performance obligation is satisfied.

Example 14-6 *Identify the Performance Obligation(s) and Revenue Recognition*

ComTech sells laptops for $570 with a free-of-charge default warranty for one year. However, ComTech provides customers with an option for an extended warranty for five years at an additional price of $30 at the time of purchase only. How would ComTech account for the cash sale of 100 laptops sold during January 20×1 if 20% of the customers bought the extended warranty?

The transaction consists of two performance obligations. A delivery of laptops to customers is one performance obligation to which ComTech applies a point in time revenue recognition. The extended warranty is another performance obligation that ComTech applies over-time revenue recognition. Because the performance obligation for the laptops is satisfied at the time of sale, ComTech recognizes sales revenue from the laptop sales. However, the extended warranty will be satisfied over the warranty period of five years. Therefore, ComTech records deferred revenue for the extended warranty at the time of sale.

Journal Entries during January 20×1:

Cash	57,600	
Sales revenue - Laptop		57,000*
Deferred revenue - Extended warranty		600**

* $\$570 \times 100 = \$57,000$

** $\$30 \times 100 \times 20\% = \$600$

14.7 VARIABLE CONSIDERATIONS

The transaction price is fixed in many cases. However, the transaction price may also include variable components. For example, a contract can be written so that the seller receives a fixed price, but the seller can also receive a bonus depending on achieving specific incentive targets set by the customer. If a contract contains variable considerations, then the seller can recognize the variable considerations as revenues using either the expected value approach (기대가치법) or the most likely amount approach(최고확률금액법). However, when recognizing the variable considerations, a constraint not to overstate revenue recognition should be applied. Accordingly, sellers only include an estimate of variable consideration in the transaction price to the extent it is "probable" that a significant revenue reversal will not occur when the uncertainty associated with the variable consideration is resolved. Indicators that a significant revenue reversal could occur include: (a) poor evidence on which to base an estimate, (b) dependence of the estimate on factors outside the seller's control, (c) a history of the seller changing payment terms on similar contracts, (d) a broad range of outcomes that could occur, and (e) a long delay before uncertainty resolves.

Example 14-7 *Variable Consideration*

On January 1, 20×1, Ibis Consulting entered into a consulting service contract with Yummy Chicken to provide professional marketing services over a six-month period. As a result, Ibis Consulting recognizes monthly revenue from the consulting services evenly over the six months.

The terms of the contract are:

On January 1, 20×1, Yummy Chicken pays Ibis Consulting an up-front fixed fee of $120,000 for tailored consulting services.

Yummy Chicken also will pay Ibis Consulting a bonus of $60,000 if Yummy Chicken's sales volume increases by more than 20 percent during the six months.

Ibis Consulting estimates a 75% chance it will achieve the target and receive the $60,000 bonus.

Required:

1. Compute the bonus amount under the expected value method for the consulting services and prepare journal entries on January 1, 20×1, and January 31, 20×1.
2. Compute the bonus amount under the most likely amount method for the consulting services and prepare journal entries on January 1, 20×1, and January 31, 20×1.
3. Assume that Ibis uses the most likely amount approach, and Ibis estimates a 40% chance that it will achieve the target on April 30. Prepare the journal entry on April 30, 20×1.

Solutions:

1. The expected value method

Bonus under the expected value method = $60,000 × 75% + $0 × 25% = $45,000

January 1, 20×1 Journal entry:

	Debit	Credit
Cash	120,000	
Deferred revenue		120,000

January 31, 20×1 Journal entry:

	Debit	Credit
Deferred revenue	20,000*	
Bonus receivable	7,500**	
Service revenue		27,500

* $120,000/6 months = $20,000

** $45,000/6 months = $7,500

2. The most likely amount method

Bonus under the most likely amount method = $60,000 (75% is the most likely.)

January 1, 20×1 Journal entry:

Cash	120,000	
Deferred revenue		120,000

January 31, 20×1 Journal entry:

Deferred revenue	20,000*	
Bonus receivable	10,000**	
Service revenue		30,000

* $120,000/6 months = $20,000

** $60,000/6 months = $10,000

3. Under the most likely amount method, it is now estimated that Ibis will not receive the bonus. Therefore, Ibis should reduce the previously recognized bonus receivable and service revenue of $30,000 ($10,000×3 months) and recognize monthly revenue based on fixed price only on April 30, 20×1. Therefore, Ibis Consulting should prepare the following journal entries on April 30, 20×1:

Service revenue	30,000	
Bonus receivable		30,000
Deferred revenue	20,000	
Service revenue		20,000

14.8 ESTIMATION OF STANDALONE SELLING PRICES

Sometimes, a contract may contain multiple performance obligations, and a performance obligation may not have a known standalone selling price. Then, three approaches are available to estimate standalone selling prices.

ⓐ ***Adjusted market assessment approach***(시장조정평가접근법). Estimate a price using the market price for a similar product or service with adjustment if necessary.

ⓑ ***Expected cost plus margin approach***(예상원가이윤가산접근법). Estimate the costs of satisfying a performance obligation and then add an appropriate profit margin to the costs.

ⓒ ***Residual approach***(잔여접근법). Subtract the sum of the known or estimated standalone selling prices of other goods and services in the contract from the total transaction price of the contract.

Example 14-8 *Estimation of Standalone Selling Prices*

Bobcat Inc. sells a product with two separate performance obligations: the Bobcat golf clubs and the NiceSwing teaching software. The club has a standalone selling price of $900. Bobcat sells both the clubs and the teaching software as a package deal for $1,000. However, the teaching software does not have a standalone selling price. Bobcat is aware that other vendors charge $150 for similar software, and Bobcat's prices are generally 10% lower than what is charged by those vendors. Bobcat estimates that it incurs approximately $80 of cost per copy of the software and usually charges 40% above cost on similar products.

Required:

1. Estimate the standalone selling price of the software using the adjusted market assessment approach.
2. Estimate the standalone selling price of the software using the expected cost plus margin approach.
3. Estimate the standalone selling price of the software using the residual approach.

Solutions:

1. Standalone selling price under the adjusted market assessment approach
   $=\$150\times 90\%=\$135$
2. Standalone selling price under the expected cost plus margin approach
   $=\$80\times 1.40=\$112$
3. Standalone selling price under the residual approach
   $=\$1{,}000-\$900$ (Golf clubs' standalone selling price) $=\$100$

14.9 SPECIAL ISSUES IN REVENUE RECOGNITION

(1) Is the Seller a Principal or Agent?

Sometimes more than one company is involved in providing goods or services to a customer. In those situations, we must determine whether a company is acting as a principal or an agent. The principal is responsible for providing the good or service to the customer. The agent arranges for the principal to provide the good or service.

We view the seller as a principal if the seller obtains control of the goods or services before they are transferred to the customer. Various indicators help determine whether a seller obtains control. Control is indicated if the seller is primarily responsible for providing goods, setting prices, taking risks associated with holding inventory, or receiving returned inventory. A principal's performance obligation is to provide goods or services. In contrast, an agent acts as a facilitator who receives a commission for helping sellers provide goods or services to customers. If the company is a principal, it records revenue equal to the total sales price customers pay. On the other hand, an agent records as revenue only the commission it receives on the transaction. Table 14-3 illustrates the accounting issues regarding the seller as a principal or agent.

Table 14-3 Special Issue: A Principal or Agent?

	Principal	Agent
Performance Obligations	To deliver goods and services (Owner of the goods)	To facilitate a transaction between a principal and a customer
Recording Revenue	Total revenue from customers	Only the commission it receives on the transaction

EXAMPLE 14-9 *Is the Seller a Principal or Agent?*

An online retailer AgenCo sold a goose-down coat made by PrinCo to a customer for $800. Let's consider accounting for that sale by two sellers: PrinCo and AgenCo:

PrinCo ships individual goods to buyers when a sale is made through AgenCo. AgenCo is a web portal where various sellers can offer their goods for sale. The manufacturers ship goods directly to buyers when a sale is made. AgenCo receives a 10% commission on each sale via its web portal.

The journal entries for the sale by PrinCo and AgenCo are as follows:

Journal Entries by PrinCo (Principal):

	Debit	Credit
Cash	800	
Sales revenue (Gross amount)		800

Journal Entries by AgenCo (Agent):

	Dr.	Cr.
Cash	80	
Commission revenue (Net amount)		80

(2) Licenses

Intellectual properties, such as software, technology, media, and entertainment, are typically traded through license agreements between a licensor and licensee. IFRS requires the seller (licensor) to recognize revenue over time only if the seller's ongoing activities affect the benefits the customer obtains from the intellectual property (IP, 지적재산). This type of intellectual property is called a 'right of access' intellectual property(접근권지적재산). On the other hand, if the seller's ongoing activities do not affect the customer's benefits, the seller should recognize revenue at the time of transfer of the intellectual property. This type of intellectual property is called a 'right of use' intellectual property(사용권지적재산).

EXAMPLE 14-10 *License of Intellectual Property*

SCMTech Inc. sells software that helps restaurants to take short-term and long-term reservations from their customers in a manner that helps restaurant businesses prepare the orders to be delivered on a timely basis, keep the ingredients fresh and run the business efficiently. Hickory Cuisine paid a licensing fee of $30,000 for a copy of the software. Although Hickory Cuisine can use the software as long as it wants, SCMTech expects that Hickory will use it for approximately five years. SCMTech does not anticipate any further interaction with Hickory following the transfer of the license. How much revenue should SCMTech recognize in the first year of the contract?

Solutions:

The license transaction is a right-of-use type transaction. Therefore, SCMTech would recognize $30,000 as revenue in the year of software transfer.

(3) Gift Cards

Sales of gift cards(상품권) are common business practices. Suppose a department store sells gift cards that can be redeemed within one year from the date of sale. Then, the department store recognizes the sale of gift cards as deferred revenue(이연수익) that is a liability. Revenue is recognized when a gift card is redeemed, or the likelihood of redemption is viewed as remote.

EXAMPLE 14-11 *Gift Cards*

Stork Department Store sells gift cards redeemable for goods either in-store or online. During 20×1, Stork sold $100,000 of gift cards, and $70,000 of the gift cards were redeemed for products. As of December 31, 20×1, $5,000 of gift cards had passed the expiration date that the cards can be redeemed.

Required:

1. Prepare a journal entry when Stork sold the gift card.
2. Prepare a journal entry to record the redemption and expiration of the gift cards in 20×1?

Solutions:

1. Journal entry for the sale of gift cards:

Account	Debit	Credit
Cash	100,000	
Deferred revenue		100,000

2. Journal entry for the redemption of gift cards:

Account	Debit	Credit
Deferred revenue	75,000	
Sales revenue		70,000
Other revenue		5,000

14.10 REVENUE FROM LONG-TERM CONTRACTS

Suppose it takes a long period to construct, manufacture, or prepare goods or services to be delivered to customers. In that case, we need to determine whether we can apply over-time recognition of the goods or services before they are delivered. IFRS allows firms to apply over-time revenue recognition to qualified long-term contracts. However, if long-term contracts do not qualify for the over-time recognition of the contract amount, firms are not allowed to recognize revenue until the completion of the project.

Long-term contracts usually have a single performance obligation because they do not meet the "separately identifiable" criterion necessary for goods and services to be considered distinct.

For the qualified long-term contracts, we recognize revenue over time according to the progress toward completion. The over-time revenue recognition method is called a POC method(진행기준법, percentage of completion method). If we cannot apply the POC method, then entire revenue recognition occurs at the completion of the contracts. The method is called a CC method(완성기준법, completed contract method).

Accounting for long-term contracts has two unique accounts: Construction in progress (CIP, 진행공사) and billing on the contract(계약대금청구). They are mutual contra accounts to each other for reporting purposes in the statement of financial position. The CIP account is an inventory account like the work-in-process(재공품) account. The CIP account accumulates costs incurred until the completion of the contract and gets derecognized when completed. In addition, the CIP account under the POC method consists of both costs and profits. However, the CIP account under the CC method consists of only costs since the CC method does not recognize revenue and profit until completed. If the CIP account balance exceeds the billings on the contract account balance at the end of an accounting period, the difference is reported as current assets. On the other hand, if the CIP balance is smaller than the billings account balance, the difference is reported as current liabilities.

Typical journal entries for long-term contracts include the following:

Journal entry for costs incurred:

CIP – Costs	×××	
Cash, materials, labor, overhead, etc.		×××

Journal entry for billing customers:

Accounts receivable	×××	
Billings on the contact		×××

Journal entry for the collection of billings:

Cash	×××	
Accounts receivable		×××

Journal entry for the recognition of revenue and profit:

Cost of construction	×××	
CIP – Profits	×××	
Revenue – Long-term contract		×××

The first step to applying the POC method to qualified long-term contracts is to determine the percentage of completion (POC, 진행률) toward completion of the contract. The most common approach is a cost-based POC computed as follows:

POC=Cumulative costs÷Total estimated costs

The POC is a cumulative percentage since the numerator is the cumulative costs incurred. With the POC ready, we can determine the cumulative revenue under the POC method by multiplying the POC by the contract amount. We need to subtract revenues recognized in the previous periods from the cumulative revenues to calculate the current period revenue. More specifically, revenue for the period is computed as follows:

Revenue in the current period
=Contract Amount×POC−Revenue recognized previously

After recognizing revenue, we also compute profit for the period by subtracting the costs of the period from the revenue of the accounting period as follows:

Profit for the period
=Revenue for the period−Costs incurred in the current period

EXAMPLE 14-12 Accounting for a Long-Term Contract

At the beginning of 20×1, the Harding Construction Company received a contract to build an office building for $100,000. Harding will construct the building according to specifications provided by the buyer, and the project is estimated to take three years to complete. According to the contract, Harding will bill the buyer in installments over the construction period according to a prearranged schedule. Information related to the contract is as follows:

	20×1	20×2	20×3
Construction costs incurred during the year	$30,000	$20,000	$32,000
Cumulative actual construction costs	30,000	50,000	82,000
Estimated costs to complete at the end of the year	45,000	30,000	0
Total estimated construction costs	75,000	80,000	82,000
Billings made during the year	24,000	40,000	36,000
Collections of the billings during the year	20,000	28,000	52,000

Required:

1. Prepare journal entries to record costs incurred each year under the POC and CC methods.
2. Compute the percentage-of-completion (POC) and revenue each year under the POC method.
3. Prepare journal entries to recognize revenue each year under the POC method.
4. Prepare journal entries to recognize revenue each year under the CC method.
5. Present the contract-related items in the statement of financial position in 20×1 and 20×2 under the POC and CC methods.

Solutions:

1. Journal entries to record costs incurred each year are the same under the POC and CC methods:

POC and CC methods	20×1		20×2		20×3	
CIP - Costs	30,000		20,000		32,000	
Cash, materials, labor, etc.		30,000		20,000		32,000

2. POC and Revenue in each period under the POC method:

	20×1	20×2	20×3
POC	\$30,000÷\$75,000 =**40%**	\$50,000÷\$80,000 =**62.5%**	\$82,000÷\$82,000 =**100%**
Revenue	\$100,000×40%−\$0 =**\$40,000**	\$100,000×62.5%−\$40,000 =**\$22,500**	\$100,000−\$62,500 =**\$37,500**

3. Journal entries to recognize revenue each year under the POC method:
Profit in each year is computed as revenue minus costs incurred in each year. Profit and costs are included in the CIP (construction in progress).

POC method (Over time)	20×1		20×2		20×3	
Cost of construction	30,000		20,000		32,000	
CIP - Profit	10,000		2,500		5,500	
Revenue from construction		40,000		22,500		37,500

4. Journal entries to recognize revenue in each year the CC method:
Revenue and profit are not recognized until the completion of the contract in 20×3. Therefore, the entire revenue and profit are recognized in 20×3 under the CC method.

CC method (a point in time)	20×1		20×2		20×3	
Cost of construction	No entry		No entry		82,000	
CIP - Profit					18,000	
Revenue from construction						100,000

5. Presentation of the contract-related items in 20×1 and 20×2 under the POC and CC methods:
Accounts receivable balances at each year-end are computed as cumulative billings minus cumulative collections. Therefore, accounts receivable balances in 20×1 and 20×2, respectively, are \$4,000 (\$24,000−\$20,000) and \$16,000 (\$24,000+\$40,000−\$20,000−\$28,000).
Cumulative CIP (consisting of cumulative costs and profits) and Billings in 20×1 and 20×2, respectively, under the POC method, are \$40,000 and \$62,500. Cumulative billings in 20×1 and 20×2 are \$24,000 and \$64,000 (\$24,000+\$40,000), respectively.

Remember that the cumulative CIP and Billings are mutual contra accounts.

Cumulative CIP under the CC method consists of only costs. Therefore, the CIP balance at the end of 20×1 and 20×2 are $20,000 and $50,000 ($20,000+$30,000), respectively. On the other hand, cumulative billings are the same under both methods.

If CIP>Billings, we report the net amount as current assets. However, if CIP <Billings, we report the net amount as current liabilities.

Therefore, the presentation of the items related to the long-term contract will be as follows:

Partial Statement of Financial Position at the end of the period	20×1	20×2
The POC method		
Current Assets:		
Accounts Receivable	$4,000	$16,000
CIP ($40,000) in excess of billings ($24,000)	16,000	
Current Liabilities:		
Billings ($64,000) in excess of CIP ($62,500)		1,500
The CC method		
Current Assets:		
Accounts Receivable	$4,000	$16,000
CIP ($30,000) in excess of billings ($24,000)	6,000	
Current Liabilities:		
Billings ($64,000) in excess of CIP ($50,000)		14,000

CHAPTER 14 Multiple Choice Questions

14.1 Which of the following is not a step used to apply the core principle of revenue recognition?

- ⓐ Determine the transaction price
- ⓑ Identify the performance obligations in the contract
- ⓒ Identify the contract with a customer
- ⓓ Ensure the sales price is fixed and determinable

14.2 Which of the following is not a key indicator in deciding whether a control has passed from the seller to the buyer?

- ⓐ Seller can identify the contract with a buyer.
- ⓑ Buyer has an obligation to pay the seller.
- ⓒ Buyer has legal title to the asset.
- ⓓ Buyer has physical possession of the asset.

14.3 Which of the following is not an indicator that control has passed from the seller to the buyer?

- ⓐ Buyer has legal title.
- ⓑ Buyer has an unconditional obligation to pay.
- ⓒ Buyer has scheduled delivery.
- ⓓ Buyer has assumed the risk and rewards of ownership.

14.4 Which of the following indicates that revenue for a service should be recognized over time?

- ⓐ The seller is enhancing an asset that the customer controls as the service is performed.
- ⓑ The seller provides services to the customer as needed.
- ⓒ The seller can estimate the percentage of work completed.
- ⓓ The sales price is fixed and determinable.

14.5 Nuthatch Co. wrote a contract that involves two performance obligations. Product A has a standalone selling price of $100, and product B has a standalone selling price of $200. The price for the combined product is $240. How much of the transaction price would be allocated to the performance obligation for delivering product A?

- ⓐ $40
- ⓑ $60
- ⓒ $80
- ⓓ $100

14.6 Gill Co. offers a promotional coupon with every product it sells. The coupon gives the Gill customers an opportunity to buy an electric drill that normally sells for $50 for only $30 (a 40% discount). The coupon must be redeemed within one year of the purchase. Gill Co. estimates that 80% of customers will take advantage of the coupon. What is the standalone selling price of the coupon?

- ⓐ $20
- ⓑ $30
- ⓒ $50
- ⓓ $16

14.7 Robin Inc. enters into a contract offering variable consideration. The contract pays Robin $2,000/month for six months of continuous consulting services. In addition, there is a 60% chance the contract will pay an additional $4,000 and a 40% chance the contract will pay an additional $6,000, depending on the outcome of the consulting contract. Robin concludes that this contract qualifies for revenue recognition over time. How much revenue would Robin recognize for the first month of the contract, assuming that Robin estimates variable consideration as the expected value?

ⓐ $2,000
ⓑ $2,666
ⓒ $2,800
ⓓ $2,400

14.8 Crawfish Consulting operates a website that links experienced statisticians with businesses that need data analyzed. Statisticians post their rates, qualifications, and references on the website, and Crawfish receives 25% of the fee paid to the statisticians in exchange for identifying potential customers. Dove Associates contacts Crawfish and arranges to pay a consultant $4,500 in exchange for analyzing some data. Crawfish's income statement would include the following concerning this transaction:

ⓐ Revenue of $4,500
ⓑ Revenue of $4,500 and cost of services of $3,375
ⓒ Revenue of $1,125
ⓓ Revenue of $5,625 and cost of services of $4,500

14.9 Which of the following is not true?

ⓐ Licensing fees are recognized over time for any license viewed as providing a right of access.
ⓑ Licensing fees are recognized as revenue over time for licenses of IP, for which the seller expects its ongoing activities to affect the benefits that the buyer receives from IP.
ⓒ Licensing fees are recognized as revenue at a point in time for licenses of IP, for which the buyer expects that the seller's future activities will not affect the benefit the buyer derives from the IP.
ⓓ Licensing fees are recognized as revenue at the end of the license period, when the seller has completed its performance obligation to provide access to its IP.

14.10 Angelfish Store sells gift cards redeemable for Angelfish goods either in-store or online. During 20×1, Angelfish sold $6,000,000 of gift cards, and $5,400,000 of the gift cards were redeemed for products. As of December 31, 20×1, $450,000 of the remaining gift cards had passed the date at which Angelfish concludes that the cards will never be redeemed. How much gift card revenue should Angelfish recognize in 20×1?

ⓐ $5,400,000
ⓑ $5,550,000
ⓒ $5,850,000
ⓓ $6,000,000

14.11 Heron Construction entered into a contract to construct a tunnel for a fixed price of $1,200,000. Heron recognizes revenue over time according to the percentage of completion. Here are some facts:

	20×1	20×2	20×3
Cost incurred	$300,000	$500,000	$250,000
Estimated additional cost to complete	600,000	200,000	0

What is Heron's percentage completion and revenue in 20×1?

ⓐ 25%; $300,000
ⓑ 33.33%; $400,000
ⓒ 37.5%; $450,000
ⓓ 100%; $1,200,000

14.12 Opossum Construction entered into a contract to construct a tunnel for a fixed price of $1,200,000. Opossum recognizes revenue over time according to the percentage of completion. Here are some facts:

	20×1	20×2	20×3
Cost incurred	$300,000	$500,000	$250,000
Estimated additional cost to complete	600,000	200,000	0

What is Opossum's percentage completion and revenue in 20×2?

ⓐ 50%; $200,000
ⓑ 66.67%; $400,000
ⓒ 80%; $560,000
ⓓ 88.89%; $666,667

14.13 Zebra, Inc. sells software that helps farmers plow their fields to prevent erosion and maximize the effectiveness of irrigation. Wildebeest paid a licensing fee of $60,000 for a copy of the software. Although Wildebeest can use the software as long as it wants, Zebra expects that Wildebeest will use it for approximately five years. Zebra does not anticipate any further interaction with Wildebeest following the transfer of the license. How much revenue should Zebra recognize in the first year of the contract?

ⓐ $0
ⓑ $12,000
ⓒ $15,000
ⓓ $60,000

14.14 Rose-moss is an artist who sells his work under consignment (he displays his work in local nail shops, and customers purchase his work there). Rose-moss recently transferred a painting on consignment to a local nail shop. After Rose-moss has transferred a painting to a nail shop, the painting:

ⓐ Should be counted in the nail shop's inventory, as the nail shop now possesses it.
ⓑ Should be counted in Rose-moss's inventory until the nail shop sells it.
ⓒ We lack sufficient information to know who should carry the painting in the inventory.
ⓓ Should be counted in either Rose-moss's or the nail shop's inventory, depending on which incurred the cost of preparing the painting for display.

CHAPTER 14

Exercises

14.1 Service revenue

Orchid Ski, Inc. operates a downhill ski area. Customers can purchase a season pass that entitles the pass holder to ski any day during the season, typically from December 1 through March 31. Orchid Ski expects its season pass holders to use their passes equally throughout the season. The company's fiscal year ends on December 31.

On November 6, 20×1, Orchid Ski sold a season pass to a customer for $500.

Required:

ⓐ Prepare the appropriate journal entries that Orchid Ski would record on November 6 and December 31.

ⓑ What will be included in the Orchid Ski 20×1 income statement and statement of financial position related to the season pass sale to the customer?

14.2 Performance obligations - Customer option

Bluefeet, Inc., a shoe retailer, sells boots in different styles. In early November, the company starts selling "Snow Boots" to customers for $70 per pair. When a customer purchases a pair of Snow Boots, Bluefeet also gives the customer a 30% discount coupon for any future purchases made in the next 30 days. Customers can't obtain the discount coupon otherwise. Bluefeet anticipates that approximately 20% of customers will utilize the coupon, and those customers will purchase additional goods that generally sell for $100 on average. The discount coupon is considered a separate performance obligation.

Prepare a journal entry to record revenue for the sale of 1,000 pairs of Snow Boots, assuming that Bluefeet uses the residual method to estimate the standalone selling price of Snow Boots sold without the discount coupon.

14.3 Variable consideration – Most likely amount approach vs. expected value approach

Coral Reef Guide Service provides guided scuba diving excursions in the South Coast areas. Ocean Tours hires Coral Reef to lead scuba diving tours for Ocean Tour customers. Coral Reef receives $1,000 per tour day. In addition, shortly after the end of each month, Coral Reef learns whether it will receive a $200 bonus per tour day it guided during the previous month if its service received an average evaluation of "excellent" by Ocean Tour customers. The $1,000 per day and any bonus due are paid in one lump payment shortly after the end of each month.

On July 1, based on prior experience, Coral Reef estimated that there is a 40% chance that it will earn the bonus for July tours. It guided a total of 20 days in July.

Required:

ⓐ Prepare Coral Reef's July 31 journal entry to record revenue for tours given in July, assuming Coral Reef uses the most likely amount approach for variable consideration recognition.

ⓑ Prepare Coral Reef's July 31 journal entry to record revenue for tours given in July, assuming Coral Reef uses the expected value approach for variable consideration recognition.

14.4 Timing of revenue recognition – A point in time revenue recognition

On July 1, 20×1, Anemone Company, a real estate developer, sold a parcel of land to a construction company for $2,000,000. The book value of the land on Anemone's books was $800,000. Terms of the sale required installment payments of $400,000 to be paid every other month, with the first payment on July 1 beginning in 20×1. How much revenue will Anemone recognize for the sale (ignoring interest), assuming it recognized revenue when transferring the land to the construction company?

14.5 Timing of revenue recognition – Over time revenue recognition

Orca Construction is constructing a building for Humpback Inc., an online retailing firm. Under the construction agreement, if Orca can't complete construction for any reason, Humpback would own the partially completed building and could hire another construction company to complete the job. When should Orca recognize revenue: as the building is constructed or after construction is completed?

14.6 Timing of revenue recognition

On July 1, 20×1, Goldfinch Tech signed a $12,000 consulting contract with Blue Jay Inc. The contract requires Goldfinch to provide computer technical support services whenever requested from July 1, 20×1, to March 31, 20×2, with the customer paying the entire $6,000 on July 1, 20×1. How much revenue should Goldfinch recognize in 20×1?

14.7 Allocating the transaction price

Cormorant System sold software to a customer for $80,000. As part of the contract, Cormorant promises to provide free technical support over the next six months. Cormorant sells the same software without technical support for $70,000 and a standalone six-month technical support contract for $30,000, so these products would sell for $100,000 if sold separately. Prepare Cormorant's journal entry to record the sale of software.

14.8 Identification of a contract

Mantis Mower entered into a contract for a $100,000 sale of mowers to the new Garden Company. Mantis only anticipates a slightly greater than 50% chance that Garden will be able to pay the amounts that Mantis is entitled to receive under the contract. Upon delivery of the mowers, assuming payment has yet been made by Garden, how much should Mantis recognize revenue?

14.9 Performance obligations – Prepayments

Antelope Fitness is an online fitness company offering access to workout routines, nutrition advice, and Antelope coaches. Customers pay a $100 fee to register on the website and then pay $20 per month for access to all Antelope services. How many performance obligations exist in the implicit contract when customers register for the services?

14.10 Performance obligations – Warranties

Osprey Fans sells ceiling fans. Each fan has a one-year warranty that covers any product defects. When customers purchase a fan, they also have the option to purchase an extended three-year warranty that covers any breakage or maintenance. Customers pay 20% less for the extended warranty if they buy it at the same time they buy a fan. How many performance obligations exist in the implied contract to purchase a fan?

14.11 Performance obligations – Construction

Hummingbird Precision, Inc. specializes in designing and installing customized manufacturing equipment. On February 1, 20×1, it signed a contract to design a fully automated Smartwatch assembly line for $2 million, which will be settled in cash upon completion of construction. In addition, Hummingbird Precision will install the equipment on the client's property, furnish it with a customized software package integral to operations, and provide consulting services that integrate the equipment with Hummingbird Precision's other assembly lines. How many performance obligations exist in this contract?

14.12 Variable considerations

In January 20×1, Thistle Asset Management Services, Inc. entered into a one-year contract with a client to provide investment advisory services. The company will receive a management fee, prepaid at the beginning of the contract, calculated as 1% of the client's $100 million total assets being managed. In addition, the contract specifies that Thistle will receive a bonus of 20% of any returns in excess of the return on the KOSPI index. Thistle estimates that it will earn a $1 million bonus, but it is very uncertain of that, given that the bonus depends on a highly volatile stock market. On what transaction price should Thistle base revenue recognition?

14.13 Principal or agent

Suppose that Lark Market, an eCommerce retailer, sells LG Gram produced by LG for a retail price of $1,000. Lark arranges its operations for customers to receive products directly from LG rather than Lark Market. Customers purchase from Lark Market using credit cards, and Lark Market forwards cash to LG equal to the retail price minus a $50 commission that Lark Market keeps. In this arrangement, how much revenue will Lark Market recognize for selling one LG Gram?

14.14 Estimating standalone selling prices

Dandelion Golf sells golf clubs. Dandelion provides complimentary club-fitting services with each sale of a full set of clubs. A full set of clubs with fitting services sells for $1,300. Dandelion sells the same clubs without the fitting services for $1,200. Similar club-fitting services are available from other vendors for $100, and Dandelion generally charges 10% more than other vendors for similar services. Also, Dandelion estimates that it costs $60 to provide the fitting services and typically earns 30% over costs on similar services.

Assume that the clubs and fitting services are separate performance obligations. Estimate standalone selling price for the club-fitting services ⓐ under the adjusted market assessment method, ⓑ the expected cost plus margin method, and ⓒ the residual method.

14.15 Licenses

Peacock Associates sold two licenses to Kim & Johnson on September 1, 20×1. First, in exchange for $100,000, Peacock provides Kim & Johnson with a copy of its property management software, which Peacock does not anticipate updating and which Kim & Johnson can use permanently. Second, in exchange for $90,000, Peacock provides Kim & Johnson with a three-year right to market Kim & Johnson's financial advisory services under the name of Peacock Associates, which Peacock advertises on an ongoing basis. How much will Peacock recognize in 20×1 under this arrangement?

14.16 Franchises

Weaver Cosmetics sells hairstyling franchises. Weaver receives $50,000 from a new franchisee for initial training, equipment, and furnishing with a standalone selling price of $50,000. Weaver also receives $30,000 for using the Weaver name and ongoing consulting services for three years. Lion's Mane became a Weaver franchisee on January 1, 20×1, completed training, and was open for business on March 1, 20×1. How much revenue will Weaver recognize for its franchise agreement with Lion's Mane in 20×1?

14.17 Consignment

Woodpecker & Associates is an artist company specializing in landscape painting. Woodpecker places four paintings with a retail price of $500 each in the Beaver Gallery during 20×1. Beaver earns a 20% commission on paintings sold to gallery patrons. As of December 31, 20×1, two paintings have been sold by Beaver to gallery patrons. How much revenue for the four paintings should ⓐ Woodpecker and ⓑ Beaver recognize in 20×1?

14.18 Gift cards

Jewelweed Store sells gift cards redeemable for Jewelweed goods either in-store or online. During 20×1, Jewelweed sold $100,000 of gift cards, and $80,000 of the gift cards were redeemed for products. As of December 31, 20×1, $2,000 of gift cards had passed the expiration date. How much gift card revenue should Jewelweed recognize in 20×1?

14.19 Long-term contract – Percentage of completion method

A construction company entered into a fixed-price contract to build an office building for $20 million. Construction costs incurred during the first year were $6 million, and the estimated cost to complete at the end of the first year was $9 million. The company recognizes revenue over time according to the percentage of completion. ⓐ How much revenue and gross profit or loss will the company recognize in the contract's first year? ⓑ Assume that, during the first year, the company billed the customer $7 million, of which $5 was collected before the year-end. Prepare a partial statement of financial position showing the items related to the contract.

14.20 Long-term contract - Complete contract method

A construction company entered into a fixed-price contract to build an office building for $20 million. Construction costs incurred during the first year were $6 million, and the estimated cost to complete at the end of the first year was $9 million. The building was completed in the second year, and construction costs incurred in the second year were $10 million. How much revenue and gross profit or loss will the company recognize in the first and second years if the company recognizes revenue upon contract completion?

ACCOUNTING TERMINOLOGY IN CHAPTER 14

a point in time 단일시점
adjusted market assessment approach
시장조정평가접근법
billing on contract 계약대금청구
commercial substance 상업적실질
completed contract (CC) method 완성기준법
construction in progress (CIP) 진행공사
contract with a customer 고객과의 계약
customer option 고객선택권
deferred revenue 이연수익
delivering goods 재화의 인도
expected cost plus margin approach
예상원가이윤가산접근법
expected value approach 기대가치법
extended warranties 연장형보증
fixed price 확정가격
gift cards 상품권
intellectual property (IP) 지적재산
most likely amount approach 최고확률금액법
over a period of time 일정기간
percentage of completion (POC) method
진행기준법
performance obligations 수행의무
prepayments 선수금, 선급금
quality-assurance warranty 품질보증형보증
relative standalone selling prices 상대판매가격
rendering services 용역의 제공
residual approach 잔여접근법
revenue 수익
revenue recognition at a point in time
단일시점수익인식
revenue recognition over time 기간수익인식
right of access 접근권
right of access intellectual property
접근권지적재산
right of return 반품권
right of use 사용권
right of use intellectual property
사용권지적재산
service-type warranties 용역형보증
transaction price 거래가격
variable considerations 변동대가
work-in-process 재공품

INDEX

[b]

[c]

[d]

[e]

[f]

[g]

[h]

[i]

[j]

[l]

[m]

[n]

[o]

[p]

[t]

[u]

[v]

[w]

IFRS
PRINCIPLES OF ACCOUNTING 5E
With Keywords in Korean

2010년 8월 30일 제1판 1쇄 발행
2023년 2월 10일 제5판 1쇄 인쇄
2023년 2월 15일 제5판 1쇄 발행

저 자 윤순석 · 김효진 · Grace Johnson
발 행 인 권 영 섭
발 행 처 (주)신 영 사

경기도 파주시 심학산로 12(출판문화단지)
등 록 : 1988. 5. 2 / 제406-1988-000020호
전 화 : 031-946-2894(代)
F A X : 031-946-0799
e-mail : sys28945@naver.com
홈페이지 : http://www.shinyoungsa.co.kr

정가 27,000원

ISBN 978-89-5501-813-4